*Praise for*
# CUSTOMER-CENTERED GROWTH

"Defining the customer as the basis for transforming your company is the best experience you'll ever have. But, as Whiteley and Hessan illustrate, without enrolling everyone in the vision, the context, and the process, growth remains elusive."

—CRAIG E. WEATHERUP, President and CEO, Pepsi-Cola North America

"Whiteley and Hessan provide the roadmap for managers to forge a trail to greatness for their firm. The authors reveal the ingredients needed to keep an enterprise mindful of its defining purpose. Tools for enhanced financial wizardry, retooled efficient operations, and energized teams abound. Until this book, there has been no guide to the dynamics of growing within your firm's marketplace."

—JEFFREY A. SONNENFELD, Director of the Center for Leadership and Career Studies, Professor of Organization and Management at Goizueta Business School, Emory University

"There is no better way to grow a company today than through customer-centered growth. Richard Whiteley and Diane Hessan will show you how. This is a must read for any conscientious manager."

—KEN BLANCHARD, coauthor, *The One-Minute Manager*

"*Customer-Centered Growth* is a springboard to action—not cold theory and concept, but a warm, well-organized toolkit created from real-life business experiences. This is a customer-centered book, smooth reading and filled with how-to's for the executive who realizes that success can come only from the customer."

—STEPHEN R. BONNER, President, Construction Information Group, The McGraw-Hill Companies

"Contains practical and relevant insights into securing growth through customer focus. A worthwhile read."

—A. COLETTE BURKE, President, Mott's North America

"Richard Whiteley has done it again. He and Diane Hessan have created a winner. By the time you are through with this whirlwind book, you are not only convinced about customer-centered growth, you are also learned in its ways. Its power is in its ability to deeply engrain its messages through a wealth of fascinating examples. It seeps into your psyche."

—STAN DAVIS, author of *Future Perfect*

"In *Customer-Centered Growth,* Richard Whiteley and Diane Hessan have hit on the formula behind today's successful companies and leaders: focusing on consumers and customers, walking the talk with employees, and having a little fun along the way. An easy and relevant fact-based read."

—WILLIAM D. PEREZ, President and COO, Worldwide Consumer Products, S. C. Johnson and Son

"Must reading for the business leader who is serious about turning rhetoric into reality and building an organization that has the capability to truly satisfy customers. Whiteley and Hessan spin a compelling story, weaving critically important principles in a rich fabric of real-world examples. *Customer-Centered Growth* is an exciting contribution to our understanding of how to make the 'voice of the customer' an automatic, everyday input into the process by which an organization makes its decisions."

—ROY D. SHAPIRO, Jesse Philips Professor of Manufacturing, Harvard Business School

"*Customer-Centered Growth* is filled with fresh perspectives and invaluable advice. Hessan and Whiteley clearly lay out the strategies that will help readers to win today and to ensure enduring prosperity as they look to their customers for answers."

—BARRY D. LIBERT, Managing Director, Real Estate Transformation Group, Arthur Andersen LLP

"*Customer-Centered Growth* provides an extensive array of practical insights and techniques for gaining customer closeness without suffering 'closeness' myopia, so common among market leaders."

—JEFFREY A. TIMMONS, Franklin W. Olin Distinguished Professor of Entrepreneurship, Babson College

"Richard Whiteley and Diane Hessan have produced a lucid, lively, and well researched book that is brimming with penetrating insights and profoundly right ideas. It should be required reading for everyone in business."

—BERNARD AGACHE, Managing Director, The Westin Stamford and Westin Plaza Singapore

"*Customer-Centered Growth* is an excellent sequel to *The Customer-Driven Company.* It is easy to read, informative, and dynamic and contains first-class ideas and examples on key areas for customer-focused companies to address. I particularly liked the sections on the critical issues of contact leadership and employee involvement."

—SCOTT BELL, Group Managing Director, Standard Life

"*Customer-Centered Growth* is a powerful antidote for the ills which often beset companies operating in global markets. This book is a wonderful tool that is clear, well written, practical, and useful."

—DR. EDSON DE GODOY BUENO, Chairman of the Board of the Amil Grupo

# CUSTOMER CENTERED GROWTH

To Karen
with best wishes,

Also by Richard Whiteley

*The Customer-Driven Company*

# CUSTOMER CENTERED GROWTH

## Five Proven Strategies for Building Competitive Advantage

RICHARD WHITELEY
and
DIANE HESSAN
THE FORUM CORPORATION

ADDISON-WESLEY PUBLISHING COMPANY
*Reading, Massachusetts   Menlo Park, California   New York   Don Mills, Ontario*
*Harlow, England   Amsterdam   Bonn   Sydney   Singapore   Tokyo   Madrid   San Juan   Paris*
*Seoul   Milan   Mexico City   Taipei*

*Library of Congress Cataloging-in-Publication Data*

Whiteley, Richard C.
Customer-centered growth : 5 proven strategies for building competitive advantage / by Richard Whiteley and Diane Hessan.
p. cm.
Includes bibliographical references and index.
ISBN 0-201-47967-2
ISBN 0-201-15493-5 pbk
1. Consumer satisfaction. 2. Competition. 3. Strategic planning.
I. Hessan, Diane. II. Title.
HF5415.3.W49 1996
658.8'12–dc20 95-51041
CIP



Cover design by Suzanne Heiser
Cover and title page art by James Kaczman
Text design by Irving Perkins Associates
Set in 11-point New Baskerville by Pagesetters, Inc.



1 2 3 4 5 6 7 8 9-MA-0100999897
First paperback printing, May 1997

To Sharon, for her insight and support, and to Jeffrey, Matthew,
and Philip, for being who they are
R.W.

To Paul, Lindsay, Amanda, Mom and Dad
for your unconditional love, for your belief that I could do
anything, and for the sheer joy you have brought to my life
D.H.

# SPECIAL THANKS

We would like to offer special thanks to the following organizations that contributed to the knowledge base from which this book was created.

3M

AlliedSignal, Inc.

Amdahl

American Airlines, Inc.

American Express Company, Inc.

American President Lines, Ltd.

Amil Assistencia Medica International

Apple Computer, Inc.

Applied Materials, Inc.

Arthur Andersen Real Estate Transformation Group

Asea Brown Boveri s.a.

Astra Merck, Inc.

AT&T Corporation

Bank of Boston Corporation

Bell Atlantic Corporation

Bell Atlantic Properties

Best Products

The Black & Decker Corporation

Borough Council of Basingstoke and Deane

British Airways PLC

Byggmeister

The Center for Strategy Research

Central Sprinkler Corporation

Channel 10 Television–Sydney

Charles Schwab & Company, Inc.

Chase Bankcard Services

Chemical Banking Corporation

China Light and Power

Ciba-Geigy Corporation

Citicorp

Citizens Financial Group, Inc.

Club Med

CNA Insurance

Compaq Computer Corporation

Coopers & Lybrand LLP

CUNA Mutual Insurance Group

David Weekley Homes

Delta Air Lines, Inc.

Domino's Pizza

The Dow Chemical Company

Eastman Kodak Company

E.I. DuPont de Nemours & Company

Eli Lilly

Federal Express

Fidelity Investments

Fletcher Music Centers

Ford Motor Company

Ford of Australia

fX Networks

Gemini Consulting
General Electric
General Motors
Gillette
Giordano
Goldman, Sachs Group L.P.
Great Plains Software, Inc.
Hewlett-Packard Company
The Home Depot, Inc.
HSM
IBM
Industry.Net
Intel
Instructional Systems Association
ITT Sheraton Hotels
John Hancock Mutual Life Insurance Company
Johnson & Johnson
Kaiser Permanente
Learning Curve Toys
Levi Strauss & Company, Inc.
Lutron
Manulife Financial
Marriott International, Inc.
Mazda Motor Manufacturing
MBNA America Bank
The McGraw-Hill Companies
MCI Communications
Microsoft Corporation
Midland Bank PLC
Milliken & Company
Moore Corporation
Motorola, Inc.
MSD AGVET, Division of Merck & Co., Inc.
NACCO Materials Handling Group
National Car Rental System, Inc.
National Starch & Chemical Corporation
Nike, Inc.
Northern Telecom, Ltd.
PCA International, Inc.
Peacock Papers
Pepsi-Cola Company
Phelps County Bank
PictureTel Corporation
Pizza Hut, Inc.
Plymouth Rock Assurance
PNC Bank Corp.
Poochies
The Procter & Gamble Company
Quaker Oats
Reebok International, Ltd.
Reynolds Metals Company
Saturn
Scotiabank
Sea-Land Service, Inc.
Sheetz Incorporated
Southern New England Telecommunications
Southwest Airlines Company
Standard Chartered Bank
Standard Life Assurance Company
Steelcase, Inc.
Sun Microsystems
Taco Bell Corp.
Texas Instruments, Inc.
Thomas Cook Travel
Tom's of Maine
Toyota Motor Corporation
U.S. Bancorp
UARCO
U-Haul International
United Technologies Corporation
UNUM Corporation
United Parcel Service
USAA
USF&G Corporation
The Vanguard Group of Investment Companies
Virgin Atlantic Airways, Ltd.
Wal-Mart Stores, Inc.
Wawa, Inc.
Westin Plaza Hotels
Westvaco Corporation
Willow Creek Church
Xerox Corporation

# CONTENTS

## Chapter 1

# THE CHALLENGE: TURNING TURMOIL INTO CUSTOMER-CENTERED GROWTH

ON A WEDNESDAY MORNING in the winter of 1991, readers of the *Boston Herald* were treated to a picture of Steve DiFillippo, normally an agreeable fellow, carving up his American Express card with a butcher knife.

The picture and accompanying front-page article marked the beginning of a business rebellion. A reporter had overheard DiFillippo, the owner of three Boston-area restaurants, complaining bitterly about the high rates he had to pay American Express each time a diner used the much ballyhooed plastic to pay for a meal. The *Herald*'s story, in which DiFillippo and other businesspeople said they found American Express both arrogant and inflexible, struck a nerve. Soon scores of other merchants in and around Boston were joining the revolt, threatening to refuse American Express cards.

Although it had been under attack for several years from Visa, which offered much lower merchant rates, American Express at the time seemed to be sailing serenely along. After all, according to *Fortune* magazine, American Express was one of the "most admired financial services institutions in the world."

But stung by defections, its stock slipping, with the buzz engendered by what would come to be known as the Boston Fee Party spreading far and wide, American Express finally decided it was, indeed, in trouble, and that it could not just wait out the storm. American Express Establishment Services, the division responsible for getting and keeping merchant relationships, went into action, its goal to address the negative perceptions it had previously ignored. And not only to woo back those merchants who had left, but to sign up thousands more.

Did American Express succeed? And how. In an era of downsizing and fierce global competition, the company—in only three years—was able to dramatically alter its fractious relationship with its merchant-customers. In fact, of all charge and credit cards, American Express, once scorned, ended up achieving the highest satisfaction ratings among merchant-customers in its industry. In the process, the company landed some 350,000 new customers, including a number of so-called mega-accounts like Sears and Wal-Mart—accounts that once had seemed entirely out of reach.

What did it do? American Express Establishment Services used the extreme dissatisfaction of its customers as a catalyst for action that not only solved the immediate problems but transformed the entire organization. The customer threw the stone in the water and the ripples spread throughout the company, which became not just customer driven, but customer centered. The change was both challenging and profound—and it enabled the Establishment Services group to simultaneously kick-start growth for short-term results and position itself for sustained growth and profitability in the long run. The company accomplished this by following a learnable and measurable process that can work for any organization, no matter what products or services it offers.

## CUSTOMER-CENTERED COMEBACKS

Just as it worked for American Express, it worked for Compaq Computer Corporation. And it worked for Sheetz, Inc., a chain of convenience stores in Pennsylvania. For each of them, being customer centered was the road to redemption and growth.

In the same year that American Express was jolted by the Boston Fee Party, Compaq Computer fell upon hard times. Sure, it made a great little PC, but other companies were making good machines and offering them for a lot less. Sales dropped precipitously, rivals stole market share, the CEO was bounced, and 14 percent of its people were laid off. Would the company, which had the fastest start-up in the history of the Fortune 500, survive?

The situation was so tentative, so precarious, said one Compaq executive, that it "felt like a stroll at midnight in the South Bronx."

But survive Compaq did, and flourish. Only two years later sales volume had doubled from the previous year to 3 million personal computers, and at the same time manufacturing costs actually dropped by $10 million. By 1994 sales had soared to almost $11 billion, and sales per employee were way up, too—zooming from $305,000 in 1991 to a glorious $805,000 in 1994. Compaq had become customer centered.

The principles that worked for a computer company served equally well in the case of Sheetz, Inc., the convenience store chain, which faced not the threat of going belly-up but a slow decline in profitability and number of customers served.

The alarm sounded for Steve Sheetz, president of the chain of family-owned stores, when an ominous statistic surfaced. The average number of shoppers per day at each Sheetz store had inexplicably dropped from 1,400 to 1,250. The probable cause was revealed in a flurry of interviews and surveys. They showed that Sheetz scored significantly below the average of other area convenience stores in a number of key categories, including "friendly service" and "fast service."

The handwriting was on the convenience store wall. Could Steve Sheetz and his company do anything about it? Indeed they could. Since 1988 Sheetz's sales have more than quadrupled, and that's with the addition of only five new stores.

Today each store in the now highly profitable chain gets 2,150 visits a day. That's a lot—on a yearly basis, to give you some perspective, that's twice the traffic of all the U.S. properties of the Disney Company.

## Customer-Centered Becomes a Reflex

American Express Establishment Services, Compaq Computer Corp., and Sheetz, Inc., became, as we have pointed out, customer centered. Sounds good. But what does it mean? How has being customer centered helped these companies grow while others have turned inward and failed to perform under the smothering effects of one organizational change after another?

Yes, these companies focused on their customers. Yes, they embraced the basic rules of providing superior customer satisfaction. But they took these rules to a new, deeper level. The customer-centered company has the willingness and ability to bring the customer to the very center of its organizational being. When this happens, customers are identified and known. Their needs are communicated throughout the entire organization, and every employee evaluates every process, every task, and every decision by asking one vital question: "How will this add value for our customers?" Whereas in some companies, the customer is "out there" and often forgotten in the trauma of organizational change, customer-centered companies are different. In a customer-centered environment, there is no prodding to remember customers, no checklists to ensure they are included, no wallet-card value statement to remind its carrier who comes first. For work on behalf of the customer there is no "should," only "is."

*Center* means "a hub of activity or influence." For the customer-centered organization this definition holds true. By bringing the customer to its hub, a company makes it easy for every employee, from the CEO to the mail clerk, to know precisely what has to be done to earn that customer's continued loyalty. This process of knowing and acting becomes like breathing—natural, reflexive, impossible to neglect.

Through this process, the company creates world-class quality and services naturally, without extraordinary effort, in any language and for any industry. And like any healthy organism, the company grows.

## HOW CHANGE BRINGS GROWTH

In the past three years, we've talked to, studied, and analyzed hundreds of organizations to find out why some remain in a muddle—confused, dispirited, unable to extricate themselves—while others achieve dramatic growth. We've found fascinating parallels in the overwhelming majority of the successes we've seen, parallels representing beliefs and practices common to those enterprises which have leveraged change into new prosperity.

What's particularly significant about these growing companies is that they are succeeding during an era of unprecedented change, change that is occurring in business throughout the world and with a greater velocity than ever before. In one survey conducted by The Forum Corporation for this book, 98 percent of the managers in nearly 150 organizations reported that their companies were undergoing reengineering or other significant alterations, and some 90 percent said their companies were downsizing.

And stability is not around the corner. A Watson Wyatt worldwide survey of managers in six major countries revealed that 66 percent thought restructuring would either continue at the same pace or accelerate.[1] A recent American Management Association (AMA) survey of over seven hundred organizations concluded the same kind of future—more firms planning on downsizing than ever in the survey's eight-year history.[2] Has all this change—cost-cutting activity and personnel churning—led to better results? Hardly. In our search for successful companies, we found a myriad of struggling firms. In the Watson Wyatt survey, only 22 percent of the managers questioned said they hit their productivity targets. Only 17 percent achieved their customer-satisfaction targets.

And the AMA survey also reported disappointing results. From a sample of over three hundred downsized companies, only 44 percent saw an increase in operating profit; only 25 percent experienced an increase in worker productivity; and a measly 2 percent saw an increase in employee morale.

Our primary research for this book painted a similar picture. In contrast with managers at the companies we'll be describing, an astounding 97 percent of other company leaders we surveyed thought their employees were "fearful." And what did the employees have to say? We found that about 85 percent of those we talked to thought management didn't respect them.

Officials in a Canadian bank came up with this truly depressing statistic: fully half of their employees come to work each day believing they can't make much of a difference in their workplace. And since there is a direct link between employee satisfaction and customer satisfaction, it stands to reason that the consulting firm Mitchell & Co. found the value of stock in companies that downsized to be 26 percent lower than the share value in similar organizations that hadn't.[3]

## Reversing the Downward Spiral

The upshot of this massive change is that the most popular phrase of the 1990s has become "corporate anorexia"—a term that indicates the extreme leanness of organizations and a corresponding weakness of spirit that renders them incapable of getting back on the growth track. The situation can best be illustrated as a downward spiral, as in Figure 1.1.

Increasing competition and price pressures lead to organizations instituting massive changes, the most common of which is cost

**Figure 1.1**
THE DOWNWARD SPIRAL

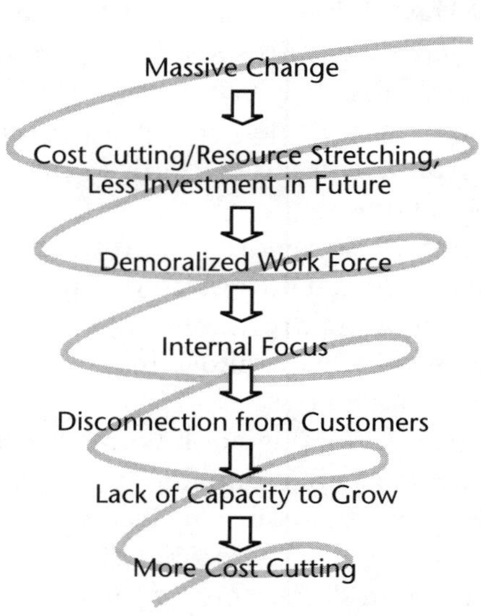


cutting because of its immediate impact on the bottom line. Lowered costs lead to stretching out of resources, lack of investment in the future, and demoralization of the workforce. This leads to a keen internal focus and subsequent disconnection from customers—and, ultimately, a lack of capacity to grow. The spiral keeps going because without the capability to grow, organizations need more cost cutting, and so on and so on.

Yet some organizations have reversed this downward spiral. They are taking steps to do far more than what the harried garment manufacturer in the 1973 movie *Save the Tiger* had as his goal: just to get through another season. These organizations are creating powerful new ways of doing business, ways that have enabled them to nourish and transform customer relationships and create dramatic revenue and profit growth.

They understand and willingly accept the idea that the beat they must march to is sounded by their customers.

## How American Express Became Humble and Flexible

When American Express faced its Boston-made Waterloo, it reacted by first making Thomas O'Neil Ryder, a company veteran, the head of the bewildered Establishment Services business unit. "We were dealing on a daily basis with very angry merchants, merchants who for the first time ... felt they had power with American Express," says Ryder.

In his first six months on the job, Ryder spent half of his time talking to these customers face-to-face. He stopped all sales calls by his business unit's demoralized marketing force, and focused the organization on improving service and researching the special value American Express brought to its customers.

The research revealed that the average bill paid for with an American Express card was 22 percent higher than that of a bank card. What's more, restaurants got extra business from corporate and foreign cardholders (who used no other card), and from the company's belatedly launched but successful program that gave free miles to airline frequent fliers. American Express found that 19 percent of its cardholders carried no other credit card; thus, merchants who refused to honor that card ran the risk of losing a big chunk of business. These were facts that needed to be communicated loudly and clearly to a restless group of customers.

Ryder and his fellow executives rolled up their sleeves. There was a great deal of work to do—work that included listening to customers and reacting to their needs (up to then not a strong point for American Express); providing persistent, clear leadership; offering exemplary service and attention; and fostering collaboration by different teams within the Establishment Services unit. "Arrogant" and "inflexible" were two words that had to go.

Establishment Services was reorganized by customer group instead of by function. Teams were established at the company's New York headquarters to service the needs of the one hundred or so merchants in each of the customer groups. A special task force targeted the mega-accounts, and another worked with the neglected small-business market, developing programs to serve these accounts effectively by telephone.

Like many other business organizations, American Express Establishment Services was forced to downsize (20 percent staff reduction, eighty-two field offices reduced to twenty), but Ryder initiated changes that yielded much more than a lean cost structure.

Reduced costs meant slightly lower fees for merchants, but more importantly, these customers no longer felt friendless and futile when dealing with the giant credit card company. Says Steve DiFillippo: "I got the rate lowered, and that helped. But most of all, the people at American Express listen to me now. They really do."

For revitalized American Express, the Boston Fee Party was no longer an issue. But it remains a somewhat painful reminder that any company that's not customer centered can fall hard and fall fast.

## HOW COMPAQ COMPUTER CHANGED ITS CENTER

When Compaq Computer began to falter, Eckhard Pfeiffer, formerly chief operating officer, was made president and CEO. His first step was aggressive cost cutting. But his long-range goal, the one he felt would not only save the company but make it prosper, was to convert Compaq from an engineering-centered to a customer-centered organization.

Compaq identified a half-dozen or so groups of customers throughout the world that it wanted to serve. It asked them questions and, most importantly, listened to the answers. Compaq focused on what each group wanted. It carefully analyzed the needs of each segment in dozens of countries. For the first time, Compaq was developing clearly defined ways to deliver the products and services that each of those segments wanted.

Compaq engineering would still be superb, but for the first time the criteria that shaped the machines and their pricing would come from users and potential users. Compaq engineers would disassemble a Compaq PC and a competitor's PC side by side, estimate what each feature added to the final cost, then bring customers in and ask them if they were willing to pay the cost for each feature. If the customers said yes, the feature stayed. No, and it was gone.

Compaq salespeople were trained to be much more of a partner to the customer. Telephone support—once offered only from nine to five only by a staff of 150—was available twenty-four hours a day from a staff of 1,000.

As it rebounded from hard times, Compaq did a lot of things right. Primarily, it became customer centered, understanding that its product must be something people really want, not just a device that gets an A-plus from engineering critics.

## How Sheetz Convenience Stores Got Its Customers Back

When Steve Sheetz saw that his stores were losing ground, he realized that his company had become expansion driven instead of being driven by the needs and likes of its customers. The Sheetz family had wanted to add 20 new stores a year to the 150-unit chain, but, family members concluded, that goal was distracting them from the key tasks of the business. New-store openings were cut back drastically.

Sheetz decided to focus the chain's entire effort on achieving excellence in the six areas that caused customers to make convenience-store decisions: location, cleanliness, friendliness of people, fast service, quality of products, and convenient hours. Sheetz learned to listen strategically. For example, he and his management colleagues learned that customers consider cleanliness "lots of light" and that white buildings were perceived as the cleanest.

Sheetz, Inc., rebuilt its stores the way customers said they liked them—white buildings, more and easier-to-use gas pumps, free air for car tires, and more aisle space. Sheetz trained employees and gave them the authority to help achieve excellence in the six key criteria of convenience store choice. Steve Sheetz taught them to use the acronym GUEST, which stands for

**G**reet every customer.
**U**niform clean and complete.
Ask, "Will there be anything **E**lse?"
**S**mile and say ...
"**T**hank you."

In addition, Sheetz instituted special shopping tours. Thirty times a year he would invite three employees from different stores to spend a day with him. They would drive to other Sheetz stores, and while the owner himself waited in the parking lot, the employees would play "mystery shopper," entering the stores as if they were customers. When the expedition found someone acting on all five GUEST principles, Sheetz would come into the store, shake the employee's hand, and take his or her picture to run in the next company newsletter. Not exactly a twenty-one-gun salute, but very effective in building morale, instilling customer-centered behavior, spreading the word, and keeping people on their toes.

Within two years of its refocusing, Sheetz, Inc., increased the share of customers who rated the stores "good" or "excellent" on all six key criteria from 75 percent to 90 percent. In 1994 the industry magazine *Convenience Store Decisions* named Sheetz, Inc., "Convenience Store Chain of the Year."

## FIVE STRATEGIES FOR RENEWAL

There is no secret formula to becoming customer centered. As we've stated, the strategies for achieving this goal are observable and transferable. We've boiled them down to five key points, summarized in Figure 1.2. This figure also shows the difference in the way successful companies and struggling ones execute these strategies. When companies follow the behavior described in the "Customer-Centered Winners" column, they grow. When their activities resemble those in the "Struggling Companies" column, they don't.

The growing, customer-centered organizations we studied come from throughout the world and span a wide variety of industries. Although their businesses were different, the strategies they were using to grow were remarkably similar. We found these successful companies using five strategies to achieve growth.

### STRATEGY 1: SHIFT FROM AN IDENTITY CRISIS TO A LASER-BEAM FOCUS

Virtually every one of the successful companies sought and found a precise understanding of how it could create a customer-centered competitive advantage. Rather than going after every potential source of revenue, these companies discarded assets that didn't add value for customers, cleaned house of bureaucratic policies and procedures, and precisely targeted the customer groups they believed they could serve best. They determined what kind of work they would and would not do for these customers and, in turn, they carefully taught themselves how to fulfill the needs of each kind of customer in their target markets.

USF&G, a large property-casualty insurance company in the United States, made a decision to target services only in the areas that its customers cared about, and sold off no less than thirteen ancillary businesses to allow it to focus on its remaining core: property and casualty insurance. Furthermore, CEO Norm Blake and his team made

**Figure 1.2**

THE ACTIONS THAT SEPARATE CUSTOMER-CENTERED WINNERS FROM STRUGGLING COMPANIES

| | Struggling Companies | Customer-Centered Winners |
|---|---|---|
| **Laser-Beam Focus** | Distracted managers and employees seek business opportunities everywhere | Managers and employees focus laser-like on being best-in-the-world at providing value for well-defined target customers |
| **Hardwiring the Voice of the Customer** | Companies invest heavily in poorly coordinated customer research and take little action on the data | Companies develop clear listening strategies and then hardwire what they learn into the company so employees predictably deliver what customers seek |
| **Universal Collaboration** | Fashionable trends like "total quality" have disrupted traditional ways of work, but no consistent new way of getting things done has emerged | Shared superordinate goals, wise investments in training, and a well-designed infrastructure produce a collaborative way of working that's visible everywhere |
| **Lasting Customer Enthusiasm** | Salespeople pressured to maximize orders; service is a "support function" treated as a necessary evil | The company develops a proprietary customer interaction process that is as much a part of what its brand stands for as the core product itself |
| **Contact Leadership** | Executives try to reposition their companies by force of their own decisions or to "go back to basics" when the basics don't work anymore | Contact leadership emerges as managers come out of their ivory towers to customer work sites and to the places in the organization where real work gets done |

a decision "to play only in areas where we feel we have an unfair advantage" and began to focus on certain customer groups in particular. USF&G's strategy of focusing has brought the firm back from the brink of bankruptcy and has created a net income in 1994 of $232 million, a 41 percent jump over the previous year.

Giordano, a retailer serving the upwardly mobile youth of Southeast Asia, expanded rapidly into the enormous Chinese market—and soon found itself losing money. Company chairman Peter Lau felt that the company had no focus, and he decided that it should emulate the trendy U.S. retailer The Gap, but with even better service. Excessive inventories led to the discovery that Giordano's buyers had been ordering clothing without careful thought, that they seemed to have lost touch with what their Chinese customers wanted. Lau's solution was to force those buyers into focusing on the company's customers by closing all but the largest of Giordano's warehouses. His staff had to squeeze all the stock into the one remaining building, and, as Lau had anticipated, the crowding forced buyers to order more carefully by focusing their buying on a profitable segment of young customers. The strategy turned $13 million of inventory into cash that Lau then used to refurbish the stores in keeping with his Gap vision. Giordano's laser-beam focus is on delivering what its customers want, and growth is extraordinary.

## STRATEGY 2: DON'T JUST LISTEN TO THE VOICE OF THE CUSTOMER. HARDWIRE IT.

Successful companies make sure that they hear the voice of the customer loudly and clearly. Whereas most companies amass an overload of information from any customer—employing all of the latest techniques—and then never use it, customer-centered companies get precise information from customers and then actually *use* the data to shape their own approaches and set their priorities. The customer voice is *hardwired* into the company—that is, it's a permanent fixture, as essential to growth and financial health as paydays, employee attitudes, and production schedules.

Johnson & Johnson's Vistakon Division, which in the last decade has grown from a tiny player to lead the world market for contact lenses, asks production employees to participate in phone calls to customers who have complaints. The company wants these employees to understand firsthand the impact manufacturing errors can have on customers. Its computer system captures every purchase, inquiry, and comment the company receives, sends the information to the relevant parts of the organization for action, and creates a readily accessible database employees can use to analyze what customers like and don't like. The system not only enables Vistakon to act promptly on individual complaints but has also helped the company to quickly change troublesome policies.

American Express's Establishment Services unit has a sophisticated measurement system that tracks all the information necessary to estimate how much a merchant's relationship with American Express is adding to that merchant's bottom line. The unit pays account managers according to this profitability measure as well as overall customer satisfaction. It's another way to make sure the entire organization is concerned about the customer's success as well as its own.

## Strategy 3: Convert Teamitis into Universal Collaboration

The business world has shifted from looking up to looking across, from vertical to horizontal. In today's environment, companies that want to be world class in how they provide products and services for customers must be adaptable and responsive. And this is impossible to achieve without superior collaboration both within and between business units.

The response by most companies to the elimination of the hierarchy has been to install teams throughout organizations, in the hope that many heads are better than one in providing excellence to customers. Although some organizations have achieved extraordinary results with teams, others are suffering from "teamitis," an ailment characterized by teams for teams' sake—bustling with activity but accomplishing little for customers or for their organizations.

The growing companies, on the other hand, were using teams well and were also going further to create environments in which people always collaborated smoothly on behalf of customers—whether they were acting as part of a formal team or not. We call this type of cooperation "universal collaboration," and anything less is what former Booz Allen senior partner John Rockwell calls "peanut butter in the gears."

In the early 1990s Ford Motor Company of Australia was in trouble. New and effective competition created by relaxed import regulations and a nervous mother company in Detroit brought it to the brink.

But President John Ogden turned the situation around in dramatic fashion. After paring thousands of workers from the payroll, he focused on universal collaboration as the way to revive Ford Australia. Using "survival" as a rallying cry, he broke apart the existing "I tell/you do" command-and-control culture. He created self-directed teams and rolled out training specifically designed to teach people how to collaborate in the new environment. One result: Its 1994 introduction of the Australian Falcon was cited as the best product launch in the entire Ford system.

Charles Knott, former managing director of the U.K. Adhesives Division of National Starch and Chemical, and now the head of its Asia Pacific operations, saw big changes coming to his industry in the early 1990s. The changes in customer requirements would mean that employees needed to work together differently—particularly since the Adhesives Group had reduced its headcount by 20 percent that year. Knott began by drastically altering the floor plan of the division's offices, to signal that the culture needed to become more cross-functional, more ad hoc and less hierarchical.

Executives, who had fought for years to get into precious offices with their names on the doors, resisted vigorously. So Knott put his desk smack-dab in the middle of the open floor plan. No more complaining. More important, this single action signaled how people were going to have to work in very different, more collaborative ways—creating immediate energy for the change. The increased collaboration stimulated by this act has enabled Knott's group to improve on-time deliveries from 65 percent to 98 percent. As he states it, "We were able to get a windfall gain instead of a windfall loss."

## STRATEGY 4: TURN CUSTOMER SATISFACTION INTO LASTING CUSTOMER ENTHUSIASM

Most companies today find that it is virtually impossible to create any kind of sustainable competitive advantage based on product alone. The upshot has been a commitment by many companies to be outstanding in interactions with customers. The idea is to beat the competition not just by having a better product but by being better in how that product gets sold, serviced, and marketed at the customer interface. Doing this successfully—going from mere customer satisfaction to outright customer enthusiasm—requires more than just finding out what the competition is doing and doing it better. It requires that companies create breakthroughs in how they interact with customers, and design a way of interacting that makes an indelible impression on customers, one that so utterly distinguishes them from others that it becomes a brand in itself.

In 1992, the leaders of PCA International, a three-thousand-employee portrait studio company, began to reinvent the way they worked with customers. Chief Operating Officer Jan Rivenbark led the mission to create a "Best Photographic Experience" for customers. PCA overhauled everything about how it treated its customers, and created a unique approach which had studio managers thinking about lifetime relationships with customers. This was in stark contrast to PCA's previous interactions, which were cursory at best, and which at worst pressured customers into buying much more than they needed in the short run. In just a brief period of time, customer complaints have declined over 60 percent and PCA's profits have nearly doubled.

In response to customer data that characterized its relationship managers more as product pushers than as customer-oriented problem solvers, Standard Chartered Bank set out to create a new approach to how it worked with its increasingly sophisticated customer base. Training was overhauled, new customer segments were selected, compensation structures were changed, and new philosophies about what the bank wanted to be for its customers were communicated. The result, in just two years, is more than a sixfold increase in the number of customers who rate their Standard Chartered relationship manager as "best in class."

### Strategy 5: Move From Facilitative Leadership to Contact Leadership

The leaders of customer-centered companies were found all over their organizations, from the executive suite to the front lines. No matter where they were, it was clear that these leaders had a different way of behaving than the old model of a facilitative leader who sat back, gave directions, and then "empowered" everyone else to do the work. Leaders in the growth companies were out with customers, on the shop floors, talking to employees, asking questions, and helping people out when they needed an extra pair of hands. Their style of leadership is about contact: working every day out in the trenches to ensure that employees are clear about what their roles are, confident about where the company is going, committed to what is important for customers, and excited about what is possible for the future.

Examples abound of leaders whose everyday, "roll-up-your-sleeves" way of working is moving their organizations to new levels of productivity: from Larry Bossidy of AlliedSignal who met with five thousand employees in his first few months as CEO and who continues to communicate with small groups of customers and employees on a daily basis; to Victoria Rickey of NACCO Materials Handling Group

(NMHG) who spends significant parts of her day working with employees to identify and remove barriers to being world class with customers; to Susan Beckmann, a highly successful MCI manager, who faces the difficult task of getting her employees to change in the midst of strong performance in order to stay ahead of the game—"a little like trying to fix the roof when it hasn't leaked"—and who reinforces the messages every day with a continuous stream of parables and analogies; or to Home Depot's dream team of Bernie Marcus and Arthur Blank, who personally train all store managers, and who spend a large proportion of their time in their stores, finding out how employees and customers think they can improve.

## MANAGE DIFFERENTLY AND *GROW*

Many organizations struggle today because they remain, despite their rhetoric, internally focused. Their unsuccessful scenario is one of business as usual but with fewer people, less cost, and diminished revenue levels. When nothing else is done, dispirited, distrustful, and fearful employees hunker down, avoid standing out, and spend extraordinary conscious and unconscious energy on their own survival. When employees are keeping their heads down, they can't see the company's customers. Maybe they don't even care.

It should be no surprise then that when Forum asked 250 groups of executives from around the world to rate their companies' performance on customer-driven practices, the lowest mark went to the statement, "Serving customer needs takes precedence over serving our internal needs."

The story for flourishing companies is remarkably different. Yes, they too may have downsized and, in the process, broken implied promises of career-spanning employment. They too may have suffered—and caused—their share of fear and anxiety. And it's quite likely that, in the midst of a business maelstrom, they forgot to focus on the all important—their customers. But these companies were different because they saw the very turmoil that was upsetting them as an opportunity. Balancing short-term survival concerns with a longer-term view of their future, they quite literally reinvented themselves.

We believe that almost any organization can find the same path to a prosperous, customer-centered existence if the methods described in this book are followed. To research it, we talked to managers and experts in nearly two hundred companies on six continents. We used Forum Corporation research that includes interviews with thousands of other managers, professionals, analysts, and specialists. We asked this question: "Given that many companies have learned the basics of how to create customer satisfaction, yet most aren't growing, what distinguishes those that grow from those that don't?" We looked for specific evidence from real experience. The concept of customer-centered growth, and the five strategies, are the result.

We weren't surprised to find these same themes appearing not only in industries and countries we knew well, but also in industries and parts of the world we knew little about. Where did we find the five strategies? Just about everywhere we found success.

So we can state with confidence that this book is about what is *actually* working. It doesn't tout some trendy theory dreamed up in academia, but represents principles hammered out on the anvil of world marketplaces. Throughout, we've done our best to support this assertion with research and real-world examples.

In this book, we will deal with each of the five strategies in turn. For each, we'll offer graphic stories that will communicate both the spirit and specifics of the customer-centered organization. We'll lay out the principles that customer-centered organizations follow, and describe the specific steps you can take to make each of the strategies come alive in your organization. We've also compiled what we call a Toolkit, excerpted from some of The Forum Corporation's most popular training programs, to help you use these strategies in your work. The Toolkit appears at the back of the book.

We believe that all over the world, businesses are at the edge of unprecedented opportunity. In *The Customer-Driven Company,* published in 1991, Richard Whiteley wrote of the daunting challenges then facing most organizations and pointed out that many would require significant reorientation just to survive.

The message of this book builds on and expands the message of *The Customer-Driven Company. Customer-Centered Growth* takes into consideration the special turbulence and disruption of the last few years and describes what's necessary to recover and grow. The message of the book is an encouraging one. It is that companies that can learn to be customer centered will have a remarkable opportunity to grow and prosper and take their well-earned place in a dynamic, powerful, and highly competitive world marketplace.

Chapter 2

# FROM IDENTITY CRISIS TO LASER-BEAM FOCUS

*You have to understand what it is that you are better at than anybody else and mercilessly focus your efforts on it.*

—ANDREW GROVE[1]
CEO, INTEL

YOU COULD SAY THAT Fletcher Music Centers and Tune Town were the retail version of the Hatfields and the McCoys. Both music stores stocked it all: guitars, portable keyboards, pianos, home organs, and sheet music—and they competed fiercely, often in the same Florida malls. Fletcher and Tune Town, along with other regional music stores in competition with them, were stuck in a game of tit-for-tat. For example, if one gave five free lessons with each instrument sold, another might up the ante to, say, seven. This game lasted twenty years—until famine struck.[2]

The 1970s were good to music stores, largely because of the popularity of home organs. Both Fletcher and Tune Town saw demand for organs swell with the introduction of integrated circuits. For the first time, customers could create impressive music almost instantly. But as the technology progressed in the 1980s, the marketplace changed dramatically.

For some reason the "improved" organs simply weren't selling. "We weren't smart enough at that point," says Fletcher president John Riley, "to realize that the one reason customers were so resistant to new organs was that engineers were building them based on technology rather than on what people wanted." Fletcher tried forcing the issue with customers, but, no question about it, the technology was simply scaring potential customers away—customers whose average age, everyone in the industry agreed, was clearly over fifty-five. Annual U.S. sales of new home organs plunged from a high in the 1970s of 250,000 units down to a mere 14,000 by 1990, and business was so slow that sales of used organs surpassed the sales of new.

What could Fletcher do? As sales of their most profitable item, new organs, declined, most music stores turned to two recently introduced products—portable keyboards and Korean grand pianos. The industry hoped that portable keyboards, which held most of the electronics of an organ in a far smaller, less expensive package, would seed the market and spark a revival in sales of full-sized organs.

But the thinking was flawed. It turned out that keyboards appealed mostly to kids, who started off tinkering but then lost interest after a few months.

Low-priced Korean grand pianos proved popular with young and affluent baby boomers just setting up their households. But pianos were a commodity—that is, produced by a number of manufacturers—and price competition was wicked. Sales of grand pianos, portable keyboards, and a number of other products pushed Fletcher's gross revenue higher and higher, but their profits, says John Riley, "were shrinking alarmingly." By the end of the 1980s the situation was more than just alarming. Fletcher executives knew something had to be done.

## FLETCHER FINDS ITS NICHE

Something was done—and to many it seemed a bizarre move. The company decided, as Riley explains, "to focus exclusively on what we do best—and that was to sell organs." Competitor Tune Town's employees were flabbergasted as they watched Fletcher liquidate its baby grands, keyboards, and other instruments. No one seemed to be buying organs anymore, and yet that's where Fletcher was betting its future.

Was it a bizarre move? No. Despite the many ups and downs in the music market, Fletcher knew, the one constant was that home organ sales continued to be its single most profitable offering. Why? Organs were a specialty marketing item. Customers needed to be convinced that they wanted one, but once they had been, they rarely haggled over price. And organ buyers were repeat buyers: As they became educated, they would upgrade to more sophisticated models which would enhance their newfound skills.

Tune Town's and Fletcher Music's lack of focus had spread them too thin. Pushing commodities such as pianos required skills different from educating consumers to the benefits of home organ ownership. Trying to offer both, the music centers failed to develop an area of expertise valuable to customers.

Fletcher understood this, and made a survival decision to focus on what it did best and what customers valued most—to the exclusion of all else. In so doing, the company found new life, a new market, and a redefinition of who—and what—it was. Profits, which had hit bottom at $300,000 prior to Fletcher's changes, climbed to $4 million annually within five years, and Riley expects to finish 1995 with a $9 million pretax profit.

## A TIGER BY THE TAIL

The critical difference between Tune Town and Fletcher Music Centers was that Fletcher looked to its customers to provide a specific, customer-mandated direction. From the time of Adam Smith, wise business thinkers have recognized that effectiveness often comes from specialization. Specialization only becomes profitable, however, when it reflects customer desires. The Fletcher–Tune Town saga provides a dramatic illustration of how choosing a customer and focusing on the needs of that customer can produce explosive growth in today's economy.

Soon after he decided to focus on organ buyers, Bob Fletcher, chairman of Fletcher Music Centers, set out to discover exactly who those customers were and what motivated them to buy. He brought in his good friend Bob Zadel, a retired music store executive and industry consultant from California, to help. One thing Zadel had noticed was that the audiences for organ demonstrations and concerts were getting grayer and grayer. He suggested to Fletcher that they consider focusing on older folks.

As Fletcher Music moved closer to customers through direct interviews and focus groups with salespeople, it uncovered three startling discoveries.

- First, customers were not just fifty-five plus. *Their average age was seventy.* According to Zadel, "We were the first to realize the exciting potential of the retired population. Not only does the elderly market control more wealth than any other segment of the population, with more time to learn new skills, it's also the fastest growing segment in the United States."
- The second revelation was that these seniors really were struggling with the technology, and no amount of sales ability would overcome that barrier. Older people were unable to read the minuscule type on the newer organ buttons; had a hard time placing their fingers on the narrow keys; were not interested in having to push three keys at the same time to make a reggae beat when all they wanted was to push one button for ragtime; and wanted an organ to look like a beautiful piece of living room furniture—not like a gadget out of *Star Trek.*
- The last startling discovery revealed through study of Fletcher's customers, according to Riley, "was that these people got really involved. It was more than just music to them. It was companionship, continued achievement, self-worth. Once we finally realized this, we knew we really had a tiger by the tail."

Responding to these findings, the company made "Lifetime Free Lessons" the cornerstone of its new package. Although Fletcher had always offered free lessons with a home organ purchase, the importance and structure of the lessons had changed dramatically. Says Riley: "Seniors started coming in not so much for music as to rub elbows with peers who had the same wants and needs. Many of these retirees had left forty years of friends and family and church to come down here to Florida. We noticed that if the wives were having a lesson, the husbands would meet together for coffee at the mall. So we started having potluck dinners, concerts, breakfast clubs. We wanted our store to be the center of social activity. We realized we were no longer in the music business; we were in the 'lifestyle-enhancement business' and the music was just a part of that."

Another problem surfaced. As sales of home organs steadily grew, Fletcher started worrying about supply. Manufacturers were slowly discontinuing the models popular with Fletcher's customers, replacing them with high-tech versions. After extensive interviews with customers and salespeople, Fletcher created the Estey, the first organ developed by and for senior citizens. The Estey was designed to be a return to an uncomplicated traditional organ. It had simple, easy-to-read buttons indicating rhythms such as big band or ragtime and discarded the more contemporary ones. With wood cabinetry, a roll top, and a padded bench, the Estey was an organ that would easily blend into a standard living room.

The company knew what it wanted but had trouble finding a manufacturer who would custom make the organ rather than just slap the Fletcher name on an existing model. After Japanese manufacturers refused, Fletcher finally found a small manufacturer in Italy to produce it to the company's specifications. How'd it do? The first shipment was expected to last one year. The Estey sold out in three months.[3]

### CLARITY OF PURPOSE CHANGED EVERYTHING

The challenge of survival forced the leaders at Fletcher Music Centers to reconceive the company's business according to the desires of its most profitable customers. This cogent strategy drove a dramatic expansion of value. And those target customers changed everything about Fletcher: *what* it sells ("life-style enhancement"); *whom* it sells to (senior citizens); *how* it sells ("educating with lifetime free lessons"); and *where* it sells (expanding to other retirement communities). Customer desires not only changed what Fletcher did, but who it was. Fletcher, since changing its focus, has become the world's largest retailer of home organs.

How did Tune Town fare? Not so well. Fletcher's rival continued to slug away trying to do everything and be everything in the music business until July of 1991, when sales had collapsed to such a degree that the company was forced to file for bankruptcy protection under Chapter 11. Two months later it was Fletcher's turn to watch Tune Town liquidate, except this time it was not just unprofitable product lines that were eliminated, but the entire company.

## CREATE A DRAMATIC EXPANSION OF VALUE BY RECONCEIVING YOUR BUSINESS

Something important happened to Fletcher during its redefinition effort. The focus on organs started out to some extent as a cost-cutting move—getting rid of unprofitable items. But Fletcher Music made this exercise a search for identity. John Riley, Bob Fletcher, and Bob Zadel asked serious questions, paradigm-challenging questions. They examined their purpose and the value they brought to their customers. The company needed a clear direction, and it had the wisdom to go directly to the source—its customers.

Fletcher's success has relevance for *every* business, particularly those that have cut back operations in the last few years. What starts out as an effort to survive or stay competitive by "getting the waste out" or "reducing cycle time" or "increasing productivity" must become a process of asking fundamental questions about the purpose of the organization and the value it brings to its customers. Otherwise you will have missed the opportunity to find the new and exciting competitive advantage that lies beyond a lean cost structure. It is a matter of starting from scratch and reexamining who you are and what you do strictly according to what your customers value.

## Large-Scale Focusing: Wal-Mart vs. Kmart

If Fletcher and Tune Town were feisty rivals, how about the competition between Wal-Mart and Kmart? These two chain stores have been slugging it out for years, and right now Wal-Mart is in the ascendancy. Luck? Superior strategy? What?

Wal-Mart sells just about everything under the sun, from suntan lotion to thermal underwear, but that doesn't keep it from being singularly focused on an unswerving strategy: value and convenience. Where Fletcher Music avoided selling products that were price-driven commodities, Wal-Mart has focused on exactly that. Value and convenience are what matter most to Wal-Mart shoppers, and therefore Wal-Mart puts its money where its customers' most critical desires are.

Wal-Mart's target customers define value as well-stocked shelves, dependably low prices, variety, and a smooth and pleasant shopping experience. Wal-Mart has responded by investing in a world-class operating system that delivers that value seamlessly. Its sophisticated computer programs keep real-time tabs on inventory, enabling the chain to keep shelves stocked and prices low. The system also prevents pricing errors at checkout.

While Wal-Mart invested in operations and technology, Kmart invested huge sums in developing its own brands and on diversification into bookstores, sports stores, office supply stores, and the like. Were these what customers asked for? No, but they obviously seemed like a good idea to Kmart management.

Because Kmart was busy buying bookstores, it couldn't deliver operational efficiencies as effectively as its rival. Kmart may have had a good brand in, say, Jaclyn Smith clothing, but it wasn't worth buying if checkout lines were bottlenecked by price checks. Advertised specials weren't worthwhile if the discount didn't ring up at the register. And Kmart wasn't worth visiting if customers feared having to stand in one more line, maybe at the service desk this time, waiting for a rain check on specials that had sold out.

Shoppers noticed that Wal-Mart never seemed to run out of anything. And that was a big draw for ex-Kmart shoppers.

### ATTENTION KMART

Recently Kmart divested itself of such irrelevant businesses as OfficeMax, the Sports Authority, and Borders Bookstores, but it took a stockholder uprising[4] and the ouster of CEO Joseph Antonini to bring about the change.

Kmart stockholders are hoping the chain can effectively play catch-up. But while Kmart has been trying to find its way back to what matters most—customer desires—Wal-Mart's customer-centered strategy has taken the chain from sales 40 percent less than Kmart's in 1987 to more than double Kmart's today.

## FIGURING OUT HOW TO BE GREAT

It is the job of leaders to discover exactly what customers value most and which of those valued products or services their organizations can deliver as well as, or better than, the best in the world. That knowledge can revolutionize everything about an organization. It can be the "on" button to set in motion a full-throttle turnaround and growth.

Why is this one effort so important? When a clear, specific, customer-driven purpose is effectively communicated to everyone in an organization, it coalesces dispersed power and direction by saying, "We know you have a million things tugging at you for attention, but these, say, three things are utterly important to our customers and therefore to us." It tells employees what may be worth worrying over and, just as importantly, what is not.

It also clearly defines for customers what specific values they can expect your organization to deliver flawlessly every time. Peter Viner, managing director of Channel 10 Television in Sydney, Australia, has increased profits fivefold within thirty months with a well-orchestrated, focused strategy aligned to its most profitable audience, viewers between the ages of twenty and thirty. Viner repositioned Channel 10 from what he called a second-rate imitator into a polished, youthful, and urbane trendsetter. This new focus and strategy have encouraged spending by advertisers because, according to Viner: "If the customers feel that you have got a strategy and the strategy is being executed well in that now you're focused and there's some stability in your organization, they're much more likely to spend with confidence."

## Get the Right Answers by Taking the Right Steps

The goal of the steps you'll find on the following pages is to enable your organization to ask the right questions, questions that will help you discover in what area your organization can become unbeatable. These questions will give you clarity of purpose comprised of:

- A laser-beam focus that springs forth from a match between the critical values of your target customers and the core expertise of your organization.
- An ever-evolving, focused strategy which continually fine-tunes that match and enables you to adapt to changing customer desires.
- An explicit, phased plan that guides and signals the stages within the strategy.

As Taco Bell chief John Martin notes, making sure your organization is on the right road is by far the most important work you'll ever do. "When you're on the right road and the wind is behind you," says Martin, "you can make all kinds of mistakes."[5] A clear understanding of precisely where to become the best will keep small mistakes from escalating into crippling errors.

The world constantly tempts businesses to do things that they can't do well. During the 1980s many companies lost focus. Advertising firms became marketing consultants. Automobile companies acquired car-rental companies. Banking and insurance companies became "financial supermarkets." Large multinational companies accumulated acquisitions unrelated to core strengths.

Today, the reverse is true. Hardly a business day goes by without some company reporting that it is shedding something not related to its core business to sharpen its direction. Jettisoning poorly chosen and burdensome business segments may help, but such an action alone will hardly put you on the growth track. The downsized companies that are growing are the ones that have learned to focus with a laser-beam intensity on what their customers need.

A business that is clear about what its customers value makes very different cost-reduction and cost-allocation decisions than a company that is worried only about making short-term budget numbers look good. The effectiveness of 10 percent across-the-board cost cutting has declined. That "solution," despite its simplicity, fails to recognize that some places have more waste than others, while some need increased funding. The executive who calls for uniform cost cuts across the organization is saying quite publicly, "I do not know how value is created in my company." It is an obsessive focus on the critical things that customers value that will keep your organization from dabbling unprofitably.

Resolving to do more of the right things is easy, of course. The challenge is to figure out what the right things are. Discovering what to obsess over is essentially a matter of following these four steps:

STEP ONE: *Identify Which Customers You Really Want*

Begin with a clear understanding of who your customers are and which ones are the most profitable.

STEP TWO: *Identify What Your Targeted Customers Deeply Value*

Get to the heart of what they are really buying (as opposed to what you think you are selling).

STEP THREE: *Discover a Laser-Beam Focus*

The area of convergence between the critical few things that your profitable customers value most and those things that you can do best is where a laser-beam focus can be found. This focus then allows you to create your value-driven strategy.

STEP FOUR: *Create an Organization-wide Obsession with Focus*

To become consistent and successful, a laser-beam focus requires an organization-wide obsession. To drive this obsession intentionally up and down the organization, create a well-signaled track that explicitly spells out stages toward the implementation of the goals. And then? Communicate, communicate, communicate.

## STEP ONE: IDENTIFY WHICH CUSTOMERS YOU REALLY WANT

*Begin with a clear understanding of your entire customer base—in particular of those customers who are the most profitable.*

Many organizations, even today, never really understand who their customers are. In England, we recently met Katrine Sporle, chief executive of the borough council of the small towns of Basingstoke and Deane. She's trying to make borough officials "customer-driven," and she declares that even the people the town is suing for back taxes are "customers."

Sound a bit silly? Indulgent? Well, maybe. But in declaring tax delinquents to be customers, Ms. Sporle is saying that even when the government sues citizens, those people are still the judges of officials' performances. She most certainly does expect the officials in the tax office to treat nonpayers with honor. Her answer to the question "Who are our customers?" is crystal clear: She really means that customers include all citizens with whom the borough council staff interacts.

### ASK, WHO ARE OUR MOST PROFITABLE CUSTOMERS?

Fletcher Music Centers revolutionized its direction and profitability by targeting those the company could serve better than anyone else, and then excluding all other markets. Fletcher executives made their choice clear with murals throughout the stores of healthy, happy senior citizens playing the organ. The identity of their customer was certain—to Fletcher employees and to their customers. By contrast, competitor Tune Town thought its customer was anyone who played any kind of music. This misconception cost the company its corporate life.

The reliable way to choose a profitable direction is to select the group or groups of customers you wish to serve, and then decide that you will meet those customers' needs in such a flawless manner that they will be compelled to do business with you.

Start by asking, Who are my most profitable customers? That is a good clue as to whom you are able to serve best.

## PRIDE AND PERCEPTION

Black & Decker is a household brand name. This, surprisingly, can be a distinct disadvantage. In fact, it allowed the company to get stuck with customers who weren't very profitable.

The company's most profitable customers—tradespeople and industrial contractors—are willing to pay two to three times the price that a homeowner will pay for a drill. But they're not willing to pay that much for something they perceive as an upper-end version of a do-it-yourself product. Tradespeople take pride in their tools. They think a tool intended for amateurs must be of lower quality.

After a decade of losing contractor sales to the prestigious industrial tool manufacturer Makita, Black & Decker decided to once again actively romance its most profitable customers. The company took some tools of superior quality out of its existing Black & Decker industrial power-tool line and reintroduced them as DeWalt, a discontinued brand the older tradesmen had known and respected as a quality product, and which Black & Decker had acquired decades earlier.

The only major difference between "high-end" Black & Decker tools and DeWalt tools is the name, the color (DeWalt's are a bright construction-hat yellow), the price (DeWalt tools are priced 10 percent higher than Makita and much higher than their Black & Decker parent clone), and where they are sold.

According to Joseph Gallie, head of Black & Decker's North American power-tool division, "Price denotes quality. If you target the do-it-yourselfer, you lose the tradesman."[6] But, it turns out, not vice versa. Quite the opposite, in fact. Half of all DeWalt sales come from do-it-yourselfers, who, like the tradespeople, equate price with quality. By paying attention to their most profitable customer, DeWalt outsold its parent Black & Decker by 100 percent ($300 million in sales vs. $150 million) within two years of its reintroduction into the market.[7] As Black & Decker continues to prosper, it will also continue to obsess over meeting the future needs of tradespeople and dedicated do-it-yourselfers.

## SEGMENTING CUSTOMERS

Segmentation is a means of grouping together similar customers. Companies can't be all things to all people, but they can be extraordinary for one or more critical groups.

Segmenting can be done in many ways—by geography, age, industry, buying frequency, or the like. Although we don't recommend ignoring these methods, they are often the easy way out. The customer-centered way to segment is to differentiate people by their different needs for the products and services they buy.

Take the classic retail bank segmentation shown in Figure 2.1.[8] On the vertical axis, you plot customers by whether or not they like coming into the branch. On the horizontal axis, you plot the customer's belief about their need for a bank.

Suddenly, customer needs become clear. "A" customers, even if they are wealthy, may be too difficult to pursue. As it turns out in most retail banks, "B" customers tend to have the least money and yet are the most expensive and time-consuming to service. "C" customers want a bank but need service. And "D" customers will buy almost anything if you figure out how to serve them. Such customers will often ask, "How does it happen that I have $600,000 in a Vanguard fund and I've never been to Philadelphia—and yet I have $4,000 in my bank and I have to come in to the branch if I need more than $300?"

Needs-based segmentation asks the key question, How can you organize your operation to meet your customer's needs? The answer provides the chance to anticipate customer needs before customers even know they have them.

---

A deeper understanding of customers revealed that U-Haul's fiercest competition was not Ryder or any other truck rental firm, it was the other 50% of the potential market—what chief executive Joe Shoen calls "the owned and borrowed" segment.[9] Shoen now focuses on those who would borrow a brother's truck or cram furniture into the back of their minivan, rather than renting. The company markets its vans as a preferable alternative to your own or your brother's vehicle.

---

**Figure 2.1**

RETAIL BANK CUSTOMER SEGMENTATION

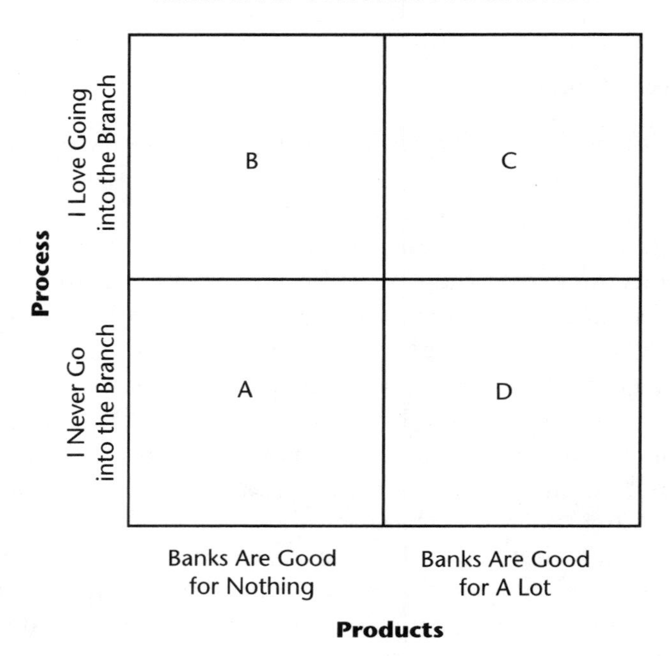


## STEP TWO: IDENTIFY WHAT YOUR TARGET CUSTOMERS DEEPLY VALUE

*Get to the heart of what they are really buying, not what you think you are selling.*

Understanding what your most profitable customers really value often becomes a fervent search for identity that has more to do with *who your customers think you are* as an organization than *what you do* specifically.

It was an inspired understanding of how their customers made travel decisions that led Southwest Airlines executives to see themselves more in competition with buses and cars than with other airlines. Consider the logic. Southwest's shorter routes meant that it acts more like a bus than a traditional airline. And like a bus it features no assigned seating, less-expensive tickets, and a relaxed, informal attitude on the part of employees. Driving a car can be a stressful, tiring experience, and Southwest tries to make each flight a relaxed, pleasant experience. In fact, Southwest sees itself as being in the entertainment business, and their flight attendants have been known to pull pranks like jumping out of overhead compartments—pranks that might not be tolerated in another, more traditional airline. (*Note: Southwest's pilots and copilots do not do this, particularly when the plane is in flight.*)

Providing inexpensive, on-time, reliable, enjoyable flights has propelled Southwest Airlines from a small regional carrier—starting with three planes in 1971—to a dominant player in the airline industry with 144 airplanes in thirty-four cities from California to Maryland. During the first four years of the 1990s, the airline industry lost a grand total of $10 billion. During the same period, Southwest netted $335 million in earnings.[10] In fact, Southwest was the only airline to turn a profit.

## You May Be Surprised by the Business You're In

Prism Inc., a Johnson Wax Company, learned from its customers that it was not so much in the pest-elimination business as in the insurance business. How's that again? As Prism sees it, the primary concern of customers such as restaurants and hotels is not pests per se, although, certainly, they don't care for creepy-crawly things. No, the biggest fear these owners have is loss of revenue. Bugs and rodents scare away customers and put boards of health in a close-down frame of mind.

Because Prism understood this, it created an extraordinary service guarantee, in essence, an insurance policy. It guarantees customers no pests. Period. Suppose the customer has kept his or her place clean but, despite his efforts, pests appear. Prism will not only refund the customer's monthly service fee during that period, but will pick up the room and meal charges of complaining guests and send them each a note of apology. If a facility is ever closed down by the board of health, Prism will reimburse the customer for the amount of the fine and provide support in dealing with the authorities. Now *that's* an insurance policy.[11]

## KODAK: START WITH A TARGET AND WORK BACKWARD

New business directions become successful when they come from the customer's point of view. To discover what your customers' deepest values are, ask:

—What are you really selling?
—What are your customers really buying?

Dig deep. For example, people don't just buy a car for transportation. They also buy it as an extension of who they are. In Hong Kong, a dog is not just a pet; it is very much an extension of its owner's image. When you walk your dog in Hong Kong, you are saying, "This is what I'm like as a person." The more expensive your dog, the higher your status.

It's been suggested, for instance, that Kodak once marketed its products by first "shooting the arrow and then drawing the target around it."[12] Yes, that's a sure way to always get a bull's-eye. But it also produces a stream of new products and services searching for customers—often unsuccessfully.

Today, Kodak starts with a target market and works backward, developing technology and products as a response to, not as a precursor of, customer preferences and desires. For example, its Consumer Imaging Division has discovered three "life-stage" market segments: youth, parent, and fifty-plus. It develops and markets products accordingly.

For the youth segment, Kodak encourages children to take photographs by targeting their needs for simplicity and success. The company created Photo fX packs for children ages eight to fourteen which include an easy-to-use 35-mm camera, batteries, and an activity album. Schools participating in Kodak's "Cameras in the Curriculum" receive a Fun Saver single-use camera and photofinishing for each student while the teacher receives a Kodak Star. The class is also invited to tour a photofinishing operation.

Parents with children eighteen or younger take 30 percent more pictures than the average household. They are interested in speed and convenience and quality, yet most are not serious photographers. Their interest is more in memories than in art. This explains the wild success of Kodak's single-use cameras, which provide reliable, hassle-free snapshots. No more worrying that the batteries are dead or the film isn't loaded. What's more, the pictures the Fun Saver Camera produces are often so good they astonish customers.

To tap the fifty-plus market, Kodak capitalizes on brand recognition. These customers have the most free time, the largest disposable income, and the most loyalty to brand names. Kodak has set up a program for retirees called Kodak Ambassador, bringing together those knowledgeable about picture-taking with those who are interested in learning. A partnership with Holland Cruise Line conducting onboard picture-taking seminars was one of the cruise line's most successful partnership efforts ever.

## STEP THREE: DISCOVER A LASER-BEAM FOCUS

*Build your future at the intersection of the critical few things that your customers value most and that you do best.*

You now have a clear picture of your entire customer base. You know which profitable customers to target and the critical few things that they deeply value. Now you are ready to figure out where to create excellence by bringing your own expertise into the mix.

### THE FOCUSING FRAMEWORK

The Focusing Framework (Figure 2.2) helps you to determine what you need to obsess over and what you can forget about. Plot what each profitable segment values on the horizontal axis of a grid similar to the one in the figure. (If you need help here, chapter 3 will contain details on how to learn what your customers value.) Next, plot your key capabilities on the vertical axis. If you can't immediately pinpoint these capabilities, try answering the question, What do you do that other companies would want to benchmark?

The matrix reveals the intersection of customer values and your organization's expertise. Each box requires different strategies.

**_Box 1: Weak Customer Value/Weak Capability_**
**_Action: Stop_**

*If it doesn't add value, stop it;*
*if it makes sense for our customers, do it.*

—BOB HARBAGE, CHAIRMAN
UARCO

**Figure 2.2**

THE FOCUSING FRAMEWORK

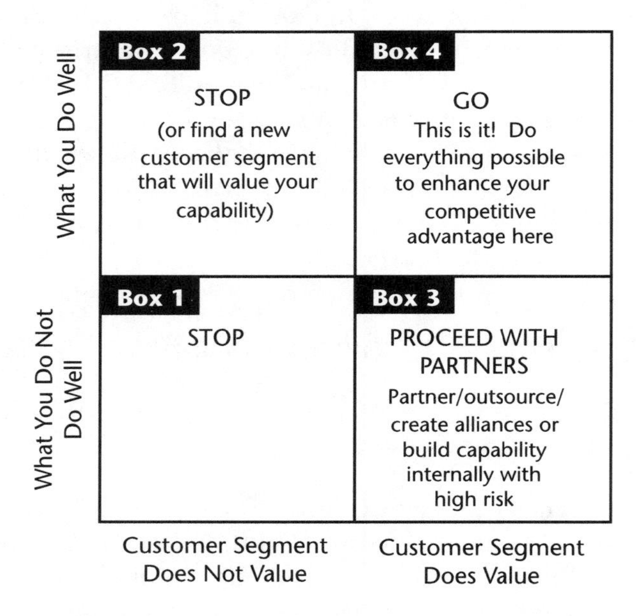


Some companies do something poorly—and customers don't want it anyway. That is a source of waste and it consumes precious resources. Consider the sad saga of Greyhound's "Trips." May it rest in peace.

Greyhound was praised by Wall Street when it announced that it would initiate Trips, a computerized operating system that promised to bring America's largest bus company into the twentieth century. Downsizing and cutbacks of personnel, routes, and fleets at Greyhound had taken their toll on customer service. But the hope was that Trips would make up for it. Computerization would allow efficient fleet scheduling, and a sophisticated reservation system would elevate bus travel standards to those of air travel. An obvious winner.

Optimistic investors helped Greyhound's stock nearly double in the six months after the announcement of Trips. But soon after the system's initial installation, the stock dived on the news that ridership had fallen 12 percent in one month.

To put it mildly, something had gone wrong. Greyhound, it turns out, was not very good at implementing a computerized system. Destinations were missing from the database, a single keystroke could take up to forty-five seconds to register on the system, and tickets could take up to five minutes to print. The six-dollars-an-hour "customer service associates" often had to write the tickets by hand.[13]

Bus passengers suffered countless frustrations. Computer-generated snafus sometimes stranded them in terminals. They waited in dreary lines while ill-trained employees tried to figure out how to solve massive glitches. At the Port Authority in New York, competing bus lines capitalized on the situation by sending over spare buses. Lost luggage piled up in terminals across the country, resulting in beleaguered customers.

Not only did Trips require Greyhound to do something it wasn't good at (running a computer system), but there was no evidence that Greyhound customers even wanted computerized reservations. Customers who use buses earn, on average, seventeen thousand dollars a year. Many don't have credit cards with which to make advance reservations even if they want to. They have a simpler system. On the rare occasion when a bus is full, would-be passengers wait for the next one. They're used to that. Low-tech, just-in-time ticketing, while imperfect, worked just fine for Greyhound customers. In the final analysis, Trips was unnecessary.

Successful focusing involves getting out of Box One: Weak Customer Value/Weak Capability. Kodak now understands this. A substantial percentage of the revenue from each little yellow box of Kodak film is profit, but forays into other markets, such as medical equipment (the Clinical Diagnostics business that Kodak sold to Johnson & Johnson), kept Kodak from concentrating on its most profitable product. In the 1980s, Kodak began to lose market share to Fuji Film and others, going from 80 percent down to 70 percent within five years.[14]

When George Fisher began the turnaround at Kodak, one of his first actions was to create a strategy focused almost exclusively on what Kodak did well and what customers valued. It focused on imaging to the exclusion of all other businesses. Fisher quickly sold off the nonimaging health divisions—Sterling Winthrop; L & F Products, and Clinical Diagnostics—which accounted for a total of 23 percent of Kodak's 1993 sales. The result: Kodak got out of Box One.

***Box 2: Weak Customer Value/Strong Capability***
***Action: Stop or find a new customer segment.***

*If it's not worth doing, it's not worth doing well.*

If you do something well that customers don't want, your task is to stop doing it or find a segment that does value your capability. Smith Corona made a good typewriter, but computers have made mechanical typewriters about as valuable as high-button shoes. Not surprisingly, Smith Corona filed for Chapter 11 in mid-1995. It's now seeking a turnaround by leveraging other areas of expertise such as its knowledge of small office equipment.

And, certainly, a strategy of bringing customers of a bank back to the branch office lobby—instead of having them use ATMs—would seem, on the surface, just as outdated as pushing typewriters in the age of computers. Yet a successful banking strategy has been built on doing just that. Citizens Financial Group in Boston knew that one of its key capabilities was its ability to deliver superior "banking the old fashioned way"—with real people dealing with customers. CEO Larry Fish went looking for a segment that would still value such a capability—people who wanted to come into the branch instead of using an ATM. He found it in "mid-market customers," customers who don't have personal investment advisers and tend to use a single bank for all their banking needs.

Fish has found that a specialty in face-to-face branch banking, "banking with a heart," has increased the number of services he can sell. Citizens has doubled assets in the last three years to $10.3 billion. Correctly targeting a customer segment that would particularly appreciate Citizen's core strengths has made an "old-fashioned" skill a modern moneymaker.[15]

***Box 3: Strong Customer Value/Weak Capability***
***Action: Proceed with partners or build capability internally.***

*We outsource all bad work. It gets us focused on innovation.*

—SUSAN CRAMM, FORMER CIO
TACO BELL[16]

As companies focus more and more on becoming the "best in class" in serving their customers' needs, they look to find partners who have capabilities they lack. They will go anywhere to increase the value customers derive from their products and services. They'll partner with customers, make alliances with competing firms, or outsource entire functions and departments. Building capabilities in-house or buying the capability via acquisitions can be risky. More often, the preferred alternative is to partner with others who can help you respond to the customer desire with excellence.

The most extreme version of such partnering is outsourcing. Today, we see outsourcing of accounting, manufacturing, information management, recruiting, and marketing. Three out of ten U.S. industrial firms outsource over 50 percent of their manufacturing activities,[17] and a Coopers and Lybrand study found that companies that outsource generate revenues 22 percent higher and have sales prospects 25 percent better than non-outsourcing counterparts.[18] But the number one reason companies outsource is to free them to focus on what they do best and leave what Susan Cramm calls "bad work," work that isn't central to what they do, to those who can do it with excellence.

**Top Ten Reasons Companies Outsource Today**[19]

1. Improve company focus.
2. Gain access to world-class capabilities.
3. Accelerate the benefits of reengineering.
4. Share risks.
5. Free non-capital resources.
6. Make capital funds available.
7. Reduce operating costs.
8. Look for cash infusion.
9. Resources not available internally.
10. Function difficult to manage.

According to The Outsourcing Institute:

> Outsourcing is nothing less than a basic redefinition of the corporation. . . . The choice of which facets of the organization to outsource and what types of outside relationships will best suit its purpose becomes critical to the ultimate goal: bringing the greatest value to the customer and the greatest productivity to the corporation itself. Seen in this light, outsourcing is a central management tool.[20]

Outsourcing is currently creating market anomalies like Nike. The powerhouse shoe company manufactures nothing. It is world class at design and marketing but totally outsources shoe production to others more capable. This frees Nike to concentrate on what it does best.[21] Because of its successes, however, Nike will not be an anomaly for long.

**Insourcing: Inviting a "Resident Expert"**

In another significant example of outsourcing, DuPont has outsourced (or as they prefer to call it, "insourced") virtually all its training and development services worldwide to us at The Forum Corporation. In effect, Forum *is* DuPont's training department.

Why? DuPont has decided that although it does many things extremely well, nontechnical training is not one of them. During the early 1990s DuPont sought ways to streamline operations and focus its assets. When executives looked at its training function, they discovered 500 employees in the Wilmington, Delaware, area alone who were spending more than half their workdays on training concerns. "We needed something dramatic," explained Ed Trolley, DuPont's training and education manager. "This was not about making incremental change."

At one time DuPont offered 1,000 courses, including 54 separate time-management courses and 20 writing courses. Now the catalog is down to 150, including 2 for time management and 2 for writing. Costs for education programs are down 30 percent, and the value of these programs as viewed by the participants has increased 16 percent. Millions of dollars have been saved. By dealing with a single partner-supplier, DuPont not only gets superior training, but it reduces costs through better management of services, travel, and worker time. It also benefits from Forum's economies of scale in purchases of other vendors' training materials. Most important, however, the DuPont/Forum relationship allows each to focus on its core capabilities.

*Add Value with New Supplier Relationships*

The technology/information explosion continues to blur lines between customer and supplier. A customer/supplier collaboration can create the opportunity to respond in a world-class way to customer values in areas outside your core capability. Bose Corporation, the Massachusetts high-fidelity company, prospers in the Japanese-dominated world of consumer electronics. One way it achieves excellent manufacturing and materials management is by inviting suppliers to station individuals full-time in Bose's corporate headquarters. Their mission: to coordinate the relationship and suggest ideas that will help solve Bose's problems. The system allows production planners and other Bose personnel to develop close, direct relationships with the supplier without working through highly paid salespeople. Wal-Mart and Procter & Gamble, among others, have created electronic data interchange so truckers making deliveries need do no paperwork. The goods move without pause from P&G's control to Wal-Mart's.

*Add Value with New Competitor Relationships*

The relationship that consultant Sam Albert calls "coopetition"—simultaneously competing and cooperating with another company—is becoming essential. In 1993, for example, all of the Big Three U.S. automakers entered into a partnership with the government to develop safer cars that are hyperefficient and gentler to the environment.

Similarly, one of the United States' largest ocean shipping companies has found that working with the competition can mean higher profits for all. In the 1970s, American President Lines (APL) abandoned European and Mediterranean markets to focus on the faster-growing Pacific trade. APL has since returned to Europe and Africa, but as a very different organization. In response to customers who are insisting that APL handle their needs worldwide, APL expanded not by reestablishing its own terminals and buying its own equipment, but by joining an alliance in Europe with four other *competing* shipping companies—sharing ships and equipment.

***Box 4: Strong Customer Value/Strong Capability***
***Action: Go—pan for gold.***

When an organization discovers the area where customer values and organizational capabilities intersect, it has also discovered its unique niche and the basis for a laser-beam focus. Once you have clearly defined what your focus should be and it is grasped and embraced by the entire organization, watch out.

Your organization will seem to take on a life of its own. It will know full well what it is about, what it isn't about, and like a thoroughbred blind to anything but the fast track ahead of it, the laser-focused organization will become energized to proceed at supersonic speed.

Willow Creek Community Church, in suburban Chicago, is one example of an organization that knows what its "market" values, and focuses on it. Willow Creek started in 1975 with little understanding of the needs and wants of prospective parishioners. It ended up becoming the largest church in America.

Before Willow Creek opened its doors, it asked non-churchgoing people what kept them home. According to Bill Hybels, Willow Creek senior pastor and cofounder, "I didn't know this community at all, so I and three others went door to door for a month, and we just asked people, 'Do you actively attend a local church?' If they said yes, we said, 'Good for you. Keep going.' If they said 'No, we don't attend a church anymore,' then we just asked the simple question, 'Would you tell us why you stopped going?' "[22]

According to a Harvard Business School case study, there were five major reasons why they had stopped going to churches:

1. Churches were always asking for money (yet nothing perceived as personally significant seemed to be happening with the money).
2. Church services were boring and lifeless.
3. Church services were predictable.
4. Sermons were irrelevant to daily life in the "real world."
5. The pastor made people feel guilty and ignorant, so they left church feeling worse than when they entered the doors.[23]

Willow Creek boldly targeted the people with these opinions. With survey in hand, church leaders created the capabilities that would move them out of Box 2 (Weak Customer Value/Strong Capability). They designed their church to be a service organization that would attract the unchurched. They segmented potential churchgoers into two groups, "believers" and "seekers," because they felt the two groups had very different needs. Then they created separate services for each one. They designed the "seeker service" to be the exact antithesis of the five complaints people had made about churches.

Willow Creek created an archetypal profile of its target customers. It called them "Unchurched Harry" and "Unchurched Mary." Although Unchurched Mary was as important as Unchurched Harry, they designed the service to appeal to Harry, a professional man between the ages of twenty and fifty, because their survey had found that men are more difficult to convince. They planned to target the toughest audience in hopes they would win over other segments in the process.

Hybels says Unchurched Harry is a "composite man who is probably in his family room with his feet up on the foot stool reading the paper or watching TV with a can of beer in his hand."[24] Everyone working in the church talks personally about "Unchurched Harry and Mary" as if they were real people.

In the seeker service, Harry is not accosted for money. He isn't made to feel like an outsider by the use of words he probably doesn't understand. He is not even expected to sing along. He is encouraged to "sit in the shadows" and observe, think, and take in the message unhindered. Though the sermons are traditional Christianity in simple language, the experience is more like theater than church. Willow Creek respects the fact that "when you aren't sure . . . you just want to be invisible."[25]

Willow Creek also has a service for the "believer" segment. Its "New Community" and small-group services specifically target believers who have a desire to learn how Christianity should affect their daily lives. The New Community service is held midweek to free up the more convenient weekend schedule for the target customers, seekers.

Results? By 1994 Willow Creek had over fifteen thousand attending on a weekend, and six thousand midweek.

Willow Creek had discovered the critical few things that its "customers" valued above all else, and as a result what exactly it should obsess over if it hoped to reach them. This understanding spurred all the leaders of the church to creatively find ways to deliver what the target audience wanted.[26]

## Creating a Unique Value Strategy in Your Niche

A laser-beam focus leads to the creation of a unique value strategy, structured to continuously adapt to changing customer desires and preemptively respond to trends affecting customers.

Keeping up with trends is partially a matter of asking the perennially relevant questions, "How can we do things faster, better, cheaper?" and acting on the answers before your competitors do. It's also a matter of becoming world class at listening to your customer, which we will discuss in the next chapter.

But to anticipate what customers will value in the future, it's also helpful to look at major trends in society today, such as the increasing needs for customization, convenience, economy, connectivity, privacy, knowledge, and social and environmental responsibility. Responding to these trends is a key to keeping the grand passion alive and relevant. It's critical to sustained market leadership.

***Trend: Increasing Need for Personalization***
***Response: Mass Customization***

Customers increasingly want it the way they uniquely want it, and the companies that figure out how to deliver it will take the lead. Mass Customization, a phrase coined by Stan Davis, author of *Future Perfect*, represents the convergence between the increasing customer need for speed and/or value and increasing customer need for a unique solution. A "market segment of one."[27] Here are two highly successful examples:

- National Bicycle Industrial Company, a subsidiary of Japan's Matsushita, fits bicycles to the specific measurements of each buyer and delivers the bike the next day.
- To produce perfectly fitting blue jeans at one of The Original Levi's ® Stores, an assistant will measure you and feed that information, along with your selected style and color, into a computer. This information will then be downloaded to a robotic cutting machine at Levi's Tennessee plant and after sewing, washing and drying, and packaging the blue jeans, they are shipped directly to your home.[28]

***Trend: Increasing Need to Control Creation of the Product***
***Response: Help Yourself***

"Our ideology is that choices, convenience, and control drive everything in our culture," says Phil Burgess, president and CEO of the Center for the New West, a Denver-based think tank. "Anything that gives people more control over their environment . . . is a good thing."[29]

Examples of pushing customer involvement further upstream—to provide more control and involvement over the delivery, often at lower prices—abound. Remember when pumping your own gas was revolutionary? Now, not only do you pump your own gas but you make the transaction as well, right at the pump with no attendant or cashier involved.

Today, it's make your own salad, do your own banking, type your own documents, place your own order, create your own sundae, and even, at restaurants like the Minturn Country Club, a steak house near Vail, Colorado, cook your own food (if this is really your thing). First you select your meat or fish from the in-house butcher shop, bring it over to a big grill with your glass of wine, and chitchat with other patrons while you barbecue your meal.

The Sports Garage in Boulder, Colorado, offers self-service for bicycle and ski equipment repairs. With a concept not unlike do-it-yourself picture framing, the Garage provides bays at eight dollars per hour as well as the tools and expertise as needed to make the repairs. They also offer training classes and sell parts and accessories.[30]

At National Car Rental's Emerald Aisle, customers with special membership cards are dropped off at the appropriate lot and told to pick out any car they would like to rent. Each car already has a key in it, so customers need merely to get into the car of their choice, drive to the exit booth, show the attendant their credit card and license, sign a form, and drive off.

***Trend: Increasing Need for Information***
***Response: Education and support***

Until recently, Central Sprinkler Corporation viewed itself mainly as a manufacturer of fire sprinkler heads and related products. Managers knew that manufacturing and distribution were core capabilities, but they were able to expand their edge by equipping their customers with the training they needed to keep up with technology in the drafting of fire protection systems.

Central Sprinkler's management saw customers struggling to make the switch from pen-and-ruler design of fire protection systems to the more efficient but initially difficult world of computer-aided design (CAD). The company became a key provider of information and skills to its best customers. The SprinkCad Partnership Program supports them with hardware, software, training, and support needed in exchange for a small monthly maintenance fee and an agreement to make Central their primary supplier of sprinkler products.

***Trend: Reducing Total Corporate Costs***
***Response: Understand the Customer's Customer***

John Hardinger is vice president of sourcing for DuPont and one of the industry's most respected purchasing managers. As he sees it, the move to running corporate purchasing like a business with experienced business people in charge, combined with an emphasis on getting results, represents a huge opportunity for companies trying to get a bigger share of the corporate pie. "I've learned that if you get into the mindset that everything you buy has to be special, you start paying phenomenal amounts of money that don't add value to our customer base. The days of differentiated products are fundamentally over . . . our best suppliers will be the ones who know how to link up DuPont's technology, distribution, and manufacturing and take costs out of our total value chain."

***Trend: Increasing Need for Convenience***
***Response: Saturation Marketing***

Au Bon Pain is known for saturating a market with many retail outlets. They have realized that in dense retail areas, such as inner cities, customers will find an extra block inconvenient when there exist so many alternatives. They open two stores on a single block if necessary as a convenience to customers, and find it's a boon to business.

***Trend: Increasing Need for Environmental Responsibility***
***Response: Green Marketing***

Hotels in the Saunders Hotel chain, such as the Boston Park Plaza Hotel, for example, have gained international recognition as an "environmental showcase." These luxury establishments conserve resources and ease customers' consciences by offering such "green" amenities as permanent dispensers for soaps and shampoos and by such eco-niceties as instructing guests that hospitality will assume that a hanging towel is still clean and in no need of washing. Of course, towels on the floor will gladly be removed for washing.

***Trend: Increasing Need for Connectivity***
***Response: Internet Marketing***

The Vanguard Group of Investment Companies and other investment firms now offer brokerage services via the Internet. Other online services include banking, shopping, magazines and newspapers, and research.

## STEP FOUR: CREATE AN ORGANIZATION-WIDE OBSESSION WITH FOCUS

*Articulate each stage of change and then communicate, communicate, communicate.*

By 1990, when Norman Blake was brought in to save USF&G, a large insurance company in the United States, it was almost too late. USF&G was hemorrhaging—$569 million that year alone. Projections showed it was close to insolvency. Blake quickly put his finger in the dike by cutting expenses radically. But that alone wouldn't turn the company around.

"When I came, there was no real strategic vision," says Blake. "Some 38 percent of the company's equity had nothing to do with the company's core strengths in insurance. The company had an identity crisis, and very quickly we had to decide what we wanted to be when we grew up."[31]

*Growing up* meant targeting services only in the areas where customer value converged with what USF&G does well. That meant Blake had to quickly sell off no less than thirteen ancillary businesses to allow USF&G to focus on its remaining core: property and casualty insurance.

But more than that, growing up meant clearly defining what USF&G was, clarifying the company's mission of serving customers, and articulating a three-phase plan that would totally reorient how USF&G delivered those services. Blake's greatest contribution was that he came up with a systematic approach to help his organization serve customers obsessively. He laid out a clear, well-signaled track for his organization to follow to customer-centeredness and growth.

The simple strategy of Blake and his team was "to play only in areas where we feel we have an unfair advantage." That meant that strategically, they were committed to getting the entire organization into Box 4 of the Focusing Framework (Strong Customer Value/ Strong Capability).

## INSPIRING THE SURVIVORS

Between 1990 and 1994, 85 percent of USF&G management was replaced; 48 percent of the staff was let go; and 31 percent of structural expenses were cut.[32] Such large-scale change, when done without a structured game plan, has been compared to setting off a bomb in a crowded room. But Blake managed it in a way that genuinely served USF&G customers and put the company back on the growth track.

Blake and his team had a clear three-stage plan that is a good example of the kind of methodical process needed to orchestrate such massive change successfully. The three stages were: 1) to Fix the Foundation; 2) to Build with Vision; and 3) to Leverage with Leadership.

During the Fix-the-Foundation stage, Blake ended the financial bleeding with sell-offs and downsizing. And while micromanaging each daily crisis, he was working on more long-term structures such as vision and core values.

The vision consisted of four components:

1. "A high performance culture"
2. "Compete where we can lead"
3. "Market-driven and customer-focused"
4. "Leverage people, capital, and technology"

In addition, Blake and his team proclaimed five core values: "Customer first. Integrity. Professionalism. Innovation. Teamwork."

Having steadied an unstable situation and established the path to recovery, Blake instructed the organization to identify its core capabilities, market, and niche and to define and refine competitive advantage and strategy. This was the stage which USF&G calls Building with Vision. The company has identified its competitive advantage as "regional specialization." They believe that the expertise that customers most appreciate is their able presence in local marketplaces. They intend to capitalize on the strength of being a larger company but with the nimbleness of a regional carrier.

Now USF&G is looking toward the growth stage, Leveraging with Leadership. Of USF&G's sixty-five hundred remaining employees, about 30 percent have been at the company for less than two years, so the task will be to focus on unleashing the new talent and meshing it with the solid foundation to take USF&G forward. USF&G is now aggressively acquiring specialty companies that are central to its strategy, such as a nonstandard auto insurance company and a reinsurance company that focuses on the growing self-insurance marketplace. During this stage they will continue aggressive cost-management efforts.

USF&G already has seen remarkable results. The strategy of building on core expertise has not only brought the firm back from the brink of bankruptcy, but created a net income in 1994 of $232 million, a 41 percent jump over the previous year.

## Communicate, Communicate, Communicate

Norman Blake believes that clarity of purpose is no good unless it is a shared purpose. What was particularly effective about Blake's three stages was how they clarified expectations for USF&G's employees. Rather than just being given an overall mandate to "cut costs," USF&G employees were told explicitly about the path forward—what would happen, even the projected dates when their company would move from one stage to the next.

Like Blake, Peter Viner of fast-growing Channel 10 television in Australia understands the importance of communicating throughout every stage, but especially in the early ones. Viner's ability to increase operating profit from $18 million to $100 million within three years came largely from creating " a very good sense of where we are going"—to go from a "poor man's imitation of our competitors" to a profitable, innovative, and well-managed station with a particular focus on younger viewers. Viner, like most managers dealing with turnarounds, had to start by cutting costs down to a "baseline" even while revamping programming. He needed a major overhaul in management structure. And he needed to explain it to all stockholders. He explains what he did:

> In the last six to eight months we broke the staff down into units of fifteen. I gave about a half an hour presentation on the environment and the direction of the company—where we were going and why. And then

there was about half an hour of questions and answers. So, even if they may not like where we're going, they had a chance to get at me a little bit and vent their spleen. And you know, it's our belief, as long as there's clarity and direction, you can live with it. You can't live with the ambiguity. You can't live with being in limbo. And if they don't like it, they have the information to make a proper choice. At least they know where they stand.

## THE FOCUSED COMPANY BECOMES ITS OWN WORST ENEMY

*With new processes and new technologies, you want to replace yourself instead of letting someone else do it. Success comes from a constant focus on renewal.*

—GARY TOOKER, CEO
MOTOROLA[33]

Domino's seemed to be the epitome of a "laser-beam focused" company. For three decades Domino's Pizza delivered absolutely nothing other than pizza and Coke, not even Diet Coke. Founder Thomas Monaghan was so zealous about his pizza/Coke formula that the only new product introduction came thirty-two years after its founding and it was, *drum roll please*... crispy thin-crust pizza.

And talk about knowing your core capability. Domino's Pizza and "fast" were synonymous. The company's classic "30-minute delivery or $3 off" trademark service guarantee was as recognizable as FedEx's "Absolutely. Positively. Overnight." Simple Stuff. And, of course, wildly successful. How then could founder Thomas Monaghan claim that Domino's brush with bankruptcy in the early 1990s was due to a lack of focus?

### OH, OH, DOMINO'S

By 1990 Monaghan had parlayed pizza, Coke, a 1960 investment of $900, and a half interest in a Volkswagen bug into an empire pulling in $2.5 billion in annual sales. He had figured out a unique value proposition that worked beautifully. For thirty successive years, growth and profit margin surpassed the year previous. One out of every two delivered pizzas was a Domino's. Monaghan had fun enjoying his hard-won wealth—wholeheartedly and ostentatiously. He'd grown up in an orphanage, so his was truly a rags-to-riches story, and what riches.

He bought the Detroit Tigers in 1983 for $53 million, an island resort in Lake Huron for $28 million, and furthered his spiritual interests by building a cathedral in Nicaragua. He indulged his architectural aspirations and fascination with Frank Lloyd Wright by acquiring $40 million in Wright furniture, artifacts, and drawings which were kept at headquarters at 30 Frank Lloyd Wright Drive in Ann Arbor, Michigan. The corporate complex was surrounded by grazing livestock and included a petting zoo and a mime center directed by none other than Marcel Marceau. Monaghan's two-story personal office suite had a silk ceiling and a leather tile floor. He spent millions of dollars on classic automobiles. According to Tim McIntyre, company spokesperson, "Our biggest concern in the 1980s was how big the corporate jet should be."

While Domino's was out acquiring things, Pizza Hut was hard at work listening to what customers wanted—and what customers wanted was more. The company pushed hard into the delivery market by offering thin crusts, deep-dish crusts, all kinds of sodas, and salads. Practically dinner. And dinner is exactly what customers had begun to want. Domino's pizza-and-Coke focus was old stuff, and rigidly focused on a target that had begun to move on.

Domino's got rich by focusing on the needs of baby boomers. They started out delivering pizza in the 1960s and 1970s, to a large captive audience on college campuses and military bases. Having a pizza delivered then was a very big deal, especially to those unlikely to have transportation. And to think you could get it delivered in less than thirty minutes. Wow! Now that was a laser-beam focus.

The problem was that those baby boomers had changed while Domino's hadn't. They grew up. They started feeding families. Pizza was no longer just a special treat for the dorm, it had become a once-a-week staple on the dinner table. Customers had begun to expect more. Even speed of delivery was no longer an advantage. It had become simply an expectation. So what competitive advantage did Domino's have over Pizza Hut? Clearly none.

Pizza Hut first began delivering in 1986, and by 1990 it had taken half the market. Domino's didn't budge. According to McIntyre, Domino's "suffered" from a bad case of corporate ego. "We didn't think anyone could touch us. Anyone who brought up the idea of expanding offerings was bluntly told 'Don't even think of it. Our niche is 30 minutes, and we don't want *anything* to slow us down. Period.'

We thought, 'these Pizza Hut people don't know anything.' We've spent 30 years perfecting our focus on convenience and speed of operations. What did they know?"

What they knew was that it didn't matter how fast you got it to customers if it wasn't exactly what they wanted. It wasn't until Pizza Hut and Domino's were in a dead heat, both selling one out of every three pizzas, that Domino's finally realized its strategic error. It had stuck too long with a focus that was no longer tied to what customers valued.

Not only did Domino's come to realize, almost too late, that it was adrift with an outdated value proposition, but the company was up to its eyeballs in assets irrelevant to customers. Domino's needed that cash to fend off bankruptcy and fund a turnaround. So the first thing Monaghan did after he woke up was to sell off everything not directly tied to what customers valued. Domino's sold the Tigers, the real estate, the cars, and the helicopters. Not only did it get rid of the corporate jet, but flying first-class by any employee became a fireable offense. Then Domino's started listening closely to its customers.

## Keep Checking the Focus

Two years after Pizza Hut entered its markets, Domino's bravely offered a customer-requested crispy thin-crust pizza. That offering surprised Domino's with its first positive sales growth in two and a half years. Customers were also saying they wanted salads, so the company test-marketed them—without much success. What they discovered in the process, however, was the fact that salads failed mainly because customers saw pizza as a social food. So it tried breadsticks and buffalo wings, and both were extremely profitable. Recently, it has added a deep-dish specialty pizza which now accounts for 25 percent of pizza orders. (Oh, yes—it now offers Diet Coke as well as Sprite.)

This customer-specified variety has increased delivery time from twenty-four minutes to twenty-eight minutes, but customers don't notice. What customers definitely do notice is that Domino's is becoming laser-focused on giving them exactly what they want. And Domino's focus is now constantly tweaked relative to customers' changing desires.

By 1994, its newfound but customer-reflexive focus on convenience, value, and *variety* produced *the most profitable year ever,* $30 million—with nary a dip in sight. "We were in limbo," says Monaghan.

"Now the word I use—and it doesn't excite anybody—is focus. A little focus goes a long way, and Domino's has had enough excitement."[34]

## ACTION POINTS

- Identify which customers you wish to serve. Eliminate those customer groups that are tempting but will produce only marginal results. Try this—Ask groups of managers and employees to answer the following question in writing and without conferring with others: "Who is our customer?" Analyze the responses. Their clarity and uniformity will indicate how clear your company is about its customers.
- Ask yourself and others in your company, "What are we selling?" Now ask your customers, "What are you really buying?" Is there a difference? We usually think we're selling products and services. But our customers are buying the benefits they get from using our products and services, things like security, improved productivity, self-image, reputation. Lesson: Customers are not always buying what you think you are selling.
- With a group from your company complete the Focusing Framework presented on page 34. What are the implications for action?
- Determine what work you are currently performing that you can reasonably outsource. What are the benefits and risks in doing this?
- Determine how you can "mass customize" your products or services to create a distinctive and competitively superior offering. What can you do to create a unique fit of your products not just to a market but to individuals in that market?
- Communicate your company's purpose aggressively and continuously. State clearly what you will and will not do as an organization. Leave no room for well intentioned but off-purpose entrepreneurial endeavors.
- When market conditions or other business factors threaten to make your focus obsolete, create a new path to excellence and follow it.

Chapter 3

# FROM "LISTENING TO" TO "HARDWIRING" THE VOICE OF THE CUSTOMER

*Achieving customer satisfaction would be impossible without a well-defined process for focusing the entire organization on the customer.*

—ROBERT SCHRANDT
VICE PRESIDENT, CUSTOMER RELATIONS
TOYOTA MOTOR SALES U.S.A.

THE 1988 MOVIE *BIG* brilliantly illustrates the power of the voice of the customer. Tom Hanks plays a twelve-year-old boy who becomes—physically—a man overnight, but retains his playfulness and childlike mannerisms. As he frolics around an F.A.O. Schwarz toy store, the president of a toy company recognizes him for what he is: the perfect toy-company employee.

Hanks knows intuitively what will appeal to children. After all, he is a child himself. So when the perceptive president gives him power over product decisions, he provides the toy company with an overwhelming competitive edge.

Imagine how employees with that kind of knowledge of the customer could benefit a real company. When they set out to improve processes, reduce waste, or cut product-development cycle time, they'd be guided by a deep knowledge of what customers actually valued. They'd immediately know how to anticipate and fulfill customer needs. Happy customers would recommend the company to their friends. Sales and profits would soar.

## LISTENING IN THE REAL WORLD

Can any real-world company serve customers that well? Yes indeed. Recently, in fact, a handful of organizations have shown that it's possible to (1) understand what customers truly value and (2) apply that knowledge so consistently that they create the same kind of competitive advantage that the Tom Hanks character did in *Big*. These companies offer better products and better services, and they turn them out faster and more economically. Bottom line: These companies make more money and grow much more rapidly.

What's the secret? No secret, really. Just the dogged, consistent application of a formula that has proven itself again and again. These winners hardwire the voice of the customer into their organizations. What do we mean by *hardwire*? In electrical and electronic work, hardwiring means creating a dependably wired pathway for electric current. When a contractor hardwires a fire alarm system, for instance, he or she connects all the smoke sensors to the building's electric power and to a central control box. The central box can set off an alarm, light an emergency light, and call the fire department.

Hardwiring takes time. As an alternative, an $8.95 battery-operated fire alarm from the local hardware store can be installed in a few minutes. But the hardwired system works much more reliably. After all, the battery-operated system fails if the battery dies, and it accomplishes nothing if no one is around to hear the alarm. A business needs to have a system in which the warning system works faultlessly.

### BUT WE SURE ARE LISTENING

What you need, of course, is to have the voice of the customer hardwired into your organization—hardwiring that yields a durable, failproof communications channel. Unfortunately, most companies' efforts to "focus on the customer" are more likely to represent the business equivalent of a battery-powered fire alarm. Take, for instance, one $30 million office services company with which we've worked. This organization made a commitment to become the most customer-driven organization in its industry, then set out to become world class at understanding its customers. Employees at all levels developed innovative ways to connect with the 550 clients of the company—focus groups, telephone surveys, mystery shopping, customer panels and conferences, high-tech customer databases. In one case, a division of the organization began a process of conducting visits at the customer site that they thought would significantly increase customer retention. But at the end of the first year of trying to connect with its customers, customer retention was down 10 percent and customer satisfaction was down 5 percent.

What happened? The company had spent close to $1 million trying to understand what its customers valued. In all, two hundred employees in seventeen different departments were involved in 105 separate customer research activities.

Sounds impressive, but unfortunately there were two major problems. First, the data collection effort was uncoordinated. Some customers were being contacted almost four times a month, and, not surprisingly, they often complained of being asked similar questions by different people for different purposes. The second problem was that the data collected in the company's $1-million effort was not being used to improve much of anything. *It just lay there.* Only 43 percent of the people who had collected data reported it to anyone but themselves. Only 39 percent said any action was taken as a result of it. Only 27 percent of the information taken from *external* customers was reported as "acted upon." It was as if most of the data so assiduously gathered had disappeared into a black hole.

## THE BLACK HOLE OF DATA

This story may seem like an exaggeration, but most organizations we surveyed for this book reported similar experiences: aggressive but uncoordinated customer research accompanied by good intentions, but with no real application. In fact, over 92 percent of the organizations we surveyed reported excitement about what customers were telling them, but admitted that the data wasn't being used in any visible way. Like the office services company we just mentioned, these companies *do* study customer needs. They do all the seemingly right things—interview customers, conduct surveys, and even (sometimes) create customer-satisfaction indexes.

By so doing, they've created the technical ability to sense the smoke—returning to our fire-alarm analogy—of customer data. But they haven't closed the loop with a methodology to ensure this data actually reaches the fire department—company management.

Companies that don't hardwire end up without a dependable pathway connecting customer information with the people who must act on that information. The result:

***Most customer research never benefits customers.***

Look at what happened to the minicomputer industry when the makers of microcomputers achieved the power to challenge the larger, more expensive machines.

A key factor was that the microcomputer companies simply knew how to listen to their customers and act on what they heard. But the minicomputer makers, accustomed to a world where it was hard to switch from one vendor's proprietary system to another, did not. Digital Equipment Corporation (DEC), for example, was technology driven. Although the organization—especially the Corporate Marketing Services Department—was collecting tremendous amounts of customer data in the late 1980s, the data was ignored by a senior management group who thought they already knew what their customers needed. CEO Ken Olsen, in 1991, stated emphatically, "We always say that the customers are right, but they are not always right."[1] DEC's decline was predicted by many of those customers, and the road back has been long and bumpy: While DEC's products might have been better engineered than those of its competitors, they didn't solve customers' problems as well. The company shrank to half its size before returning to profitability in 1995, a profitability created in large part by dramatic downsizing.

## "The Gap of China" Asks for Complaints

On the other hand, when you see a company that has effectively hardwired the voice of the customer into its systems, the benefits are obvious. Giordano is a case in point. As one of the fastest growing retailers in the Asia/Pacific region, Giordano has seen its sales increase from $7.7 million in 1986 to over $450 million today. But in 1993, revenue growth had translated into losses of over $15 million in its China operation.

Peter Lau, the new chairman, took a number of actions to improve profitability, aiming at becoming outstanding with customers and at becoming "The Gap of China, having 1,000 stores in China by the end of the decade." Although the company already had a strong service reputation, the largest neon sign in China was erected on the Pearl River, saying "Giordano means service," and Lau and his team engaged in a number of activities that helped the firm turn out a profit two years after its crisis.

One highly leveraged activity was Giordano's commitment to not only listen to its customers but use the data to improve how the company worked. Giordano conducts customer surveys twice a year and has an innovative program in which staff members play "mystery shopper" to put themselves in the customer's shoes.

In Hong Kong, which represents 26 percent of the group's total sales, Giordano made an even more visible attempt to get connected to customers. It ran newspaper advertisements in Hong Kong asking customers for complaints, and offered a free T-shirt for every one submitted. Over forty thousand customers responded.

After synthesizing all of the data, Giordano took action. One of the most frequent complaints was related to size availability. Customers were complaining that shirts were too large. Giordano responded by adding an extra-small size in the polo and crewneck T-shirt line. In the end, extra-small crewneck T-shirts constituted 12 percent of crewneck sales—and Giordano believes that the majority of these buyers are new customers.

The data also taught Giordano that its customers believed salespeople to be overly zealous. Digging deeper, Giordano found that many of its Chinese customers were more conservative and felt uncomfortable when sales associates were overly friendly. The company taught its sales associates how to deal with different types of customers, and the next year won *Next* magazine's Best Service Award in the boutique category. And in 1995, it won the Hong Kong Retail Management Association's Best Service Award in the specialty sales category.

Peter Lau has many stories about successes that resulted from using customer data, including a recent decision to cater more fully to female customers. Says Lau, "We also have had a few false starts when customers had good ideas that weren't quite good enough, but clearly each one of our successes could pay for dozens of failures."

## PictureTel's Customers Are Solid Gold

We recently visited PictureTel, marketer of videoconferencing equipment (cameras, monitor screens, transmission devices and controls) that allows people in different parts of the world to hold live conferences through video connections.

At PictureTel we found a company that nurtures a worldwide independent user group through direct interaction with the group's officers and board of directors, and through committees dealing with specific customer issues. A Standards and Technology Committee deals with technical issues; a Relationship Committee examines how PictureTel can improve how it works with its customers.

PictureTel's product development people consistently listen to users, track their feedback, and add user-recommended improvements to PictureTel products within months. For instance, a user suggested that the company add an option for presenters to control the video camera from across the room without walking back to the system keypad. By pushing a nearby wall button that switches the camera position to focus on the presenter, meeting leaders or presenters can feel free to roam without worrying about straying out of camera range. The new feature, called the Look-At-Me-Button, or LAMB, was implemented in systems and announced in April 1995, shortly after the critical suggestion was made.

Separately, PictureTel conducts random-sample surveys of customer satisfaction. "Information from our customers is vital to our business," says Anne Barrett, the company's liaison with the user group. "If we did everything every customer asked for, we would just be constantly fixing things and not working on major product releases." But Barrett goes on to add that PictureTel's hardwired voice of the customer helps the company's designers detach from what's not important and focus on what customers really need.

When it gets a clear customer directive, PictureTel will swing into action quickly. For example, in 1994 users returned a survey to the company on a Friday. Because PictureTel had already been working with the user group, the following Tuesday a company announcement was issued, addressing many of the things the customers complained about. "The head of the Relationship Committee was blown away," recalls Barrett.

The result of this kind of tightly coupled relationship between customer voice and organizational action? PictureTel holds a strong lead in the videoconferencing market. Sales have risen from $37 million in 1990 to $255 million in 1994. And close ties with users have had another benefit as well. PictureTel people, reminded regularly that their products and services are hardly perfect, have managed to avoid resting on their laurels—an often comfortable but precarious place for any company to find itself.

Companies like PictureTel have hardwired the voice of the customer into their organizations by precisely and durably crafting the customer-company connection, to ensure that customer requirements are fulfilled. They have created a systematic ability to solicit, hear, and act on customer needs.

## TAKING THE STEPS TO HARDWIRING

If your company's like most, you already have reams of customer data in every file drawer in every hallway. The challenge is to use it. Below are the key steps for developing a strategic listening and hardwiring process:

1. Create a listening strategy.
2. Collect, organize, and display your information.
3. Create dynamic scorecards.
4. Drive team and individual behavior with the voice of the customer.

The steps overlap, and the starting point is often overlooked. Organizations inevitably begin collecting and organizing data (Step 2) and even try to drive behavior with the voice of the customer (Step 4) before they've completely worked out a listening strategy (Step 1). But for an organization that has developed a clear direction and identified who its customers are, the steps represent a complete approach to hardwiring. Implementing them *will* produce an organization that not only hears, but also acts.

---

**Be Sure To Include These People in Your "Customer Pool"**

Too many companies think only of *current* customers when they ask, "Who is the customer?" That's a trap. Also include

- lost customers
- lost prospects
- potential customers
- competitors' customers

---

## STEP 1: CREATE A LISTENING STRATEGY

The key to taking a *strategic* approach to listening is to be intentional about why you are listening in the first place. This step is the hardest and the most likely to be neglected, so we'll outline it in some detail.

Take Toyota Motor Sales U.S.A. This organization decided to place its emphasis on getting an in-depth understanding of what its existing car buyers think of its cars and its service. Ultimately, the strategy was to understand how these customers would make their *next* purchase decision. Here are three key questions that we've found help elicit this information and some methods Toyota has used to answer them:

1. **What product and service characteristics matter most to you?** Toyota captures customer concerns largely by having well-trained people staff its national 800 number, and also through techniques such as focus groups. These give customers a chance to list as many concerns as they wish. Such a process is important because without direct customer input it's difficult to know what characteristics *might* turn out to be key.
2. **How well are we doing in delivering the product and service characteristics you want, relative to your expectations and relative to our competitors?** Toyota asks customers to indicate what level of preference they put on each of the characteristics they've mentioned and what level of performance they expect in each area. Then it asks how it's performing on each characteristic. Toyota has used two surveys regularly: a new vehicle sales-and-delivery survey of customers who've just bought a car, and a Toyota service survey of customers who've just received warranty service.
3. **What do you find to be wrong or missing?** At Toyota, the Customer Research group conducts focus groups and other studies to answer this question.

### "TUNE IN" TO THE DATA YOU ALREADY HAVE

Just as you can't hear radio waves without a receiver, chances are you're probably not hearing a lot of the customer information that flows into your organization. Neither you nor your organization is completely tuned in.

Consider what happened to CUNA Mutual Insurance Group, an organization founded by America's credit union industry in 1935 to provide business insurance for credit unions and personal insurance for credit union members. CUNA Mutual employees care deeply about supporting the credit union movement, and feel pride in doing so. But for decades, they failed to hear the frustration contained in some of the data flowing into their organization.

The company had long known that a huge number of its customers called the company for help in filling out CUNA Mutual paperwork. But no one considered that fact to be important. Executives just assumed that when customers called, customer service representatives would resolve any problems. They weren't tuned in.

Former chief executive Dick Heins helped the organization get the right station and right frequency. He commissioned focus groups with customers and had them videotaped. He played recordings of customer complaints at key management meetings.

### *Shocking Results*

The videotapes changed the attitude of CUNA Mutual managers. "Customers were crying for improvement," says Steve Goldberg, vice president for corporate quality. On the tapes, customers declared they couldn't understand CUNA Mutual instructions and brochures. And they said they frequently couldn't even reach customer service representatives at the company's Madison, Wisconsin, headquarters when they called for help.

After watching the videos, executives for the first time began to treat incoming telephone calls as important data. First, they checked how many customers were reaching service representatives when they called. The result was shocking. Some 24 percent of callers weren't even reaching a representative. What's more, the majority of those who reached someone had to wait on hold for seventy-five to ninety seconds.

### *Drastic Action*

CUNA Mutual set out to make life easier for its customers. Now that the company was listening, it seemed obvious that if a large number of people called for help with a particular piece of paperwork, either the instructions, the form, or both were hard to understand. So

CUNA Mutual carefully tracked which forms were generating the most calls. Then the forms were revised. In some cases, such as credit disability claims, the number of forms customers had to complete was drastically reduced. The company also reorganized the staffing of the phone system and gave service representatives more training.

As it turned out, redesigned forms made life easier for customers and sharply cut the number of phone calls. The changes paid off with a noticeable increase in customer-satisfaction ratings within a year. The percentage of callers who reach a representative has risen to 98 percent, and the average wait time has fallen more than 75 percent. Thanks in part to the changes Heins launched, CUNA Mutual beat back challengers for its market niche in the 1990s. It's now achieving record surplus growth.

That's typical of what happens when people start to listen carefully to the data that's already flowing into their organization. In developing a strategy to answer the three key questions about your customers and to improve processes, be sure and tune in to each of these three types of existing data:

1. **Formally collected data**—information from surveys, comment cards, focus groups, and other deliberate efforts to record the customer's voice.
2. **Inbound communications from customers**—information from customer requests, complaints, product returns, and application forms—data your business collects in the normal course of business.
3. **Casual customer contacts**—information from meetings with customers that aren't held as part of formal research. These include meetings with customers in the parking lot, on the golf course, and during sales calls.

## Be Open to the Incoming and the Informal

Christopher Samuels, managing director of The Center for Strategy Research, believes that some of the best opportunities come from data collected during inbound calls to sales and service centers. He compares organizations to a room with two doors. One door is closed (because the company is not asking or listening) and the other door is open and the company keeps looking out. Certainly you need to look out the open door—to solicit the views of customers who never call.

What amazes Samuels is how many companies ignore the chance to address more questions to customers who are knocking anyway. "How about starting with simple questions such as, 'What's the best thing about doing business with us?' or 'What are other companies doing for you that we should be doing?' The opportunity is found in the continuous dialogue between companies and customers," he states.

Customer-centered companies are learning to take advantage of inbound calls by responding to inquiries and also asking callers for additional data. Suppose telephone customer service representatives (CSRs) ask 10 percent of their daily callers, "What are some other companies doing for you that we are not doing for you?" These organizations would then have a highly valuable system—with the telephone CSR acting as the "ears" of the company. Federal Express (which gets 380,000 calls per day) and NationsBank (which gets 80 million calls per year) both have these types of systems.

Pay special attention to casual customer contacts too. Informal channels often pick up key concerns that formal research fails to capture. Successful companies work hard to promote such contacts. The roller-bearing maker Timken assigns its executives a different open-ended question to pursue in their contacts with customers each quarter. And in our own organization, Forum, a robust "customer-in" system captures comments that salespeople hear from customers—as many as fifty comments per week are logged in so that management can take action.

An illustration of the kind of idea that formal research rarely captures is a change that British Airways made in its New York-to-London first-class service. Employees working on the airline's highly profitable transatlantic route told management that the number one customer request they were hearing was for a change in meal service. In particular, many first-class passengers, a good percentage of whom are executives needing to conduct business from the minute they leave the plane, valued uninterrupted sleep time more than lots of drinks and gourmet meals. British Airways polled these customers for more specifics, and the result is that passengers now have the option to eat dinner on the ground during the dreary period between check-in and boarding—and then snooze for the five-and-a-half-hour flight. (Of course, if you request food-and-beverage service, British Airways is delighted to provide it.)[2] Conventional surveys probably would never have revealed this customer need. But employees can often pick up such ideas in informal conversations.

## Create a Strategic Mix of Tactics for Capturing the Voice

Your existing data will answer many questions, but it probably won't answer all of them. Select techniques to fill the gaps in your understanding carefully. And pay special attention to opening enough channels for subtle information that questionnaires typically miss.

As we discussed earlier, Toyota Motor Sales U.S.A. has a powerful strategy for capturing the voice of the customer and hardwiring that voice throughout the organization. Key elements are a nationwide 800 number staffed with highly trained people; a new vehicle sales-and-delivery survey of customers who've just bought a car; and a Toyota service survey of customers who've just received warranty service.

### *I Thought You Liked Me*

John McLaughlin, Toyota's national customer administration manager, says that before it developed a listening strategy in the 1980s, Toyota and its dealers hadn't really known how customers felt. "The dealers thought, 'Customers really like us,'" McLaughlin says. "And they thought that because they talked to their managers or they looked at the letters they received or they talked to their friends, who probably got good treatment because they were friends."

Learning what customers *really* thought has made a big difference for Toyota. Today the overall satisfaction scores of its worst twenty dealers have increased to just a few points below the levels of average dealers at the start of the program. Increased satisfaction has helped Toyota increase its share of the U.S. market from 5.5 percent in 1986 to 8 percent today, and this at a time when the rising yen has forced continual price increases for anything the company imported from Japan.

Toyota is adding a new element to its strategy. In hopes of more effectively demonstrating to dealers the advantages of good service, Toyota has launched the Ownership Experience Survey, which regularly studies people who bought Toyotas one to six years previously. What really causes a customer to come back and buy another Toyota? What leads a former Toyota buyer to purchase a Ford? What do these previous buyers really think—and want? That was the missing element Toyota felt it had to add to its data collection in 1995.

***The Three Key Questions***

Hewlett-Packard is another organization with a strategic approach to listening. Figure 3.1 summarizes HP's customer listening strategy. You can see clearly how this strategy, if well executed, addresses all three of the key questions and also helps HP executives gain a feeling for their customers. HP's customer feedback system answers the question, "What product characteristics matter?" The customer satisfaction survey asks and answers, "How are we doing?" The feedback system and the customer visits together tell, "What's missing?" and also help employees gain a feeling for their customers.

Toyota Motor Sales and Hewlett-Packard don't necessarily do more research than other companies. The Forum Corporation recently conducted a study in association with the Society of Consumer Affairs Professionals in Business (SOCAP) that showed 76 percent of large

**Figure 3.1**

THE HEWLETT-PACKARD
CUSTOMER INFORMATION SYSTEM

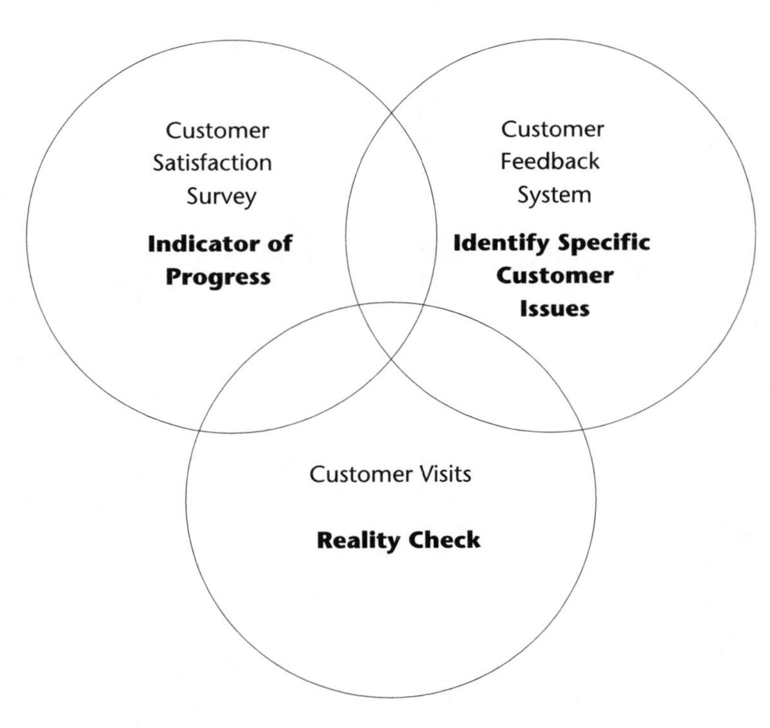

firms were using *eleven or more* different methods to gather information on customers. "Virtually everybody collects a lot of data," says Toyota's McLaughlin. "We could fill rooms with computer reports that nobody reads." Toyota's and Hewlett-Packard's systems are powerful because they are strategically designed: Both companies carefully thought through what information they needed to know to serve customers well. They collect that information—and they deliver it to the right people in an effective way.

Hardwiring is rarely problem free, and we'll see some of the difficulties Toyota encountered below. But CUNA Mutual, Toyota, and HP are each approaching the problem of listening strategically. Because of this, their listening efforts provide a real foundation for improving their service to customers.

## Increase Your Ways of Collecting Data

To help you consider the alternatives so you can create your own strategic approach to data collection, Figure 3.2 lists the most common research methods and their uses and dangers. This tool was created by Dr. William Fonvielle, a Senior Vice President of Forum, who has pioneered many of the concepts and methods presented in this chapter. For some of these approaches, it is valuable to get the customer's permission to capture the data on audiotape or videotape, because you will probably be hearing information that you will want to convey firsthand to others.

As you'll see in this chart, different listening techniques each play different roles. You'll find that:

- Techniques such as focus groups, customer panels, and individual interviews are most important to answer the question, "What product and service characteristics matter most to your customers?" They're the techniques that let the customer drive what is said.
- Surveys are most helpful to answer, "How well are we doing relative to customer expectations and relative to our competitors?"
- Techniques like customer visits and observation, customer tours, and toll-free numbers are most helpful in enabling customers to tell you what's wrong or missing.
- Techniques like customer visits and observation also play a powerful role in helping you understand your customers' latent needs.

**Figure 3.2**

TOOLS FOR HEARING THE CUSTOMER

| Tool | Nature and Purpose | Advantages | Disadvantages |
|---|---|---|---|
| **Focus groups** | Small groups (of customers or any target group) are invited to meet with a facilitator to answer open-ended questions. | This is the single technique found *most useful* in our research. It gives an intimate view of customers and allows them to tell you things they wouldn't mention in surveys. | Small group of customers may not represent your whole customer base. If it is inconvenient for customers to travel, you can use virtual group technique. See pages 70–72. |
| **Customer panels** | Like a focus group, a customer panel consists of a small number of customers invited to answer open-ended questions. However, a customer panel is a group that meets on a regular basis. | Regular meetings create even greater intimacy than focus groups. Customers who think about your problems over the long term may come up with especially good ideas. | Customer panels require considerable management effort. |
| **Face-to-face individual interviews** | Personal interviews provide nuances of different customers' thoughts. | In groups, customers influence one another's responses. Individual interviews may enable customers to articulate more idiosyncratic thoughts. | In groups, customers help each other to articulate thoughts that may not be clear at first. In individual interviews, you lose that. |
| **Visits to customers and observation of their product use** | Thoughtful study of customers in the setting in which they actually use your product probably provides the greatest intimacy of any technique. | This is probably the *most underutilized* method. When people who know what the product is designed to do see how people are actually using it, they get ideas for improvement that customers themselves could never have proposed. | This method has fewer disadvantages than you'd expect. Many customers are delighted to be visited. Visits, however, require planning. Establish a systematic idea of what you're looking for before you go. |
| **Customer tours** | Invite customers to visit your facilities and discuss how you can serve them better. | Customers offer excellent ideas while at your site. | Customer tours won't provide comprehensive understanding of customer views. |

| | | | |
|---|---|---|---|
| **Meeting customers at trade shows** | Setting up a booth in a place where customers will congregate is a cost-effective as well as time-honored method of hearing the customer. | You can meet more customers per dollar expended than with other methods. | There is little time to talk; the atmosphere is artificial. |
| **Toll-free numbers** | Companies attach telephone numbers to products or to their literature. | This is an effective method of gathering data from customers at the time when problems are actually being experienced; it also improves satisfaction and generates add-on sales. | This method can be expensive. |
| **Surveys by telephone or mail** | Surveys ask a fixed menu of questions of a large number of people; they are most useful to obtain opinions on closed-ended questions, the importance of which you've already established by asking open-ended questions in other settings. | If well-managed, they can provide scientifically valid information on what customers as a whole think. (Meetings in small groups can't reliably represent what the customer base as a whole thinks.) | You will obtain little information on anything other than the specific questions you ask. (The question, "Do you have other suggestions?" while worth asking, seldom produces extensive responses.) |
| **Mystery shoppers** | Professionals visit your business posing as customers and report on how they were treated. | They give accurate information on the service you provide. | They may cause employees to feel they're not trusted. |
| **Debriefing of frontline sales- and service-people** | Ask frontline people in a relaxed setting about their experiences to obtain insight into what the customer faces and what he or she wants. | This method taps the vast pool of data your organization already possesses. | This is not a complete solution, but it has little downside risk. |

(continued on next page)

**Figure 3.2 (cont.)**

TOOLS FOR HEARING THE CUSTOMER

| Tool | Nature and Purpose | Advantages | Disadvantages |
|---|---|---|---|
| **Customer contact logs** | Ask customer contact people to report when customers say something interesting or significant. | These capture data from the place to which many customers are likely to go first with a problem. | Frontline people perceive many "customer contact reports" as bureaucratic nuisance. You must evaluate logs on quality of information and show you're acting on the data if you want to get good information. |
| **Customer serviceperson's hot line** | This ia a phone number customer service people can call to report problems. A voicemail box may be sufficient. | A hotline not only provides information, but gives an extra sense of power to the front line. | Data must be managed carefully to be useful. |
| **Competitive win/loss debriefings** | These are special interviews with the customer at the time you win or lose a piece of business. | They catch the customer at a time when he or she has had experience thinking through his or her most important needs and comparing you to competitors. They are a big help to salespeople when conducted by an objective party (e.g., senior management). | Debriefings are the same as other interviews: The customer may not be articulate in one-on-one situations. |

***Reebok's Strategy For Listening***

To listen to its customers in the United Kingdom, Reebok used a number of techniques which all linked to one another. Interviews formed the basis for focus groups; and the results of focus groups were the foundation for customer surveys.

Feeling confident of the strength of its brand and its ability to design footwear for its end consumer, Reebok managers chose to focus on their intermediate customer, the independent retailer. They reasoned that by understanding and acting on the needs of this link in the customer value chain they could create additional competitive advantage.

Reebok U.K. implemented a three-pronged plan for eliciting the voice of the customer. First, they used interviews and focus groups to obtain an in-depth understanding of twelve retail customer groups. Five of these groups, currently high-volume buyers, participated in "Partnership Meetings"; three of the groups, representing organizations that would be valuable for Reebok to cultivate, were involved in "Potential for Partnership Meetings"; and four focus groups were conducted with independent smaller retailers, selected from a total customer base of three thousand. The interviews were facilitated with Reebok in attendance and covered strengths, weaknesses, and other areas of concern.

In the second phase, the information was synthesized. From a list of over five hundred possible customer preferences, the analytical process identified the twenty-eight preferences most important to these customers. From this list a questionnaire was designed using the exact terminology the selected retailers used. After it was field-tested with those same customer groups, the third phase was undertaken. That was to mail the new questionnaire to all three thousand customers.

The results delighted Reebok when a whopping 38 percent of the customers returned the completed questionnaires! Compared with the usual 7 percent response, this was a major success in and of itself. But just getting questionnaires returned, even a lot of them, isn't very valuable. So Reebok went to work analyzing and hardwiring what they heard. They completed a "gap analysis" which enabled them to classify items both by how important they were to customers and how Reebok U.K. was performing. The result was a list of top improvement priorities. Some of these were easy targets for immediate action and were duly taken. Others required longer-term solutions. In both cases Reebok closed the loop with its customers by reporting to them what they had found out and what actions they were taking. All in all, 112 suggestions were made by customers, and Reebok expects to implement most of them.

The process has been so successful in Great Britain that Reebok is replicating it in nineteen countries across Europe, North America, South America, and Asia. Duncan McWilliam, customer satisfaction director for Reebok International, Ltd., who led this effort, attributes Reebok's success to a number of factors, but especially the company's strategy of 1) testing the process before rolling it out worldwide; 2) going direct to retailers for in-depth information, rather than asking internal Reebok executives for their perspectives; and 3) asking customers what was most *important* to them. Says McWilliam, "In the past, we had been concerned with how we compared to the competition, independent of the customer. But, trying to be better than one's competition in areas the customer doesn't care about is how you add a lot of cost without any impact on customer satisfaction."

**Capture Crucial Moments**

It's a marketing axiom that the customer is "smartest" right after a major purchasing decision. That is when the customer has the clearest sense of his or her own needs and expectations. Moreover, at this point the customer knows what's available in the marketplace, has made competitive comparisons, and has thought about competitors' strengths and weaknesses.

This is why you're most likely to get an especially high payoff from interviewing a customer right after you've won or lost a major piece of business. Particularly if you've lost. You'll not only collect exceptionally good data, but also impress the customer with your seriousness. And maybe have a shot at a future sale.

Another excellent time for an interview is immediately after a troubled period in your relationship with a customer. Interviewing a customer immediately after you've fixed a problem will both give you a chance to determine whether the problem is truly fixed and help you to hear what alternatives the customer considered when it appeared you weren't doing your job.

***A New Technique for Powerful Group Thinking***

Forum has designed a new method of gathering customer data that bears special mention. It's a way to capture input from people too busy or too far away to attend a focus group, and at the same time promote more careful thought than focus groups can accomplish in a one- or two-hour meeting. The method is called the Virtual Group Technique.

As shown in Figure 3.3, a virtual group is created by recruiting people to respond to a series of faxes on specific days. The process begins when the organizer faxes each participant a very brief questionnaire, perhaps containing only a single open-ended question. For example, you might fax the simple question,

**Figure 3.3**

VIRTUAL GROUP TECHNIQUE: THE FLOW

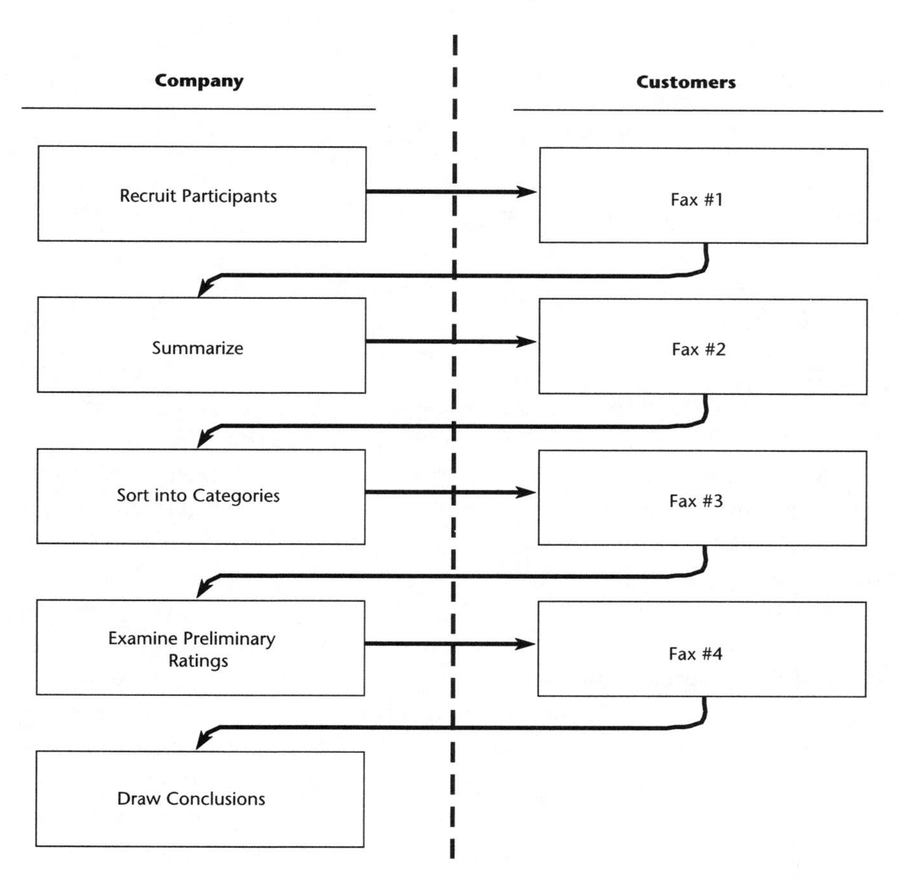

When you think of excellent service from *X*, what comes to mind?

After the participants have faxed back answers, the organizer prepares a list of the key points participants have made. Then, for Round 2, the organizer faxes the list to the participants with a cover note saying,

Here is a summary of Round 1. Is there anything that was missed?

The cover note also asks for clarification of the meanings of any unclear words participants used in Round 1.

Next, the organizer takes the data received from the second round and sorts the replies into categories that reflect common themes. In the third round, he or she faxes the replies in their categories, asking whether the categories accurately summarize the participants' ideas.

You can also ask about the relative emphasis that participants place on each of the factors they've mentioned. Continue the process with appropriate questions until you're sure you have a clear sense of the group's opinions. You can also telephone participants for further clarification.

The result of a full execution of the Virtual Group Technique is a clear report on the thoughts of people who have never been in the same room during the process.

### *NMHG's Lesson*

If you asked the average employee at NACCO Materials Handling Group (NMHG) what mattered most to their customers—forklift buyers—they'd tell you it was keeping the initial purchase price low. But Victoria Rickey, new managing director of the twenty-five-hundred-person organization in Europe and Africa, decided to challenge all assumptions about customers. In addition to a customer satisfaction index and senior-officer calling program, NMHG conducted twenty-five small focus groups and a virtual focus group with its dealer network. They found that the most important buying factor—58 percent of the proposition—was service. What mattered more than initial purchase price (which was only 15 percent of the buying proposition) was their customers' ability to keep their trucks running; the customer loses money for every minute the truck is down. NMHG now thinks of its trucks as "mission critical." If customers can't do business because of lack of service, their total economics change.

This one data point has led Rickey and her team to totally redefine their business—a business which is now experiencing double-digit growth.

## Finding Out What the Customer Doesn't Know Yet

With the fierce competition that virtually every product or service faces today, companies must continually scramble to stay ahead and retain the loyalty of their customers. Faced with ever increasing options and variations and the "have it your way" impact of mass customization, consumers are constantly bombarded with the latest product wrinkle that is designed to lure them away from their current supplier. Indeed, "newer," "fresher," "cheaper," "faster," and "better" have become the grist for advertising copy designed to create this switch in loyalty.

To be competitive, then, as we have pointed out, one need only ask customers what they want and then give it to them plus a little more. Focus groups, questionnaires, response cards, and interviews are the primary tools for such inquiry. And they work well, usually leading to product enhancements and sometimes even to new products which ensure continued customer loyalty.

But what about those needs of which your customer is unaware? In this case, you don't just listen—you watch.

### *Learning by Observing*

*Observing* means going to your customer's place of business and noting how your products and services are used. See how the business is run. Follow your products around. Notice where users have problems. Understand the customer's strategy and goals. In short, get to know them as well as they know themselves. What is their behavior? How do they make decisions?

Such scrutiny leads to many kinds of success. First, it can lead to the creation of new products. This worked for Steelcase, the office furniture manufacturer. With the business world having moved to the extensive use of teams of all kinds, Steelcase, alert to this significant trend, examined how office furniture could enhance team effectiveness. Rather than ask people what they needed, they actually set up video cameras in companies and then taped teams in action. After studying the tapes carefully, they created a new product called the Personal Harbor which met the unique requirements of team members to have both individual and common space for maximum effectiveness. The product was an overnight success.

Joban Kosan, a Japanese spa and resort, was concerned that lines for checking in were too long. It understood that first impressions color a guest's entire visit, and, therefore, that the checking-in procedure is vital to a pleasant stay. But if you ask people how long they are willing to stand in line, you will get a wide range of answers. We have tried this with audiences and usually get times that vary from zero to five minutes. Since zero is impractical, what should be the standard for check-in? Joban Kosan had a similar dilemma and solved it not by asking but by observing. It was simple. They put a video camera behind the reception desk and taped guests waiting to check in. They then varied the length of the line and watched carefully for the telltale behaviors that would indicate impatience. Such behaviors as looking at a wristwatch, sighing, shifting weight, and fidgeting were clear signs that the wait was longer than should be allowed. Armed with this information, the people at Joban Kosan simply never let any guest stand in line longer then the limit indicated by their observations.

**Benefits from Going to the Customer**

PULSE (Product Use in a Local Site Experience) is a program designed to immerse 3M health care employees in their customers' hospital environments. It was designed based on the belief that customers are closer to the product than 3M is and that the customer perspective is best understood by living where the customer lives. Under PULSE, 3M people visit customers on-site—sometimes for several weeks—and observe their products being used. The program was initiated in 1990 for 700 employees of 3M's medical plant in South Dakota and gives all employees—from production-line workers to senior executives—a chance to see how what they make is actually used. The hospital staffs have been giving the company an unsolicited wish list of future products, which 3M has been evaluating. And, on occasion, 3M staff are able to explain new product features to their customers. "Most important," says a manufacturing engineer from the plant, "this face-to-face interaction has made every worker at the plant, and at other PULSE factories, more conscientious about delivering a great product. We get literally to feel the pulse of our customers. We see their problems and frustrations up close."

In one case, work teams observed that some products' packaging was difficult to open, and others', designed for reuse, could not be easily closed. They suggested to 3M's product development people that a zip-lock-type opening and closure would make their customers' jobs easier. The suggestion became reality within a few months.[3]

Employees who have participated in PULSE claim they have a much fuller grasp of their customers' needs and 3M has seen increases in product improvement suggestions as a result. In addition to the success of the program in helping employees learn about their customers, PULSE has become a superb vehicle for strengthening customer relationships.

### *Hidden Dissatisfiers*

Another benefit of observing is your ability to identify customers' "hidden dissatisfiers." A hidden dissatisfier is something that annoys you as a customer but about which you do not complain. Strange as it may seem, because we don't expect impeccable service, we are willing to put up with less. And we do so without complaining.

What are examples of hidden dissatisfiers? How about the rolls of plastic bags in supermarket produce sections? You buy some apples and want to put them in one of those infamous bags. Problem number one? You can't isolate one bag from the entire roll. Problem number two? You can't figure out how to open it. We have used this example in speeches around the world and have yet to find a country where this is not a problem. The key point here is that this is a hidden dissatisfier because you have not complained about it. We find that although virtually everyone we talk to is aggravated by this bag problem, only about 2 percent have formally complained about it.

## Maybe the Next Big Thing

Of course, the now classic example of this customer mind reading is the Sony Walkman. People weren't clamoring for a little tape player that could accompany them while they were jogging or in the shower, but when the product was introduced, it was an overnight success. Other such products are a matter of record. Who was whining about not having Post-it Notes? How about the fax machine or microwave ovens? Wasn't it FedEx founder Fred Smith's professor at Yale who panned his idea for an overnight delivery service?

**Look for the Silent Voice**

Mazda Motor's staff developed an important new method of hearing the silent voice of the customer. They went to junkyards to see what was most often worn out or broken in junked cars. One discovery was a lot of broken rearview mirrors. Yet customers had never complained about broken mirrors. Why hadn't they? Mazda theorizes that customers felt that *they* had broken the mirrors and were responsible for the problem. One result of the junkyard tours was that Mazda developed a mirror that could reliably hold its position for decades. A big deal? Maybe not. But customer satisfaction comes from many factors, some big, some not so big—*all* important.

Wealth awaits the enterprise that can successfully tap into these latent customer needs. *Fortune* magazine estimates that while the resulting product breakthroughs account only for 10 percent of new products (the rest are line extensions), they contribute a disproportionate 24 percent of the profits. While this payoff is great, so is the risk. Through research, customers expressed a desire for New Coke, pump baseball gloves (a spin-off of pump athletic shoes), and McLean diet hamburgers, but when these products were brought to market, they flopped. Some pundits interpret this to mean that it is useless to ask customers what they want because they will answer the question but not purchase the resulting product. While the products mentioned above are exact testimony to this phenomenon, it is going too far to cite these failures as an excuse not to involve the customer. Certainly these products will not be the last to surprise their researchers with unanticipated failure.

What this indicates, of course, is that the business of researching and introducing new products and services is not an exact science. Asking the wrong questions of customers or collecting data from customers who are not representative of your target group are typical mistakes that companies make. As is the manipulation of data. Many companies confess, in retrospect, to being biased in their efforts: Instead of being open to a pet idea being rejected by customers, management skews the process to get the answer that it wants.

What customer-centered companies are trying to do, then, is *shift the odds of success in their favor.* And you don't do that by ignoring your customers. You do it by creating an atmosphere that fosters intelligent, objective listening. Such an atmosphere is fertile ground for innovation.

## STEP 2: COLLECT, ORGANIZE, AND DISPLAY YOUR INFORMATION

Data collection produces enormous amounts of information. But even strategically collected information won't serve customers unless employees understand it. As you collect information, organize and display it so the key messages are clear to the people who have to act on it.

A tool like a customer expectations map (Figure 3.4) can summarize data in just such a way. The map shows at a glance all the key customer expectations an employee needs to understand.

The Wawa convenience store chain in eastern Pennsylvania (Wawa, Pennsylvania, of course) created the map from which Figure 3.4 is excerpted, as it began a total quality management (TQM) program. Wawa was already an exceptional chain, with large, well-kept stores, friendly people, and some of the most satisfied customers in the convenience store business. Executives noted that many TQM training programs for senior managers had simply led managers through collections of case studies dealing with other companies whose relevance for them remained unclear. The executives decided to do something different: They conducted focus groups with Wawa's customers and created a complete customer expectations map *before* the first TQM seminar.

On the right side are the key expectations that customers expressed in the focus groups. Customers want prices visible and correct, clerks who provide correct change, and so on. But a mere list of those quality characteristics wouldn't help Wawa employees. To make them useful, Wawa had to classify them into manageable groups and indicate something about their relative importance.

### WHAT CUSTOMER EXPECTATIONS MAPS CAN DO FOR YOU

Wawa has divided the messages from its customers into three categories: Service Quality, Product Quality, and Cost. Figure 3.4 shows

**Figure 3.4**

A CUSTOMER EXPECTATIONS MAP:
CUSTOMER DESIRES FOR A CONVENIENCE STORE

**SERVICE QUALITY**

**Reliability**
includes dependability, meeting promises, continuity of personnel, and consistency of performance.

| | |
|---|---|
| **Accuracy (2)*** | • Prices visible and accurate<br>• Clerks provide correct change |
| ***Items I need are in stock* (4)** | • Well-stocked/I find the item I go in for<br>• Advertised specials in stock |
| **Reliable equipment (3)** | • Equipment works, is properly maintained<br>• Working soda fountain with right lids and straws<br>• Beverages are cold<br>• Telephones work (2) |
| **Consistent layout (2)** | • Same/standardized layout from store to store (2) |

*The numbers in parentheses indicate the number of focus groups mentioning the expectation. Italicized categories were selected as "important" by two or more focus groups.

Reprinted with permission of Wawa.

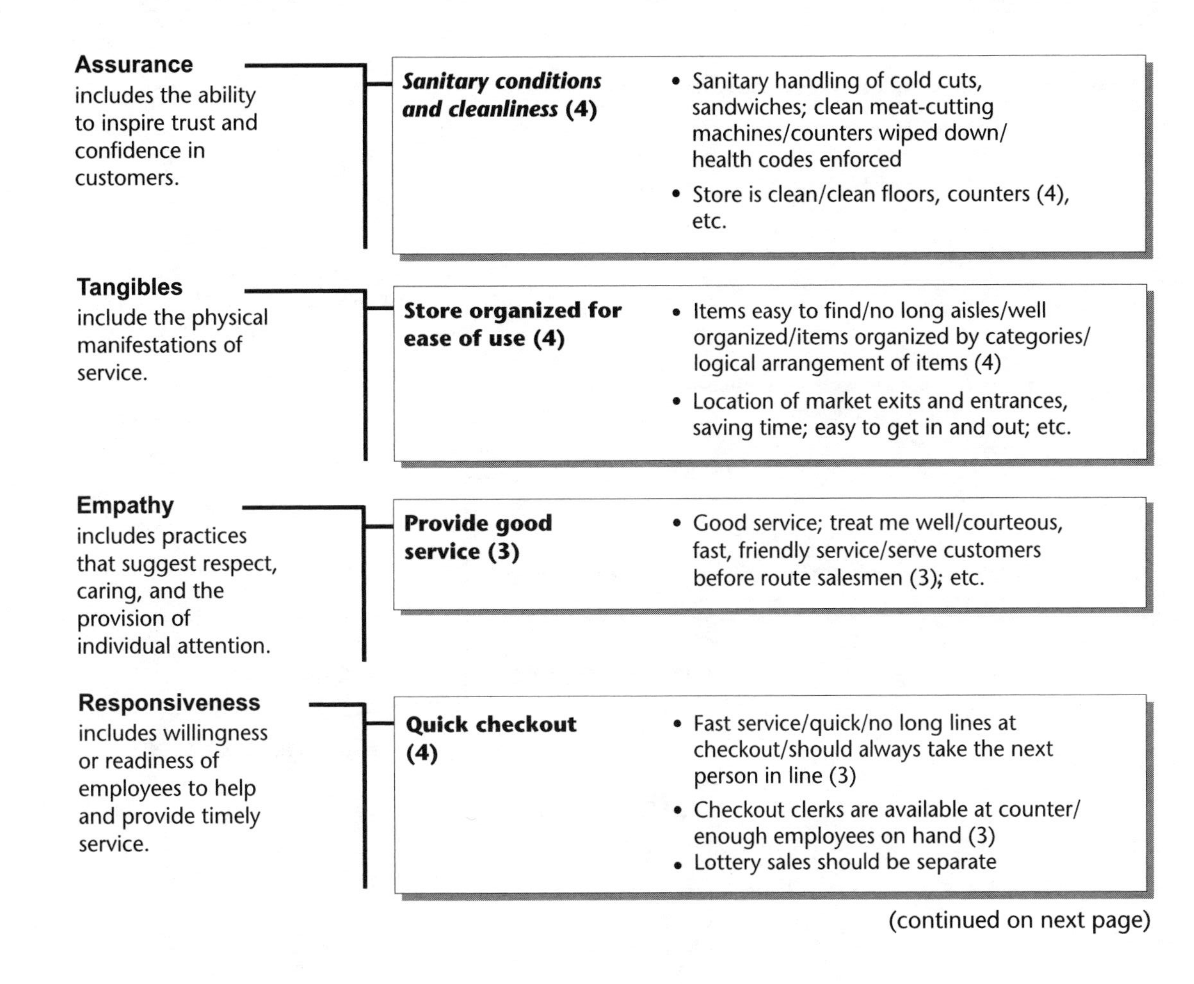

|  |  |  |
|---|---|---|
| **Assurance** includes the ability to inspire trust and confidence in customers. | ***Sanitary conditions and cleanliness* (4)** | • Sanitary handling of cold cuts, sandwiches; clean meat-cutting machines/counters wiped down/ health codes enforced<br>• Store is clean/clean floors, counters (4), etc. |
| **Tangibles** include the physical manifestations of service. | **Store organized for ease of use (4)** | • Items easy to find/no long aisles/well organized/items organized by categories/ logical arrangement of items (4)<br>• Location of market exits and entrances, saving time; easy to get in and out; etc. |
| **Empathy** includes practices that suggest respect, caring, and the provision of individual attention. | **Provide good service (3)** | • Good service; treat me well/courteous, fast, friendly service/serve customers before route salesmen (3); etc. |
| **Responsiveness** includes willingness or readiness of employees to help and provide timely service. | **Quick checkout (4)** | • Fast service/quick/no long lines at checkout/should always take the next person in line (3)<br>• Checkout clerks are available at counter/ enough employees on hand (3)<br>• Lottery sales should be separate |

(continued on next page)

**Figure 3.4 (cont.)**

A CUSTOMER EXPECTATIONS MAP:
CUSTOMER DESIRES FOR A CONVENIENCE STORE

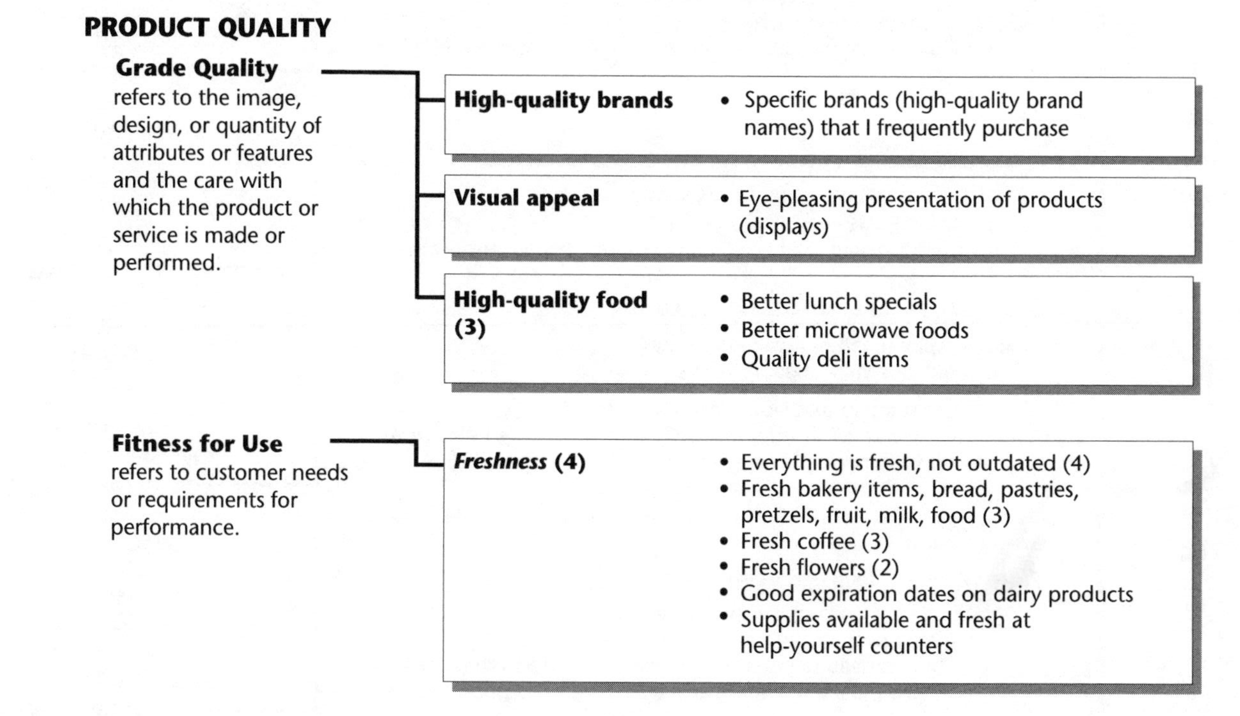

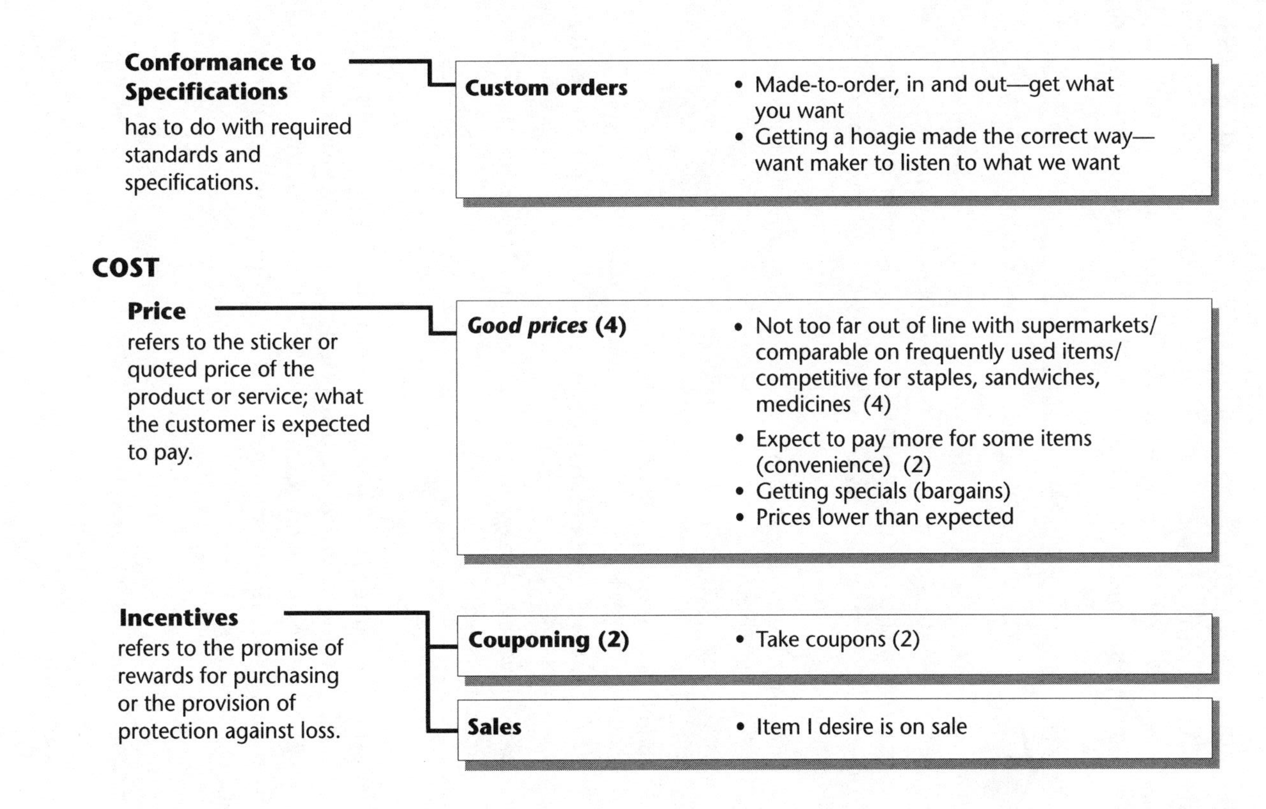
Conformance to Specifications
has to do with required standards and specifications.
Custom orders
• Made-to-order, in and out—get what you want
• Getting a hoagie made the correct way—want maker to listen to what we want
COST
Price
refers to the sticker or quoted price of the product or service; what the customer is expected to pay.
Good prices (4)
• Not too far out of line with supermarkets/comparable on frequently used items/competitive for staples, sandwiches, medicines (4)
• Expect to pay more for some items (convenience) (2)
• Getting specials (bargains)
• Prices lower than expected
Incentives
refers to the promise of rewards for purchasing or the provision of protection against loss.
Couponing (2)
• Take coupons (2)
Sales
• Item I desire is on sale

portions of the map for each category. In the Service Quality section of the map, Wawa has classified expectations according to the RATER dimensions of service quality developed by Texas A&M researchers. The RATER dimensions are *reliability, assurance, tangibles, empathy,* and *responsiveness.* This process made it much easier for all employees to grasp the meaning of thousands of pieces of customer data.

**The RATER Dimensions of Service Quality**

Because quality of service is hard to quantify, companies often fail to learn their customers' opinions about it. But a good guide is a structure developed by researchers at Texas A&M University. They determined that a customer's experience of service quality could be described in five dimensions summarized with the acronym RATER:

**R**eliability, the ability to provide what was promised, dependably and accurately

**A**ssurance, the knowledge and courtesy of employees, and their ability to convey trust and confidence

**T**angibles, the physical facilities and equipment, and the appearance of personnel

**E**mpathy, the degree of caring and individual attention provided to customers

**R**esponsiveness, the willingness to help customers and provide prompt service

But the most important part of the map for Wawa employees is the next level: the specific expectations that the focus group participants had, which lay out "the customer psyche." This is the most actionable information. Within the dimension "Reliability," for instance, the key expectations are:

- accuracy,
- needed items in stock,
- reliable equipment, and
- consistent layout.

The map also indicates what Wawa knows about the relative importance of these expectations. Next to each expectation, in parentheses, is shown the number of focus groups in which customers mentioned it. Those expectations that two or more focus groups called "important" are highlighted in italics.

With this kind of display, customer data can have a powerful impact. Employees will know what customers expect and direct their improvements toward actually delivering it. They can design the right kinds of processes, develop the right kind of training, eliminate waste that represents things customers *don't* want, and deliver what's wanted efficiently.

You can begin hardwiring the voice of the customer into your organization by creating a customer expectations map for each major group of employees in your company. This map will graphically show what customers expect from them.

## Another Approach to Displaying Information

AT&T Network Systems maps customer expectations with charts that represent an alternate approach. Figure 3.5 shows an example. With a sophisticated customer survey methodology and statistical analysis, AT&T determines not only the most important factors in customer satisfaction, but the weights customers put on these factors. Then for each key customer expectation, the company picks an internal measurement that gauges whether the company is delivering what the customers want.

Linking customer expectations to an internal metric is a powerful example of hardwiring the voice of the customer. Now AT&T's quality teams can focus on improving the processes that affect that particular measure or result.

For example, the chart says that 6 percent of customer-perceived quality is attributed to whether the product itself (which accounts for 30 percent of the total rating) is easy to use (20 percent of product value). (You get 6 percent by multiplying 20 percent by 30 percent.) By keeping track of the percentage of customers who call for help and why they call, AT&T can make the improvements that reduce the number of help calls and thereby improve ease of product use. In this way the teams are assured of working on important issues. They avoid the woeful waste of improving things that don't matter to customers. In fact, the customers are actually telling the teams what to work on. And the teams can monitor the internal measure without continually going back to the customer and asking, "How are we doing?"

**Figure 3.5**

LINKING CUSTOMER EXPECTATIONS TO BUSINESS METRICS

| | Business Process | Customer Need | | Internal Metric |
|---|---|---|---|---|
| Total Quality | 30% Product | Reliability | (40%)* | % Repair Calls |
| | | Easy to Use | (20%) | % Calls for Help |
| | | Features/Functions | (40%) | Functional Performance Test |
| | 30% Sales | Knowledge | (30%) | Supervisor Observations |
| | | Responsive | (25%) | % Proposal Made on Time |
| | | Follow-Up | (10%) | % Follow-Up Made |
| | 10% Installation | Delivery Interval Meets Needs | (30%) | Average Order Interval |
| | | Does Not Break | (25%) | % Repair Reports |
| | | Installed When Promised | (10%) | % Installed on Due Date |
| | 15% Repair | No Repeat Trouble | (30%) | % Repair Reports |
| | | Fixed Fast | (25%) | Average Speed of Repair |
| | | Kept Informed | (10%) | % Clients Informed |
| | 15% Billing | Accuracy, No Surprise | (45%) | % Billing Inquiries |
| | | Response on First Call | (35%) | % Resolved First Call |
| | | Easy to Understand | (10%) | % Billing Inquiries |

*Source*: AT&T Network Systems

* Not all customer needs are included in this table. Therefore, numbers may not add up to 100%.

Both Wawa's customer expectations map and AT&T's chart carry the same fundamental message: Display customer data in a form employees can understand, and you'll find employees will be able to use that data to help customers.

## Showing Your Priorities

One of the simplest and yet most powerful ways to display customer data is through a priority matrix. Figure 3.6 shows an example from Bell Atlantic Properties, a real estate subsidiary of Bell Atlantic, which manages all of the company's properties, along with a host of tenants that are not affiliated with Bell Atlantic. Like Wawa, Bell Atlantic Properties conducted focus groups and created an expectations map, but then Bell Atlantic went further. For each key type of customer—decision makers, users, and brokers—Bell Atlantic created a matrix that compared the importance level of each expectation with how well they were perceived as performing against it.

Figure 3.6 shows the perceptions of "users," the group of people who actually worked in the buildings managed by Bell Atlantic Properties. As the chart demonstrates, some expectations were more important than others; and likewise, Bell Atlantic's performance on

**Figure 3.6**

BELL ATLANTIC PROPERTIES: USER'S PRIORITY MATRIX

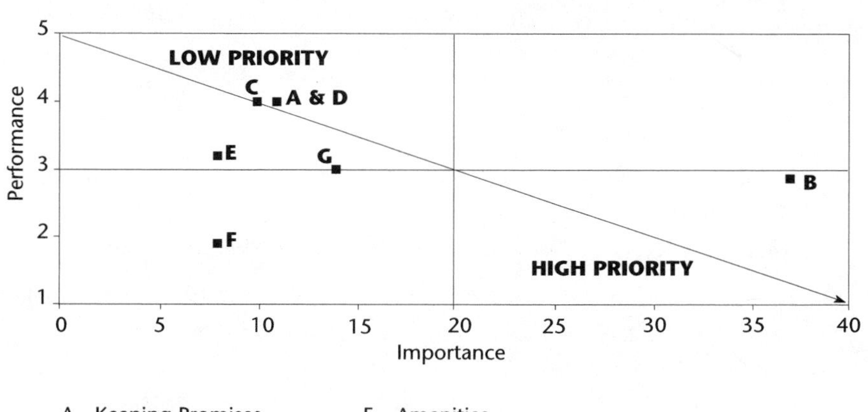


A Keeping Promises
B Safety
C Good Communications
D Helpful Attitudes
E Amenities
F Proper Building Systems
G Cost Containment

Reprinted with permission of Bell Atlantic Properties

some expectations was better than others. Specifically, it clearly shows how item B, Safety, which comprised customers' feelings about building security and fire systems, was by far the most important of all customer requirements, and yet was an area where Bell Atlantic's performance was rated as only average. Contrast this with item C, Good Communications, which was comprised of customers' feelings about proactive contact with building tenants. This expectation had relatively low importance, despite the fact that Bell Atlantic's performance was perceived to be excellent. Obviously the priority for action was in the area of safety.

In response, Bell Atlantic Properties upgraded many of its building security systems and decided to explore what safety really meant in more depth. The company surveyed tenants as they came to work and promised giant candy bars to anyone who returned the questionnaires before lunch. The result was a very high response rate and valuable information from tenants about how they defined safety. In essence, the company found that the major reason customers felt unsafe was poor exterior lighting—a true revelation, because most of Bell Atlantic Properties' staff were not near the buildings at night and thus had not experienced the problem. By investing in improved

---

**Is 4 out of 5 Good Enough? No!**

If a customer gives you a 4 on a 1–5 scale, it means "you're okay." It also means you're a sitting duck for a smart, aggressive competitor. Here's how to interpret scores on a 1–5 scale:

5—You're great.
4—You're okay.
3—Call me. Things aren't great.
2—I will never do business with you again.
1—I will actively go out and bad-mouth you to everyone I know.

The difference between getting a 4 and a 5 is dramatically illustrated in Figure 3.7, which shows the difference in the percentage of those "very willing to repurchase" an AT&T product depending on whether the customer rated AT&T "good" or "excellent." Of those who called AT&T "good," 60% were very willing to buy again. In other words, 40% would possibly go to competitors. But of those who rated AT&T "excellent," fully *90%* intended to buy from AT&T again.

---

**Figure 3.7**

"GOOD" ISN'T GOOD ENOUGH

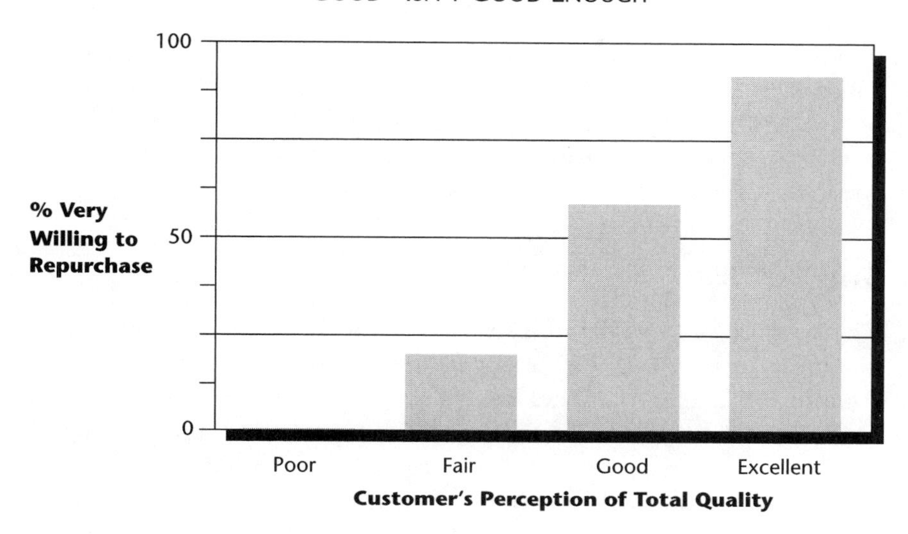


*Source:* Ray Kordupleski, "The Right Choice—What Does It Mean?"



lighting, customer ratings escalated. Says Vice President of Portfolio Management Carol Chiodo, "When we collect information, make it easy to understand, and then act on it, it benefits everyone."

## STEP 3: CREATE A DYNAMIC BUSINESS SCORECARD[4]

*Financial accounting, balance sheets, profit-and-loss statements, allocation of costs, etc., are an x-ray of the enterprise's skeleton. But much as the diseases we most commonly die from—heart disease, cancer, Parkinson's—do not show up in a skeletal x-ray, a loss of market standing or a failure to innovate do not register in the accountant's figures until the damage has been done.*

PETER DRUCKER[5]

If your company is like most, the bottom line is still the only line that matters. This is especially a problem when it comes to hardwiring the voice of the customer into your organization. Despite all of the work you do collecting customer data, displaying it, or even taking action, the ultimate indicator of whether customers really matter is whether your customer data becomes as important an indicator of performance as profit is.

Solely using traditional financial measures falls short in at least three ways. First, they may not capture all of a company's strategic objectives. For example, Ciba-Geigy Corporation, in its Vision 2000, lists environmental stewardship and social responsibility as two of its strategic objectives.

## TOO LATE NOW

The second and usually more serious shortfall is the fact that financial measures are *after the fact.* By the time you find out you are in the swamp and up to your backside in alligators, you probably have already surrendered chunks of flesh to the predators' teeth. Since financial measures are results that are recorded well after the actions and decisions that lead to them, they are indicators that arrive too late to help prevent problems and ensure organizational health.

How do senior executives typically respond to the appearance of bad news? Budgets get slashed, headcounts get frozen, or organizations get right-sized. Investments in research and development or improvements in customer service get sidelined. And not much gets done to address the real causes of the problems. We all know the drill.

Which leads to the third shortfall with financial measures, which is that they are not very diagnostic. They can tell you that you are in the swamp, but usually tell you little about how, or why, you got there.

To address these shortfalls, a number of companies are balancing bottom-line measures with operational measures related to customers, employees, and product/service offerings. Taken together, these measures constitute a business scorecard—a highly effective tool for managing the business. As Robert Kaplan and David Norton noted in the *Harvard Business Review,* scorecards are "like the dials in an airplane cockpit."

Companies have taken many different approaches to creating scorecards. Most are what we call *generic* scorecards, so called because they ask employees to accept some standard measures at face value as the critical measures. Examples of this type of scorecard can be found in many popular business publications.

In Forum's experience, the best scorecards are *customized,* linked both to the results the organization must attain and the drivers of those results. These scorecards, which we call "dynamic business scorecards," represent a company-specific model of the business. In other words, the model actually predicts bottom-line results. Customer data is not in a dynamic scorecard because it seems like a good thing to do; rather, it is there because the organization has been able to demonstrate how becoming customer centered links to better business results.

## A Dynamic Scorecard

Figure 3.8 shows the basic elements relevant to a dynamic scorecard. A company's people and processes create its product and services offering. The offering in turn drives customer behavior. And customer behavior drives business results. Figure 3.9 shows more detail: specific issues that a dynamic scorecard should track. Figure 3.10 shows detail on which measures one of our clients has incorporated into its dynamic business scorecard.

There are many ways that companies are using scorecards. Hewlett-Packard divisions track eighteen to twenty "business fundamentals." Corporate headquarters dictates a few of the fundamentals that all divisions will track, such as employee and customer satisfaction,

**Figure 3.8**

Dynamic Business Scorecard: Overview

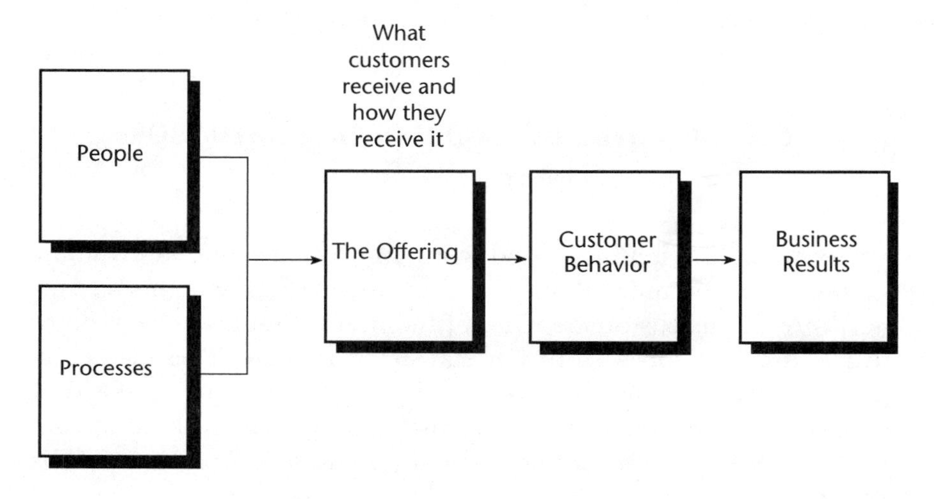

**Figure 3.9**

DYNAMIC BUSINESS SCORECARD: MEASURES

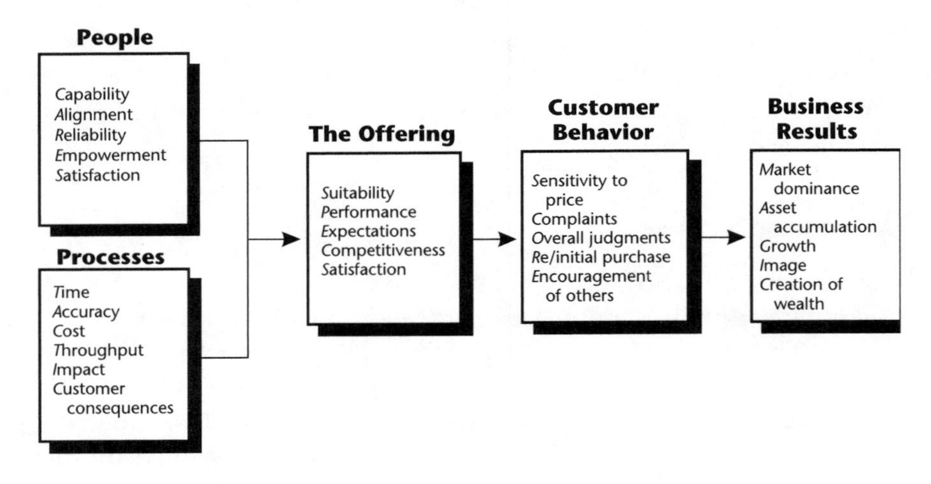


financials, and on-time delivery. The divisions pick the rest depending on their own businesses.

Although not all customer data needs to be reflected in a dynamic business scorecard, one that is well conceived helps provide a clear business purpose for improvement activities. Rather than improving a process solely to make customers happy, people can see its relationship to the performance of the business. Priorities become easier to set, and the logic of the business becomes clearer.

## STEP 4: DRIVE TEAM AND INDIVIDUAL BEHAVIOR WITH THE VOICE

With strategic listening, good communications, and a dynamic scorecard, an organization is ready to create a business that's really hardwired to its customers. One of the best examples we've seen of this is the Johnson & Johnson start-up, Vistakon. This new company's executives learned about hardwiring when in the 1980s they took on the daunting task of introducing a radical new kind of contact lens into a market dominated by Bausch & Lomb and Ciba Vision.

## What? Just Throw Them Away? After All These Years of Trying to Find Them?

Johnson & Johnson had broken into the business by buying a small contact lens maker in the early 1980s. But it remained a small player. Then a sales representative in Europe heard about a striking new technology that was allegedly capable of producing much less expensive, soft contact lenses—lenses that might be so inexpensive they could be thrown away after a week. Johnson & Johnson executives believed the new lenses could be more comfortable and more convenient. But research showed the technology was primitive. It produced many misshapen lenses that were unusable. And Johnson & Johnson executives expected that eye care professionals might resist the idea of disposable lenses.

The Vistakon division not only achieved dramatic improvement in the quality of the lenses before it introduced them, but it also developed an impressive listening strategy, communicated what customers were saying to their employees, and created measures that were tied precisely to what the customer wanted. In short, Vistakon provided every employee with an in-depth knowledge of customer needs.

Vistakon began with a careful analysis of the contact-lens value chain. Bernie Walsh, Vistakon's president at the time, realized it would be futile to make the best contact lenses in the world for consumers if eye care professionals refused to prescribe them. "You have to understand that neither eye care professionals nor consumers had asked us for a disposable contact lens," Walsh noted just before he was promoted to company group chairman at Johnson & Johnson in 1994. "Contact lenses sold to the doctor for about $15. Now we were introducing a lens at a fraction of that price. Consumers and eye care professionals needed to be convinced of the quality of the product."[6]

In dealing with its challenge, Vistakon started by creating an advisory board of leading eye care professionals. These people informed the company of many of the difficulties it would face, and they helped the company determine approaches that would satisfy its customers.

Vistakon's new lenses, called Acuvue, would be worn for a week and then thrown away. Patients would buy a three-month supply at a time. But professionals knew Johnson & Johnson mostly as the marketer of over-the-counter products like Band-Aids and Tylenol. Sales in Florida, the first market where Vistakon's Acuvue lenses were introduced, fell significantly below targets.

**Figure 3.10**

DYNAMIC BUSINESS SCORECARD: DETAIL

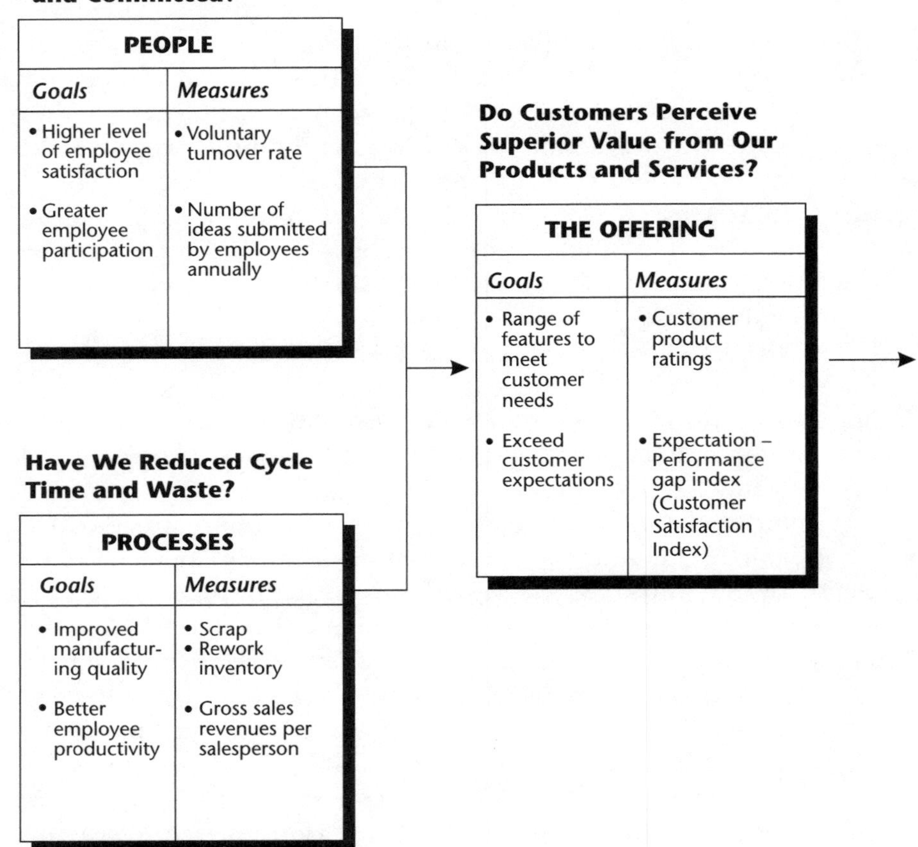


Vistakon took time to understand what the market was saying. "We asked very basic questions," said Walsh. "Most of us were new to the contact lens field. We weren't experts. We didn't tell the doctors they were wrong to be concerned. Instead we listened and asked questions."

## CONCERNS ADDRESSED

To address customer concerns that it wasn't committed to the eye care professional, Vistakon adopted an innovative strategy that had

**Figure 3.10 (cont.)**

DYNAMIC BUSINESS SCORECARD: DETAIL

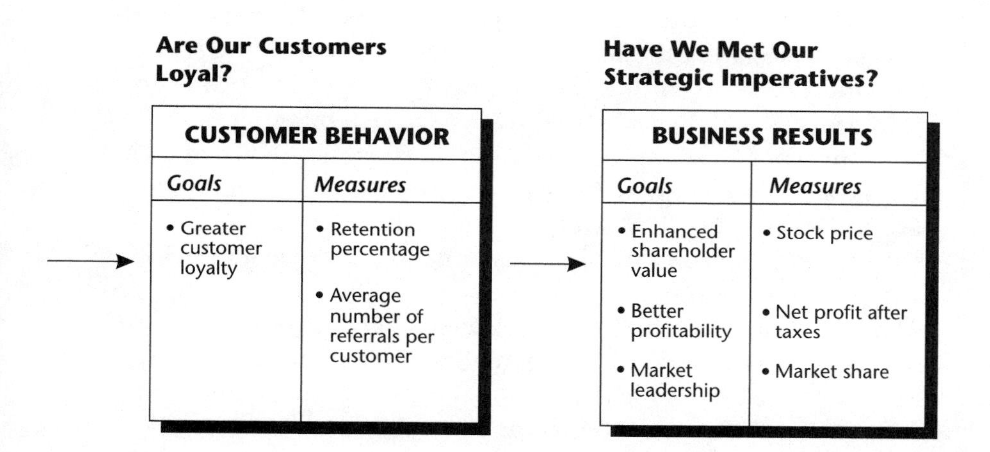


at least three major parts. First, Vistakon made a clear commitment that it would distribute its products only through eye care professionals. It wouldn't take mail orders or develop other alternative channels.

Second, it decided to build its business on a partnership between the company and its professional customers. Most contact lens marketers sold their lenses on consignment. If the lenses didn't sell, the company would take them back. To create an especially strong relationship between lens maker and eye care professional, Vistakon promised an exceptionally high level of support and, in return, required eye care professionals to purchase an initial inventory of Acuvue products before they could sell the lenses. The purchase requirement meant Vistakon sales staff had to spend even more time with potential "marketers" before they would join the team. But it sent the message that Vistakon wanted a serious, long-term relationship with a select group.

Third, Vistakon used the knowledge it gained from talks with its advisory board and other customers to develop a sales and service organization uniquely attuned to the needs of eye care professionals. Walsh worked with the sales staff to ensure each member understood the concerns of these professionals and could deal with them. Telephone service representatives received extensive training on eye care before they could answer the phones.

Today, after eight years in business, Vistakon is the leader in its field, having zoomed past its competitors to over $600 million in sales. And Vistakon has a powerful listening strategy that addresses the needs of each part of its value chain and each segment of its market. Figure 3.11 shows the market segments about which Vistakon gathers separate data through surveys, focus groups, and other means.

### *Vistakon: A Clear View*

Initially, Vistakon focused primarily on private eye care practitioners, especially the most influential. It created an advisory panel including some of the best-known optometrists and ophthalmologists in the United States and set them up to use Acuvue on a trial basis. This gave the company a clear view of how top professionals saw its products. Later, Vistakon expanded its focus to major retail chains and distributors who would service small eye care practices.

Through these channels, Vistakon initially focused on contact lens wearers eighteen to thirty-nine years old. "We wanted to be sure everything would be right, and that we had patients who would be motivated properly," says Bob Breslin, director of quality improvement. Teenagers were less reliable in following doctors' orders than older patients, while older patients often had complex problems that the first generation of Acuvue lenses couldn't treat. Later Vistakon designed special products to serve these markets and carried out special research to understand them.

Perhaps Vistakon's most powerful channel for listening to the cus-

**Figure 3.11**

VALUE-CHAIN THINKING AND SEGMENTATION AT VISTAKON

Portions of the market for which Vistakon collects separate customer data

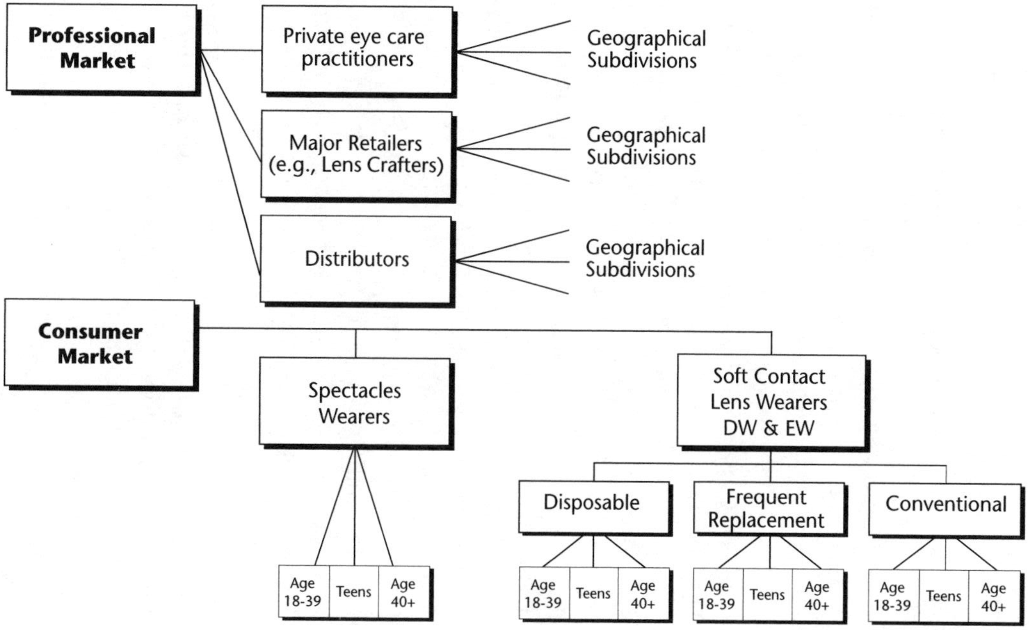

**Professional Market**

Private eye care practitioners
Geographical Subdivisions

Major Retailers (e.g., Lens Crafters)
Geographical Subdivisions

Distributors
Geographical Subdivisions

**Consumer Market**

Spectacles Wearers
Age 18-39
Teens
Age 40+

Soft Contact Lens Wearers DW & EW

Disposable
Age 18-39
Teens
Age 40+

Frequent Replacement
Age 18-39
Teens
Age 40+

Conventional
Age 18-39
Teens
Age 40+

tomer, however, is its computerized Customer Closed-Loop Action and Satisfaction System ($C^2$LASS), developed after benchmarking systems at IBM Rochester, Xerox, and Federal Express.

### *The $C^2$LASS System*

The $C^2$LASS system automatically captures the phone numbers of inbound callers before a customer service representative answers their call, and brings up a screen that describes their history with Vistakon on the service representative's computer screen. When the customer makes a purchase, inquiry, or comment, the system captures it. $C^2$LASS dispatches information to the part of Vistakon where it should be acted on. And it stores the relevant facts in a database where employees can easily analyze them.

The system makes watching trends easy. For example, when Vistakon entered the contact lens business, it had established generous quotas for the number of free lenses it would give to eye care practitioners so that they in turn could let patients try them. In the early 1990s the company, believing its quotas so generous that they encouraged waste, cut them back. Customer service representatives were trained to tell eye care professionals requesting free lenses in excess of the new quotas that their Vistakon sales representatives would call them to discuss their needs. The $C^2$LASS system would instantly dispatch a message to sales management, requesting a prompt telephone call. Vistakon considered the new system a responsive yet cost-effective way to deal with the situation. And by most standards it was.

But some eye care professionals didn't agree. A considerable number responded to the customer service representatives' promises with comments like, "That stinks"; "I shouldn't have to wait for my sales rep"; or, "Will he call back today? What am I supposed to do with the customers who are coming in?"

"In the past when we heard customer complaints, we would go to the marketing manager and say, 'We're getting a number of complaints on a specific issue,'" says Fran Mirmina, director of customer and distribution services at Vistakon. "He would ask, 'How many are you getting?' A typical response from customer service representatives would be, 'Well, we got a couple' or 'We got a lot.' The next question from the marketing manager would be, 'What's a lot?'" It was not quantified. Under traditional systems, no one could make a data-driven decision until the new policy had been in effect long enough to cause considerable customer unhappiness.

The C²LASS system changed that. Whenever an eye care professional made a negative comment, the customer service representatives simply had to touch a single "hot key" to call up a screen customized for recording complaints and sending them to the appropriate part of the organization. Each time a complaint was received, the PC on the Marketing desk would beep, and the complaint would appear on the screen.

Within days, Vistakon knew it had a problem and changed its policy. Customer service representatives were authorized to allow eye care professionals an "overdraft" of free lenses above their quota. When the quota is exceeded, a message goes immediately to the eye care professional's sales representative, and if the overdraft is significant the sales rep checks on why the overdraft was necessary. But the new system doesn't slow down an expanding optometrist who loves Vistakon's product.

### *Listening to More Than the Words*

This effectiveness typifies Vistakon's work. It carefully communicates what it knows to its employees and teaches them how to act promptly on the customer's voice. New customer service representatives get eighty hours of training on everything from eye anatomy to the company's Quality Education System to service policies before they can take phone calls. Teams of customer service representatives, with access to all Vistakon's research, designed Vistakon's guidelines for handling calls. The guides teach representatives to recognize whether a customer is "comfortable," "indecisive," "irate," or "insistent," and they teach separate techniques for handling each customer type. The company's "Close to the Customer" program wires the voice of the customer to production employees in a literal way. It gives them a chance to participate with customer service representatives in taking customer calls.

The results are exactly what one would expect from an organization hardwired to the customer. Vistakon quickly became tops in customer satisfaction, and in only five years it became the largest contact-lens maker in the world. Vistakon also won the Johnson & Johnson Signature of Quality bronze-level award, an award similar to the Malcolm Baldrige National Quality Award, given to Johnson &

Johnson divisions most effectively managed for their customers. Today the company sells lenses in over fifty countries.

Though Vistakon was blessed with an important new technology, it's also true that a long list of companies have started with an important technological advantage and suffered defeat by competitors who acted on the customer's voice more effectively. By hardwiring the voice of the customer into every part of its organization, Vistakon found the path that turned a technical edge into market dominance.

---

**The Five Whats**

Hardwiring the voice of the customer into an organization takes more than just top-down communication. It also means that every employee must know how to hear the customer's voice. It means that people need to get beyond statements about customer desires—both statements from customers themselves and statements from people within your organization.

A good technique for ensuring understanding is the "Five Whats." Just as employees should sometimes ask "Why?" five times to find the root cause of an operational problem, they should ask "What?" five times to fully understand customer needs. For example, if someone says a customer wants "total quality," it's appropriate to say, "*What* do you mean by that?" If the response is, "Rapid response to my problems," it's appropriate to respond, "*What* do you mean by rapid response?" If the questioning process is continued five times, you and your customer will be able to define the exact nature of the attribute in question. Figure 3.12 shows a Five Whats Worksheet filled in with answers to questions on service expectations.

---

There are other notable examples of hardwiring.

The Westin Stamford and Westin Plaza Hotels in Singapore have installed a "Fast Feedback" process which, on a daily basis, makes sure the voice of the customer is heard by management. Bernard Agache, Westin's managing director, is passionate about listening to customers through his twenty-four-hours-a-day hotline, which is staffed by highly trained employees with the authority to resolve guest problems on the spot. The Fast Feedback results are reviewed each morning at a meeting with Agache and General Manager David Shackleton—and any required action is taken. Over the past year, customer satisfaction has risen 5 percent, and occupancy rates surpass all of Westin's competitors in the Singapore market.

**Figure 3.12**

FIVE WHATS WORKSHEET

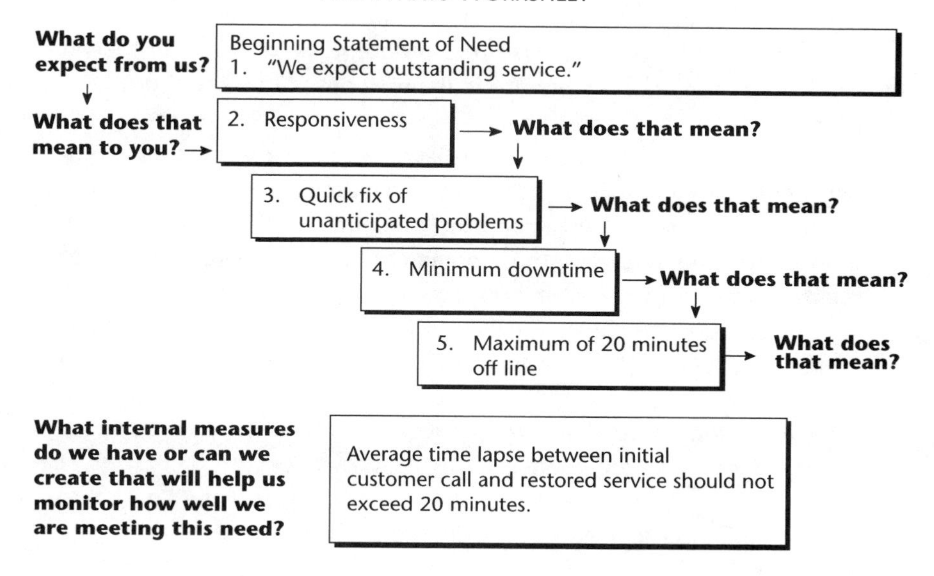


### A Barrage of Input for Midland

When Midland Bank in England set about to improve its customer service, its first step was to send a letter from its CEO to over 4.5 million customers. In it he described the journey that Midland was about to undertake, stated that he knew it would take time, and asked for each customer's help in completing a questionnaire that would indicate what they needed to do better to improve service. There was a very high response rate, and after receiving and analyzing the questionnaires, the CEO wrote back to his customers summarizing the results and outlining actions Midland would take as a result. These communications received *10,000 unsolicited responses* of praise and support. And as a result of the actions taken, customer complaints decreased by 50%, compliments were up by 75%, account attrition was reduced by 25%, and market share increased.

Simply by listening to the voice of their customers and responding with appropriate action, Midland Bank was able to create impressive improvements in its relationship with customers.

**The Company Customers Created**

High-tech entrepreneur and industrial management professor Don Jones practices what he preaches. He tells his students at Carnegie Mellon Graduate School that customers are the very best designers of products because, although you may believe you have created a wonderful product, if customers don't agree, that belief doesn't mean a thing. His company, Industry.Net, is the direct result of hundreds of surveys and focus groups with high-tech customers who told him that they needed a way to keep plugged in to all of the product changes that were occurring at breakneck speed. Industry.Net brings together buyers, specifiers, and sellers at a World Wide Web site that provides product and industry information on demand, 24 hours a day. Not only was Industry.Net a customer-created service, but its almost daily evolution is the result of intense hardwiring of customer desires. According to Jones, only 4% to 5% of employees at most companies actually talk to customers, but at Industry.Net everyone does and that information is hardwired back into the product. Industry.Net, says Vice President David Mawhinney, is "driven by users. . . . They tell us what they want and we try to make it happen."[7]

And make it happen they do. Industry.Net is the first and largest on-line marketplace for business-to-business information—currently 100,000 buyers and 3,300 manufacturers and distributors represent $1 billion in industrial products per year. Industry.Net (http://www.industry.net) is also the fastest-growing site on the Internet, with double-digit growth in subscriptions each month.

## CLUB MED'S BAROMETER

Guided by its motto, "Happiness is our Business," the French company Club Méditerranée, or Club Med, has long understood the importance of direct lines of communication with its guests. As early as 1967, the Club's leaders created a central computer system that collected and analyzed guest feedback from locations all over the world. Called the "barometer," the sophisticated system evaluates more than a quarter of a million guest responses each year. This rich data bank enables both headquarters and local management to modify or create new Club services. And this, Club management knows, helps to continually delight customers.

In addition to information provided by the barometer, the Club uses other methods to stay in touch with its customers. All letters—bouquets or brickbats—are carefully analyzed. In addition, postvacation focus groups are conducted, and even intermediate customers like travel agents are queried for suggested improvements.

Reactions and opinions are solicited from selected guests (without being intrusive, of course) during their actual stays at the Club. And as a means of gathering more casual data, the Club's staff is trained and encouraged to be alert for and fix and report any issues which occur during a guest's stay.

From all these sources was developed Club Med's Quality Charter, a statement of the top ten requirements for its guests. These requirements included: to live without worry or risk; to have freedom of choice; to learn new skills; and to experience ease in using the Club's facilities.

From the Quality Charter came service standards, which are used to assess the performance of current Clubs, manage and train staff, and provide guidance for new start-ups. In effect, Club Med has not only used multiple channels to gather vital guest information, but has hardwired the enterprise in such a fashion that guests, more than anyone else, are responsible for determining what services they receive and how they receive them.

---

**The Internet Net**

When Ford Motor Company's Explorer design team ventured on-line to plug into the voice of their customers, its members were, quite literally, stunned by what they discovered. The group collaborated with the *Detroit Free Press* and CompuServe On-line Services to open up a 12-day on-line forum that asked CompuServe members to "Help Design the Next Explorer." The design team expected a dozen or so messages a day, but by day three the team posted this reaction to an overwhelming response: "Wow! Now we know what it feels like to go over a cyber-waterfall in a barrel. It's not the fall that gets you, it's the data stream that keeps pouring over your head once you reach the bottom."

They were flooded with 700 often emotional, often technical, high-quality responses from all over the world. According to Rick Ratliff, associate director of the *Detroit Free Press* on-line site, "I had expected broad-brush comments . . . But people [were] critiquing everything from the dipstick placement to how far down on the windshield the wipers rest."[8] The biggest complaint Ford found was lack of a V-8 engine. According to one CompuServe member, "I bought the Bronco because of Explorer's lack of power . . . but I would trade it in a heartbeat if I could get a V-8 in the Explorer." This member as well as hundreds of others like him were heard loud and clear by Ford. The team is now redesigning the Explorer with an optional V-8 engine as well as making other more minor changes in direct response to this cyber "data stream." The team is also looking at other ways to use the Internet as a literal net for catching its customers' voices.

## FINAL THOUGHTS: ABUSES OF THE VOICE OF THE CUSTOMER

Toyota used its excellent customer research to drive behavior and achieved great results. Reports provided data on each salesperson and each service adviser. Dealers and their staffs developed a profound concern for what the surveys contained. They responded to these surveys by making appropriate changes, and satisfaction ratings rose rapidly.

But hardwiring demands constant work. Murphy's Law often comes into effect. Companies can create excellent systems and then people can find ways to misuse them. A good deal of that has happened in the automotive industry just in response to the pressure of topping J. D. Power Customer Satisfaction ratings.

Automotive dealers improved the quality of their service, but it soon became apparent that not all the improvement in the service indexes was genuine. There was some tinkering going on. Many customers started to get letters like the one below.

(This is an actual letter that an associate of ours received. Only the names have been changed.)

> Dear Mr. Smith,
>
> Thank you for choosing Whoville Motors as your automobile dealer. Your decision to purchase from us demonstrates great confidence in us and the product.
>
> Our headquarters office will call you soon to ask you some questions regarding your purchase experience. Your responses to their survey are very valuable to us. To each question you will be asked to choose one

of the following responses: STRONGLY AGREE, agree, disagree, and strongly disagree. The only positive response is STRONGLY AGREE.

If you answer all the questions with STRONGLY AGREE, we will receive a 100% score. As a small token of our appreciation for a 100% score, I will gladly send you a coupon for a free 3,750 mile interval service!!

So please remember, when Headquarters calls, just say . . . STRONGLY AGREE!!!

Warm regards,

John G. Doe
Sales Manager

Toyota was candid enough to tell us that a few of their customers were getting the same treatment from some Toyota dealers. The surveys were becoming a game. And some of the tactics used to manipulate the numbers were quite counterproductive. Toyota's McLaughlin says some dealerships had "negative pay plans." Dealers actually would dock their salespeople a few dollars for every negative survey. Sometimes that meant salespeople pleaded with customers to fill in the survey in the "right" way. Some regional offices which found that their combined customer satisfaction numbers didn't compare well with other regions decided that the fastest way to improve was not to help poor dealers do better but to visit already *good* dealers and urge that they push their scores still higher.

This is typical of the unintended consequences of linking a customer-satisfaction index to financial rewards. Customer-satisfaction statistics are best used to help people understand how they are doing and what to improve on. After all, most employees want to serve customers well. But when incentives start to push in the wrong direction, the entire system gets corrupted. Toyota, for one, faced a serious problem.

And Toyota took action. The company actually stopped reporting customer satisfaction statistics by dealer for the first five months of 1995. This was done to force dealers to end their counterproductive pay programs. It also stopped the pushing and shoving for ever higher customer-satisfaction index scores. While it will still look closely at low-scoring dealers, Toyota doesn't give awards for the highest scorers, at least not right now. Toyota Motor Sales also started a telephone survey that asks customers whether the dealer has given them any suggestions about how to answer surveys.

Most important, Toyota is working to shift emphasis to the new ownership experience survey, which will track exactly how much repeat business each dealer receives. In the past, few car dealers have known what share of their customers came back to them to buy their next car. Toyota tracks its customers' "intent to repurchase" just after customers buy their first car. Customers who felt they were treated well were far more likely to say they intended to buy their next car from the same dealer than customers who felt they were treated poorly. Ninety percent of customers who had a good sales experience and a good service experience said they would come back. Only 46 percent of those who said they had a poor sales experience and a good service experience said they would come back. And only 3 percent of those who said they had both a poor sales experience and a poor service experience said they would come back.

Toyota Motor Sales wants to hardwire a commitment to customer satisfaction into dealers—not with rewards and punishments from Toyota but with facts, by showing that customer satisfaction is profoundly in the dealer's own interest. That, the company believes, will be durable hardwiring. The ownership experience survey, which will track to what extent customers actually did go back to the same dealer three, four, or five years after the initial purchase, can be powerful. Recently, Toyota informed one dealer that only 17 percent of his customers were returning to purchase cars after their initial buy. At other dealers a short distance away with better service, the percentage of customers returning was as high as 50 percent. "Our feeling is that the best way to get dealers swung around to customer-satisfaction thinking is to show them the benefits of customer loyalty," says McLaughlin.

Certainly, as Toyota has discovered, efforts to drive behavior with the voice of the customer need constant vigilance. By taking a new tack, Toyota stands a good chance of advancing its continuously improving program a good deal further.

## AVOID THE MISTAKES THAT MUFFLE THE VOICE

While hardwiring the voice of the customer into an organization provides overwhelming benefits, it is a sad fact that most organizations gain little from the customer information that flows into them. How can that happen?

It occurs because companies make some common mistakes:

- *No one is assigned overall responsibility.* Each part of the company collects the data it thinks it needs, and no one ever integrates it into a coherent picture.
- *There is no systematic effort.* The idea that everyone should be involved in collecting customer data is allowed to result in uncontrolled duplication, with no high-quality coordinated analysis. The result is no clear agreement on anything like a customer expectations map, and too much confusing "noise."
- Responsibility is given to staff who use *traditional market research tools* inadequate to the task. Collecting demographic statistics on your customers, for example, may be interesting, but they are almost useless in zeroing in on what customers really expect and will pay for. They tell *who* and *where* your customers are, but not what they want.
- *Data is gathered from only some of your customers.* No one has adequately segmented the customer population. The voice, while accurate, reflects the actual needs of only a small fraction of the people you wish to serve.
- *Data on customer satisfaction is gathered, but it's not compared* with a customer expectations map or any other measures that help identify top priority issues.
- *Noncustomers* who can articulate the needs of real and potential customers *aren't included* in the data gathering. Among people who should be included are salespeople, service providers, lost customers, lost prospects, and competitors' customers.

Two other kinds of failures, however, are the worst.

First, some companies do all the technical steps of data collection right, then *fail to share the information throughout the organization.* Someone in the organization knows what the customer wants, but the people making the decisions that control what the customer will get, don't. They never get the data they need.

Second, in some companies *the information is shared, but it's hardly used.* Managers collect lots of nice binders full of survey data, but hardly anyone ever takes any action based on what's in them.

These failures are the worst because a tremendous, potentially valuable investment has been made without payoff. It's comparable to doing all the work to research and manufacture a product, then making it with defects and never shipping it.

Employees don't fail to use customer data because they don't care. They fail to use customer data because it isn't communicated to them with clarity and consistency. When companies like that begin to really listen and to hardwire, it's a turning point that transforms them.

## ACTION POINTS

- Create a customer listening strategy for your company. Ensure that you hear specifically from all your target customer segments. Also hear from lost customers, lost prospects, potential customers, and competitors' customers.
- Use customer data to answer three key questions:

  1. What product characteristics matter?
  2. How are we doing?
  3. What's missing?

- Use all three channels to gather customer information: formal, inbound, and casual. Match the channel used with the information needed. Remember to stop using channels that are unproductive and tune into ones that are available but not being monitored.
- Identify "hidden dissatisfiers" by observing your customers actually using your products and services. Then delight them by meeting their needs before they have expressed them.
- Create a customer expectations map and use it to hardwire the voice of the customer throughout your entire company.
- Expand your measurements to create a dynamic business scorecard. Measure four key voices: customers, people, processes (quality), and business results (financial).
- Caution: Often, too much emphasis is placed on achievement measures, like customer satisfaction indexes (CSIs). An unintended result can be that rather than serving customers better, employees spend time, resources, and creative energy trying to figure out how to manipulate the ratings, since they are rewarded when ratings are high. In some cases this actually inconveniences customers. Audit your reward systems. Could this be happening in your company?

# Chapter 4

# FROM TEAMITIS TO UNIVERSAL COLLABORATION

*The greatest challenge is putting the same dream, not my vision but a group vision, in everyone's mind to create one voice and one unique culture.*

—DR. EDSON DE GODOY BUENO
CHAIRMAN/TRAINING MANAGER
AMIL ASSISTENCIA MEDICA
INTERNATIONAL

DISASTERS CAN TURN PEOPLE into superb collaborators. Richard Whiteley learned this when he was only nineteen. He remembers:

> *My friends and I had crammed into two separate cars and headed out to another friend's house. The lead car rounded a curve a bit too fast. Without warning, it skidded and then rolled over, not once but five times.*
>
> *We reacted viscerally. We were out of our vehicle before it came to a stop. The upside-down car was a mangled sheet of metal that smelled of leaking gasoline. In seconds we all began to help. The division of labor was almost automatic.*
>
> *Someone called each passenger's name, one by one. Yes, everyone was alive and able to move. Another car pulled up. Someone told its occupants of the situation. A passenger jumped out to help us, and the driver sped off for professional aid.*
>
> *Our mission was clear: Get our friends out fast—the car just might explode. We got the doors open and removed the injured. By the time the ambulance arrived, they'd been extracted and covered with coats, ready for medical care.*

That was teamwork in an especially pure form—natural collaboration. The boys were unified by an urgent, clear, overarching purpose:

to save their friends. They helped them from the car quickly and efficiently. Miraculously, the victims suffered only cuts and bruises.

## THE COLLABORATION GAP

Why do people find it so hard to collaborate under more ordinary circumstances? And why do business programs aimed at promoting collaboration so rarely produce the kind of teamwork that we all know, deep in our hearts, could make life far better for employees and customers alike?

These are particularly poignant questions today because the ability of people in an organization to collaborate has become a key factor in whether it will flourish or fade. Today businesses face a clear shift in the balance of power from the producer to the consumer, from a seller's to a buyer's market. In her book *World Class: Thriving Locally in the Global Economy* (1995), Rosabeth Moss Kanter describes this shift as one of the most significant recent changes in the business world.

Today consumers have choice. In many countries, domestic competitors have become ever more numerous, aggressive, and adaptable. And with the easing of trade restrictions and the birth of trade agreements like NAFTA, the Maastricht Treaty, and Mercusur, hoards of new offshore competitors are invading formerly protected domestic markets.

The result: intense, focused, worldwide competition has given customers more and more alternatives. With more options, customers have the newfound luxury of sitting back and watching people scrap for their business. Customers today are flexing their purchasing muscles and saying: "We want it our way, *now.*"

What's required for success today is customer-responsive flexibility and agility. And this is impossible to achieve without superior collaboration both within and between business units in a company.

What have businesses done about this? They've downsized and flattened. They've embraced total quality and reengineering. While these actions have often protected earnings, they haven't necessarily improved companywide collaboration.

What they have done is put greater emphasis on cross-functional cooperation as a vehicle for breaking down barriers and building up collaboration. And a key vehicle for achieving this has been the deployment of teams throughout an entire organization. With people representing different functions as members, and with the customer in their sights, such teams have been able to cross traditional boundaries effectively. Some of these teams have clearly demonstrated that people in organizations really can collaborate like the boys at the accident site. And when this happens, astonishing results can occur. For example, a Cadillac team saved $52 million by redesigning a part of a car's rear compartment. A DuPont team significantly improved market share and profitability by developing nutritionally enhanced corn that sells for 33 to 40 percent more than competing products. A team at an Amway factory cut setup and changeover time in half on a packaging machine and ultimately raised the machine's productive time 47 percent.

Unfortunately, these are exceptions. A survey by the Carlisle, Massachusetts, firm Benchmark Communications indicates that less than 15 percent of large companies in the United States are making real progress toward their business goals with the teams they've organized. The situation is just as bad in most other countries.

Rather than creating effective collaboration, the majority of total quality initiatives and team programs have produced an ailment we call "teamitis"—the indiscriminate and poorly thought-out commissioning of teams to solve virtually any management or operational problem. Teams appeared to be a way to circumvent the bureaucracy. But, ironically, they often led to the creation of a new bureaucracy: teams for teams' sake.

Success in business today certainly requires effective teams, but it also demands far more. It requires a behavior we see emerging in successful companies, a behavior that we call **universal collaboration**.

In these organizations virtually everyone has the attitude and competence to behave in an effective team-oriented manner *whether or not he or she is on a team.* In a sense, the entire company becomes a united, effective team, and employees are permanent members.

Perhaps the greatest cause of teamitis is the unjustified search for a simple method that will create the collaborative organization. But universal collaboration *can* be achieved in any organization when its leaders and members understand its nature and conclude that it's worth doing.

## COLLABORATION AND HOW IT DISAPPEARS

Universal collaboration occurs most naturally in business during a start-up. Everything is on the line, and while the challenges aren't as dramatic as an automobile accident, the group fights for survival daily. The entire organization gets caught up in working together: The president makes coffee; the secretary does accounting; the shipping clerk sells to customers during a pickup. If it needs to get done, it gets done.

If the company is good or lucky, it grows. And then an odd thing usually happens. It loses the sense of urgency, the fun, the pioneer spirit. The only overarching purpose for coming to work is to get paid or simply to keep a job. The collaboration of the "good old days," which used everyone's talents efficiently, is dismissed as a condition that "grown-up" companies just can't re-create.

But collaboration doesn't have to disappear. And when it *has* disappeared, it *is* possible to re-create it. The results engendered by collaboration can be positively mind-boggling.

## AMIL: SMALL-COMPANY SOUL, BIG-COMPANY BODY

Can you imagine a company that has been around for eighteen years, generates close to a billion dollars in annual revenue, and yet has all the drive and desire of a start-up? It's Amil Assistencia Medica International, a major provider of health care services.

Amil sees no contradiction in being both one of the largest companies in Brazil and the fastest growing, with a staggering growth rate of 62 percent a year. The company believes this kind of performance is the natural outcome of having what G.E.'s CEO Jack Welch describes as a "small-company soul inside a big-company body." The obvious question: How is Amil able to maintain that small-company soul despite having five thousand employees, a million customers, operations in four countries, and the kind of overwhelming success that almost always satiates instead of motivates? Its people collaborate. Amil believes that when two otherwise equal organizations compete head-to-head, the organization best able to fully utilize all the talents of its people will win every time.

In fact, the word *employee* is no longer in Amil's vocabulary. It has been replaced by *collaborator*. Similarly, managers are called *coordinators*, because what they do is not about bossing (commanding) subordinates (followers), but about coordinating the collaborative efforts of others.

Amil doesn't want individual heroics or superstars. Employees who are good at working well with others are the "champions." According to Michael Lund, director of international operations, "You are always told not to go off on your own, to deeply respect and seek out the opinions of others when you make a decision, and if they disagree with you it is your job to sell the idea to create consensus. It is not a matter of who wins or loses. It is about how we work together so that we both win. This is repeated time and time again."

### *The Drivers of Growth*

The company was founded by Dr. Edson de Godoy Bueno, a onetime Rio de Janeiro shoe-shine boy who worked his way through college and medical school. It's built around a baseline belief in the abilities of people and the personal development of their myriad talents as drivers of growth. According to Dr. Bueno, his vision is to be "the biggest, best, and happiest company in South America." And he believes that is only possible with an investment in people. And he invests perhaps more heavily than any major organization in the world.

Amil's collaborators spend an average of eighteen days a year in training, far more than even training-intensive Motorola. The company has established a highly respected, highly selective in-house MBA program that is taught by Amil executives, and modeled on the Harvard Business School case-study approach. Dr. Bueno believes that the job of leadership is to equip the collaborators to build the business. This belief in people development is evidenced by his business card, which reads "Chairman/Training Manager."

### *Total Involvement*

Amil fosters collaboration by involving everyone in just about everything. At quarterly meetings called "Amil 2000," coordinators meet to study one current management book. The task is to take an existing problem Amil faces and try to solve it using the wisdom the book contains. The discussion of various solutions fosters a cross-pollination of ideas.

This cross-pollination occurs in a number of ways. For example, at Amil 2000, coordinators present the last quarter's results to the group and then the floor is wide open for discussion regarding those results—and ideas that may help to bolster them. No turf is out-of bounds. A member of Amil's pharmacy, for example, is welcome to criticize a member of its health care division.

Our research has revealed that one of the primary reasons for the turnover of frontline service providers is that they are not cross-trained. Cross-training expands the skills base so that employees are able to back each other up. Amil takes cross-training to another level. It actually rotates jobs every three years, reasoning that job rotation fosters cross-pollination of ideas as well as fostering an openness to new ones. It also creates a spirit of lifelong learning. Says Dr. Bueno, "When someone accepts a position, he or she signs a black book that says that they understand they will be in this position for no more than three years."

The belief at Amil is that employees will treat internal and external customers as they themselves are treated. To that end, the company has created an internal customer review structure. Every month, each internal "customer" evaluates his or her "supplier." Bonuses are affected by internal customer satisfaction ratings and the measurements of that satisfaction are based upon the internal customer's mission and what has been done to create added value toward that mission.

### *The Result*

José Salibi, founder of the outstanding international seminar company, HSM, states, "Amil has the most motivated and eager-to-learn workforce I have seen in the world." This spectacular success is the result of a vision— one that celebrates collaboration and the human spirit—pushed through the organization by Dr. Bueno. It is his belief in people and what they can accomplish that has seen him move from the mean streets of Rio to the proprietorship of a giant international organization serving millions of patients every day.

## SEVEN PILLARS OF UNIVERSAL COLLABORATION

So how do you create or preserve universal collaboration? Our research suggests you'll find it when an organization develops the following seven pillars to support it:

1. **A powerful overarching purpose.** The people in a truly collaborative organization believe in a purpose that is bigger than individual jobs or functions. To achieve this purpose, they are willing to abandon self-centered interests for the good of the overall organization.
2. **Involvement in decision making** of people at all levels of the organization. Successful companies encourage processes that let the people who will be affected by a decision contribute before the decision is made.
3. **The internal-customer process.** Collaborative companies teach their people to treat not just the end user as a customer, but also the next person in line who will receive their work. This creates a clearly defined network of internal customer/supplier relationships and responsibilities that stimulates collaboration.
4. **Collaboration skills.** Collaboration requires specific skills such as the ability to encourage others to express their ideas. Often the skills that people use to create success in the hierarchy are not the same as those required for effective collaboration. Effective organizations find ways to ensure that their people have those skills.
5. **Effective deployment of teams.** Collaborative organizations don't just commission teams to solve problems. They create an intelligent process to manage teams and develop team leaders who understand that the central part of their job is not so much to manage the people on the team as to manage the linkage between the team and the rest of the organization.
6. An **organizational structure** designed for serving customers. Rather than organizing themselves principally by functional groups such as "sales," "manufacturing," or "finance," the members of collaborative organizations group themselves into clusters of people who can serve customers better by working together.
7. **Infrastructure** that promotes and supports effective horizontal work. Communications systems, physical layout, technology, compensation, and recognition systems all have to work together to support collaboration. Rather than serving as freestanding business processes, they combine to build a platform that promotes and sustains effective cross-functional interaction.

## FORD OF AUSTRALIA: SURVIVAL THROUGH COLLABORATION

Ford Australia had to learn universal collaboration to survive.

Until the 1980s, Ford Australia enjoyed a secure and easy life. Tariffs and quotas protected Australia's auto market. Only the local subsidiaries of Ford and GM made the large rear-wheel-drive cars that Australians preferred. It was a seller's market.

But starting in the 1980s, Australia liberalized trade, and there was little doubt this would bring brass-knuckle competition from beyond its borders. Ford headquarters in Detroit began to ask whether Australia's design group and most of its manufacturing shouldn't be eliminated. Australia, after all, has only 16 million people—about the population of greater Los Angeles. Why not import and assemble kits of cars designed in a larger country? Ford could easily have eliminated most of its Australian employees.

The Australian subsidiary had few strengths that would suggest it was likely to survive. Today, its people describe its old way of working as a "JFDI culture." Supervisors gave orders and, if questioned, would say, "Just f—ing do it." The company was filled with waste.

Jack Nasser, Ford Australia's president, recognized just how radically the company had to change. He downsized the organization and set about improving the product development and manufacturing process. Those who remained went through a massive struggle of redesign and retraining. The changes that Nasser and later John Ogden, president in the 1990s, introduced were profound.

Today Ford in Australia is highly profitable, a gem in Ford's international network of facilities and a company bursting with universal collaboration.

To understand how such a transformation could occur, consider how Ford Australia has implemented each of the seven pillars of a collaborative organization:

**A powerful overarching purpose.** After the competitive crisis hit and ominous rumblings from headquarters were heard, Ford Australia president Nasser rallied the organization behind the most compelling overarching purpose possible: survival. He clearly described the radical changes it would take to continue existing as more than just a marketing division. He made the painful cuts. And he began developing a positive purpose for Ford Australia in the context of Ford Motor Company's global system. Today the Australian Ford units have an "imperatives process" that clearly defines for all members their place in a worldwide Ford system designed to provide the best automotive products in the world for every major market. From this fight for survival, Ford Australia has become a center for the design of rear-wheel-drive cars, not just in Australia, but worldwide as well.

**Involvement in decision making.** Ford units in Australia consider participatory decision making fundamental to success. Why? Consider product development. The most difficult design goals in today's cars involve minimizing cost and weight while retaining world-class quality. The cheapest, most durable, and lightest parts can only be designed if each individual working on them takes a strong initiative. Ford Australia found that when team members looked up to managers as "bosses" rather than across to other members of their teams as partners, they just didn't deliver their best. In fact, to ensure involvement Ford has created a guideline that a decision can't be made until those affected by the decision are consulted.

**The internal-customer process.** Ford Australia revolutionized the relationship between product development and manufacturing through the internal customer process. Today the company not only treats manufacturing as a customer of product development, it also teaches each team working on designing part of a new car to treat the teams working on adjacent parts as customers. In this way, the team designing the horn of the next generation Falcon is the supplier to the team designing the steering column in which the horn will be installed, and the team designing the steering column is the customer of the team designing the horn. This has profound implications. Each must now work to satisfy the other, rather than waiting for some "coordinator" to reconcile the two designs.

**Collaboration skills.** Ford Australia understands that people haven't learned to collaborate naturally in a "JFDI" environment. To create and instill the requisite collaboration skills, the company has designed special seminars and workshops to retrain employees to work effectively across organizational boundaries.

**Effective deployment of teams.** Ever since the 1980s, Ford Australia has had a constantly improving system for deploying natural work teams, registering improvement projects, and ensuring teams get the support they need. From teams that basically protected turf and tended to their own business in the 1980s, a new approach has arisen. Today's teams are self-managed, and when required, link smoothly and effectively with other teams in the company.

**Organizational structure.** Under Nasser, Ford Australia broke up its traditional functional structure. In the old days the product development department, for instance, designed cars in isolation from the manufacturing department that would build them and the marketing department that would sell them. Today, each of the 160 teams that will design the parts of the next Falcon includes not only designers but manufacturing people, purchasing people, and in many cases suppliers.

**Infrastructure.** Understanding that new behaviors are required to reinforce newly learned collaborative behaviors, leaders at Ford Australia know that more than involvement and training are required. To sustain collaboration and support such a major shift in culture, they realized they had to change many of Ford's core business processes. Accordingly, they created a sophisticated computer communication system, redesigned physical layouts of buildings, introduced new computer design tools, and implemented a major reward and recognition program to support collaboration.

By learning to collaborate and, through this, producing outstanding results, the Australians proved their organization deserved to survive. And not just survive. In 1994 Alex Trotman, president of the parent Ford Motor Company, called the introduction of the 1994 Australian Falcon the best Ford system product-launch that year. And in 1994 Ford Australia won the Gold Award, its country's top award for quality. Because of this, Australian design and manufacturing units are contemplating a future in which they'll become major exporters. In mid-1995, Ford corporate headquarters announced that it had approved $1 billion in new investment for Ford Australia, including the money to complete the new Falcon design. New president John Ogden called it "a vote of confidence in the operation and a recognition that commitments made were met." It was also a declaration that a once uncollaborative culture can transform itself into a smooth-functioning, "seamless" customer-pleasing juggernaut.

Let's look at each of the Seven Pillars of Universal Collaboration in more detail.

## 1. A Powerful Overarching Purpose

A powerful purpose, shared by all members of the organization, probably represents the most important factor in the achievement of universal collaboration.

But many companies have a "vision statement," and only a handful have become truly visionary. Why?

The answer, our research suggests, is that too often a vision statement is something promulgated from on high, sometimes with just a few hours of senior-management attention. In cases where the vision has truly become the purpose of the organization, the development of the vision has usually involved people from throughout the entire company.

Consider the story of U.S. Bancorp, one of the largest bank holding companies in the Pacific Northwest. By late 1993, U.S. Bancorp's earnings had diminished, in part because it had expanded far too rapidly in the late 1980s. Its efficiency ratio (expenses divided by revenue) was a shocking 74.5 percent, about twenty points higher than the industry leaders. The threat of a takeover loomed. Bold action was called for. And bold action was taken.

The redemptive activity started with the appointment of CEO Gerry Cameron, a thirty-nine-year bank veteran. He initially adopted the slogan "Focus 59," emphasizing that by 1997 the bank would reduce its efficiency ratio to 59 percent. Under this motto, Cameron closed or sold nonessential assets. Some twenty-five hundred employees took early retirement or received pink slips, including many Cameron had spent his career with. "These are men and women who helped build the bank," he told a newspaper reporter. "Telling them there's no longer a place for them, that's been the hardest part."[1]

The slashing saved $100 million in annual costs and kept the bank alive. Within a year the expense ratio had dropped to a more respectable 63.3 percent. U.S. Bancorp's stock price started to climb.

But some analysts remained skeptical. "All the low-hanging fruit has been picked," said one. The bold actions left employees feeling shocked and dispirited. "Focus 59" was seen as a signal that more bank employees could lose their jobs.

Cameron had intended the motto to connote increasing revenue as well as cutting costs. But what most employees saw was their workmates cleaning out their desks.

At regularly scheduled leadership training sessions a new theme emerged. Managers expressed concern about where the bank was going. One complained about "low clarity among the executive team as to where we're all heading." Where was Cameron taking the bank?

### *The Entire Organization Creates the Vision*

At this point, Cameron and his team set about answering this question. What they did refocused and enlivened their company.

Based on the feedback from the leadership training program, Cameron decided to develop an overarching view of what the bank was trying to do. The resulting effort had a powerful impact that demonstrates what a difference clear purpose can make.

Developing a vision statement took U.S. Bancorp four months. And an essential reason for the company's ability to emerge from the downsizing turmoil was its success in achieving strong shared purpose. It was the executive team's willingness to involve the entire organization in this process that differentiated it from other companies and made it work.

During its first meeting on vision, the executive team came up with:

> "Superior Service with Dedicated People."

It sounded good. But rather than locking in that vision and promulgating it, the executive team established a vision task force consisting of five of its members. They were to take the proposed vision to the organization and test it. After all, it was really for the employees, wasn't it?

In interviews and focus groups and through electronic mail, over one thousand employees critiqued the vision. What the executives learned was eye-opening. Employees liked the concept "Superior Service." They believed that was why they were hired. But the phrase "with Dedicated People" made them feel patronized. It hinted that they had not been dedicated prior to the creation of the vision.

Working with this feedback, the team modified and created a new vision:

> "Working Together, Delivering Superior Service to Our Customers."

U.S. Bancorp's vision statement appears in Figure 4.1. Note that the vision has been signed by each senior officer. This vision truly helped U.S. Bancorp give purpose to the organization beyond cutting costs to increase shareholder wealth.

Although the statement might apply to any service company, it worked at U.S. Bancorp for two reasons. The first is that the words

**Figure 4.1**

U.S. BANCORP VISION STATEMENT

Working together, delivering superior service to our customers

*In support of our new Vision, we are pleased to introduce our new Corporate Mission and Objectives and our redefined Core Values. We thank you for your participation in their development and hope you share our excitement about our Vision for the Future, the direction we have set with our Mission and Objectives, and the Core Values we have agreed on to guide us in our daily activities and relationships with each other, our customers, and our communities.*

themselves had meaning for employees, because they helped create them.

An effective vision-creation process, like the one at U.S. Bancorp, involves the employees throughout the organization. As they become involved, they become participants in creating their own purpose and destiny. The old axiom "I own what I help create" holds true.

Imagine the problems U.S. Bancorp would have faced had executives not tested the vision with employees. It might well have been viewed as a patronizing statement created by an out-of-touch executive group. But because these executives gave every employee a chance to be heard, and then listened and adapted, U.S. Bancorp's vision had meaning for its people.

The second and most important success factor for U.S. Bancorp is *how the vision is actually lived.*

When it came time to "roll out" the new vision, the executive team communicated it to the entire organization over satellite TV. Not only did management speak of the vision and the process by which it had been created, but each senior officer also stated what he or she would do to make it a reality. Next, every manager in the company was asked to meet with each of his employees within thirty days to clarify the vision and values and help employees relate it to their own work. Special meeting guides were created to assist them in this effort.

So far the senior team had executed the process well. But employee feedback indicated concern that under the shadow of "Focus 59," executives might not really be serious about providing outstanding service.

But the executive team was already acting quickly and visibly to back up the talk with specific behavior. They created four task forces under the direction of several executives, including Phyllis Campbell, president and chief executive officer of U.S. Bancorp's U.S. Bank of Washington subsidiary. These task forces addressed important customer-relevant issues like eliminating internal barriers to service and improving customer service itself.

Within four months, one group had already completed its analysis and made recommendations. They were far from cosmetic. And they were approved on the spot.

For example, one barrier to service was that corporate lenders and branch calling officers often served the same business customer. This led to concern about who would get credit and compensation when the customer took out a loan. The customer wouldn't much care, but could be confused with two points of contact. Moreover, when a loan was closed, the bankers would waste time sorting out who deserved what credit.

Action recommended: Create an incentive pool for both corporate and branch officers that would induce them to work together. If deposit volume increased, both sides' incomes would increase. With this solution everyone wins—the customer, the calling officers, and the bank.

When task force leader Jim Kemmish presented his team's recommendations, executives made on-the-spot approvals so quickly that Jim exclaimed, "Gee, are we done?" By their behavior, senior management was tangibly demonstrating a strong commitment to making the achievement of the vision the real purpose of the bank.

U.S. Bancorp has taken bold steps toward universal collaboration. Managers' actions, visible to the entire organization, speak loudly. They say: "We believe this. . . . It is important. . . . It is our overarching purpose as an organization. . . . We are willing to listen and adapt. . . . We are willing to go first." And when management and employees believe in the vision, good things happen. One of them is increased collaboration.

For U.S. Bancorp, so far the news is good. Year-to-year third quarter net income is up 29 percent, return on average equity rose 3.05 percentage points, noninterest expenses dropped 17.5 percent, and the overhead ratio is well below the 59 percent goal, at 57 percent. Says Gerry Cameron, "Serving the customer has never been more important. . . . Many actions we are taking to better serve the customer have the dual benefit of making our operations more efficient. This is reflected in our results for third quarter 1995 and will be reflected in the future performance of U.S. Bancorp."[2]

### *How Purpose Creates Collaboration*

It is said that people work hard for

- money,
- a leader, and
- a cause.

But the weight of these three differs. A leader motivates more powerfully than money, and a cause motivates more powerfully than a leader. One only has to think of the concept of freedom to understand to what lengths people will go to create and protect something they believe in. In business, the overarching purpose is your cause. It can bring people together, unite them.

Massive change, whether from a merger, downsizing, or any other reason, turns an entire organization inward. Almost without exception, companies told us that employees' number one reaction to cost cutting was fear. Employees become utterly preoccupied with what will happen to them. They ask: "When will the next layoff occur?" "Will I be part of it?" One executive graphically described a downsizing process by saying: "It was musical chairs and when the music stopped, not everyone had a chair." In a Darwinian, "survival of the fittest" atmosphere, collaboration is hardly a priority project for anyone.

To look outward rather than inward in times of trouble, companies need to create a sense of purpose. A thoughtfully crafted vision is the most obvious way to begin doing this.

The power of this process need not be limited just to companies that are downsizing. For any company, a clear sense of purpose is essential to strong collaboration.

To an employee, the vision should represent something important, something everybody will see as worth working a little harder to achieve. It becomes a key link between a person and the people with whom he or she must collaborate. It is a cause that both serve. In the traditional hierarchical organization, the road to success has been about accumulating power—a new title, more pay, a bigger office—not giving it up. In such an environment, employees often see peers as competitors for power; they're instinctively wary of collaboration. But under an overarching purpose, an employee will be more likely to share power to achieve such a purpose—and expect that others will too.

### 2. Involvement in Decision Making

U.S. Bancorp's experience shows how much the extensive involvement of employees in vision-setting can mean. It's essential to the creation of an overarching purpose.

But once your overarching purpose is widely shared, you'll find employee involvement in all kinds of decisions pays additional big dividends and is vital to the achievement of universal collaboration. The principle is simple. Involvement creates ownership. Ownership creates dedication to success. And when success is dependent on collaboration, one is more likely to collaborate. Moreover, when people affected by a decision are involved in making it, they collaborate and contribute knowledge that leaders could obtain in no other way.

Evidence strongly suggests that companies succeed when they're participative at every level. Consultant Dennis Kravitz selected 150 successful and unsuccessful companies based on financial results. He found that 70 percent of the most successful actively involved their employees in decision making and problem solving. Only 4 percent of the least successful did.[3]

Consider Texas Instruments' Defense and Aerospace Group, a winner of the Malcolm Baldrige Award. A "participative leadership style" is a key imperative of its management system. The group argues that when you *include the time it takes to implement the decision,* participation not only leads to better decisions and greater collaboration, but actually takes less time. As Figure 4.2 illustrates, the consensus decision wins, hands down. When people from different functions participate in the making of a decision, they are more likely to collaborate in its execution.

You can start to involve your entire organization in decision making without an inordinate investment of time. The now famous

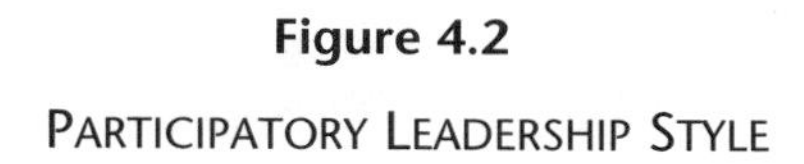

**Figure 4.2**

PARTICIPATORY LEADERSHIP STYLE

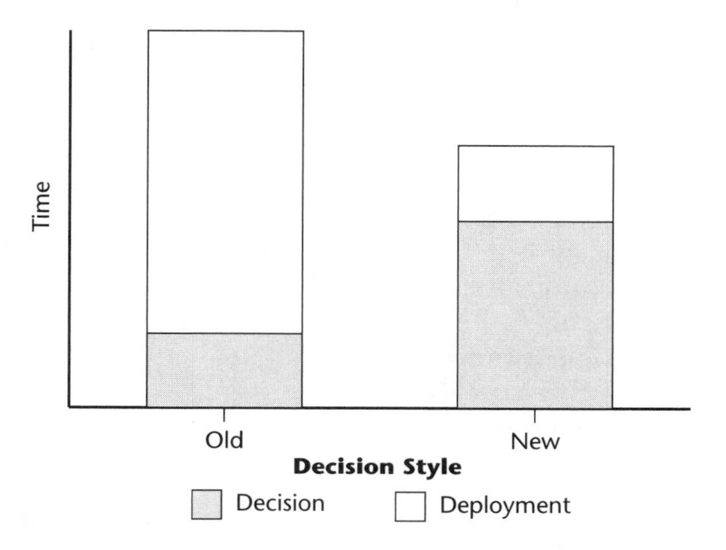


Note: Even though a participative decision takes longer, the total deployment time is much shorter in the new way of thinking.
*Source*: Texas Instruments

General Electric "workout" process, in which teams of employees gather in a large room with senior managers and facilitators and propose ideas for process improvements, takes hours—not days.

An organizationwide participative decision-making process takes more than time—it takes a strong communication system. Executives at PNC Bank Corp., the Pittsburgh-based financial services company, have identified "Network Leaders" throughout the company: twenty-two hundred managers and supervisors representing every functional area within each line of business and each geographic market.

Initially, the Network Leaders were catalysts for focusing PNC on the goal of becoming an exceptional marketing company. They carried the company's strategic objectives and plans to the front lines and then channeled vital employee input right back to the top. The result? A powerful participative force that rapidly instilled a sales and marketing culture throughout the vast PNC Bank organization.

Close to the front lines, these Network Leaders serve as credible representatives of management to employees. And, because they are accessible to management and "plugged in" to corporate initiatives and progress, they provide valuable ongoing support to organizational initiatives.

In addition to their corporate responsibility as Network Leaders, many of these same individuals participate in the monthly Management Information Meetings held within each geographic market of PNC Bank. Here the Network Leaders play a key role in communicating both corporate and local information to each line of business and staff area, simplifying the flow of information in what would otherwise be a maze of matrix management.

As PNC grows through mergers and acquisitions, it now has an additional competitive advantage: a participative system that expands easily—enabling the bank to gain efficiencies quickly with virtually no energy-sapping disruption.

### 3. THE INTERNAL-CUSTOMER PROCESS

Another powerful method of creating universal collaboration is formalizing the internal-customer process. This occurs when the organization helps each individual and group to treat the next person in line in the process of serving customers as an "internal customer." Your internal customer is the person to whom you pass your work. And it is your responsibility to help your internal customer create value for external customers. When this occurs, an organization reorients itself horizontally and collaboration flows.

> Sheraton customer-service training is not just for the company's guest service attendants (GSAs). Sheraton trains everyone—from room attendants to internal staff members—to believe that when colleagues treat each other as customers they will have the energy and momentum to treat "external" customers well.

Today many organizations talk about the internal-customer concept, but most fail to bring it to life.

One organization that practices the internal-customer concept is the Saturn Division of General Motors. One year before Saturn manufactured its first car, it hired middle-level supervisors and began their training. Education in internal "customer and supplier relations" was central to the training.

Each supervisor spent time meeting with his or her customers and suppliers, both within Saturn and outside. And as a result, relations in Saturn are as smooth and collaborative as you'll find anywhere. When Lisa McClain, the supervisor of a welding unit, heard from a transmission assembler, her internal customer, that welding flux had been splattered on a group of parts the assembler had received from her team, she worked out a way to ensure it wouldn't happen again. McClain not only stopped a quality problem dead, she actually called to thank the transmission assembler for the complaint. She said she felt the call was important, "so that they understood we appreciated it and we didn't feel that they were, you know, just giving us a hard time." How many people in your organization would call someone to thank them for a complaint?

---

At Midland Bank in England the internal-customer concept is alive and well. Internal departments consider the bank's branches to be their customers. Each branch regularly rates the quality of service it receives from each department on a 5-point scale, with 1 as the top rating, 5 as the lowest. If an internal service provider receives between a 4 and a 5 he or she must actually call on the branch to learn where the problems lie.

Midland's service quality director Andy Stephens says these calls are very productive. Through empathy and perhaps a little fear of embarrassment before one's colleagues, the internal reporting and subsequent calls stimulate much greater collaboration.

---

CUNA Mutual also uses the internal-customer concept effectively. The company's mail room staff, for example, has interviewed "customers" in the Claims Divisions and asked how quickly the divisions need mail in order to meet commitments to their external customers.

Charts on walls throughout CUNA Mutual colorfully track how each unit is serving its internal customers. These charts are designed and hand drawn by the individual department and come in varying sizes and configurations. In the pensions department, for example, is a chart with Roadrunner and Wile E. Coyote. If performance falls close to the minimum acceptable level, Wile starts nipping at the Roadrunner's heels. Throughout the organization, such charts, which are updated monthly by each department, indicate thoughtful alignment between CUNA Mutual internal and external customers.

**The Customer-Centered Training Department**

Most training departments work for a senior staff manager. Too often that gives line managers the feeling that they are out of touch. When Jim Shields became vice president of training at Scotiabank in Canada, he decided to do something about that.

Shields set up a new structure. Instead of employing a staff to develop the training the head office wanted, Shields created an "account manager" assigned to each department. The account manager's job is to work with each department and ask, "What kind of training do you need?" Scotiabank is now developing the training that the different parts of the bank consider critical to their success, and the perceived value of the training department among the line managers has increased enormously.

Perhaps the most important success factor in bringing the internal customer concept alive in any organization is the spirit with which it is undertaken. In our organizational lives, most of us are conditioned to avoid meddling in other peoples' business. We are often reluctant to point out a peer's problems, no less make them visible to all in the form of an internal-customer rating. And we are even more reticent if the customer is someone above us in the hierarchy. The problem is that without facts and data of internal-customer relationships reported openly, the entire process will fail. Indeed, it might even increase waste as people go through the motions of rating but don't tell the truth.

Two factors are critical in overcoming this natural reluctance.

First is the overarching purpose. Without a sense of purpose, candid feedback often feels more like tattling; in the context of a vision and values that speak of customer enthusiasm, continuous improvement, collaboration, and the like, people are more willing to provide candid feedback because it means they are supporting the company rather than blowing the whistle on a peer.

The second factor is how the internal customer feedback is handled. If people are criticized publicly and punished, there will be little candor in the system. If they are appreciated as team players who are trying to improve, the system begins to work.

The principle at work here is for each employee, as an internal supplier or internal customer, never to accept or pass on a defect. This was best exemplified during a study mission to Japan that a number of

Forum executives took. At a Komatsu plant where heavy earthmoving equipment was being manufactured, we were told that if any worker found a defect he or she could push a button that would stop the production line immediately, an act that would surely cause Henry Ford deep chagrin were he alive today. Although this occurs infrequently, when it does, the *other workers on the line cheer.* Why? Because even though a mistake has been made, it will never be experienced by a customer.

---

**Customer Confusion**

Some companies are reluctant to use the term *internal customer.* The fear is that the external customers will be ignored while groups of internal customers go about the business of making each other happy.

Pepsi-Cola had such a concern, so the company changed the labels. Its external customers are the people who actually drink the product. Pepsi calls these people "consumers."

Its intermediate customer is the trade, or supermarket. Pepsi calls this group "customers."

Pepsi believes in the internal-customer process but doesn't want any confusion as to who is ultimately to be served . . . its consumers and customers. Pepsi's solution? Don't use the label "internal customer." Rather, the company calls its own people who must serve one another to create external quality "performers."

A key point here is to change the labels, but don't change the internal-customer concept.

---

## 4. Collaboration Skills

*It is impossible to estimate how many good ideas are abandoned each and every day, the result of difficult-to-manage lateral relationships.*

—John Kotter, Professor, Harvard Business School

Universal collaboration often means learning a new way of working, or doing what comes unnaturally. People are asked to accomplish results in informal partnerships with others they neither manage nor report to. Because this is relatively new for most people, they need both new attitudes and new skills.

In this situation, many of the skills that effective performers have relied upon for past success are useless. For example, employees who are preoccupied with gaining influence with superiors may actually have hoarded information that would make them look knowledgeable even when that same information might benefit another department. No more. Now that same employee must communicate what he or she knows.

In addition, people have to unlearn authoritarian habits. In the workplace, people often act in subtle but destructively autocratic ways ("Look, the customer wants the project done this way, just do it!"). This demeans the person being spoken to. But in addition, research shows that such behavior limits the amount of information shared. The communication is one-way, a directive. As a result, people don't really know what's going on. Ultimately this means that they can't serve internal or external customers as effectively as they might.

When people live in a culture that uses such authoritarian approaches, they normally spend a great deal of time currying favor, protecting turf, or maneuvering for the limelight . . . none of which adds value for the customer.

One recent study revealed the chilling price of applying power and authority in the medical world. Assessing the performance of hospital intensive-care units, a Northwestern University research team found that when staff unquestioningly followed the lead of the physician in charge the units had *twice the patient death rate* found in units that functioned as a team of colleagues, all of whom were free to offer opinions that might benefit the patient.

### *Deprogramming Old Habits*

Many approaches have been used to deprogram old hierarchical habits and replace them with the specific skills of collaboration.

One effective way to create universal collaboration is to have groups that need to improve their working relationship attend a workshop with a facilitator who understands the dynamics of real collaboration. Rather than learning "theory," people learn by working on real-world problems. At a large East Coast bank, for example, a new executive recently arrived to run the retail branch operations and found extraordinary levels of competitiveness, fear, and disrespect among the staff. The climate, in short, was the opposite of collaborative. The bank launched a training program to help employees change.

Area managers were the first group to participate—and they showed up angry and threatened because their new leader, having established an overarching purpose of creating exceptional service for the customer, was granting more power to the branch managers who reported directly to them. During the first day, the group was nasty, combative, and rude. The facilitator was eventually able to "hold a mirror up" to such dysfunctional behavior and the group gradually settled down. With the workshop leader's help, the area managers began to examine ways they could reengineer their jobs in support of the new leader and create a better customer experience. By the second day, the area managers had loosened up considerably. Members were actually collaborating effectively. Laughter was even heard from inside the meeting room!

Surprisingly, the people in this group had no idea how ineffective, abusive, and uncollaborative their behavior actually was. It was normal behavior in their culture, and therefore not seen as dysfunctional. It was simply the way their old culture had allowed them to behave. After several more groups in the bank attended similar sessions and a combined workshop was held for everyone, the collaboration started flowing. Lessons learned? First, we are often oblivious to our own uncollaborative behavior. Second, bringing people together and confronting such behavior can break the logjam of noncollaboration.

Adventure learning programs are another way to create universal collaboration. Often dubbed "rocks and ropes," these workshops use the outdoors as a classroom. As part of an eight-day Global Leadership Program, for instance, senior managers from Thomas Cook ventured into the hills for a day, where they experienced challenges and exercises designed to force collaboration among people who needed to work together effectively. The focus of such programs is not to expose one's vulnerabilities, like a fear of heights or weak triceps. Rather it is to enable the team to combine strengths and collaborate for results.

Often, through teamwork, the groups accomplish feats that even amaze themselves. ("All team members scale that twelve-foot wall and only one team member can use a rope to assist in climbing.") And discussions after the exercises bring out the important dos and don'ts of effective collaboration and how executives actually treat each other in their real work environment.

### *Learning Influence Skills*

Ford of Australia took advantage of another opportunity. Its successful training program sought to improve collaboration by teaching the specific skills required to collaborate.

For the past fifteen years Forum has studied outstanding collaborators and the skills that make them effective. We refer to these as influence skills. Our research reveals that the effectiveness of influencers is determined by a distinct set of practices in which they engage. There are twenty-one influence practices, described in the self-test contained in the Toolkit at the back of this book. (See "How Good Are Your Influence Skills?" page 255.) You can complete this self-test, identify where you are strong and where you need development, and then consult the accompanying tactics guide for hints on how to improve.

Executives estimate that they spend over 80 percent of their time seeking to achieve results with others over whom they have no direct control—the type of situation that calls for influence skills. With flattened organizations, self-directed teams, and a requirement to work laterally, such skills are vital. But they are unnatural and unknown to most of us.

The majority of people, when put into a situation where effective influence is required, will react in one of two ways, neither of which is effective. Some will try to persuade or coax others to see the strength of their ideas. Others will opt for a softer approach and try to get what they want by being nice. Research indicates that neither works well. And the reason is that there is no real collaboration. Neither coaxing nor being nice involves much sharing of ideas. And because the people being influenced wind up learning little about the situation, they can't fully utilize their own unique human capabilities to address it. Each of these instinctive reactions, the active and the passive, is born of the old competitive idea that you should try to get people to "come to your side."

Forum research has found that the rate of innovation rises markedly if people approach such situations with a spirit of inquiry rather than with a goal of persuasion. In one study, 91 percent of the people on "highly innovative" teams rated themselves high on learning from one another.

Take, for example, the strategy Kodak pursued to increase the rate of innovation and patent submissions from its research and development lab. The company created a cross-functional team of attorneys, engineers, scientists, and R and D managers to help increase the odds that their findings would be patentable. The result? The lab's patent submissions are up 60 percent, and the number being issued has doubled. What worked here was attorneys and scientists collaborating and learning from each other.

The influence practices are clustered into three groups. One group helps people *build* influence, another helps them *use* influence, and the third helps them *sustain* influence. One of the practices that enables the building of influence, for example, is "encouraging others to express their ideas." Sounds obvious, doesn't it? But we are continually amazed at how often this doesn't happen, as in the poor-performing hospital intensive-care units studied by Northwestern University.

The Kodak innovation story is an excellent example of one of the "use" influence practices, "demonstrating competence by bringing relevant knowledge and skill to the work to be done."

An example from the "sustain" cluster occurred when PowerGen, a United Kingdom utility, charged each unit in the company with creating its own charter. Working together, members of each unit shaped a statement of purpose, defined how they added value, and outlined their personal responsibilities. This encouraged the practice of "contributing suggestions aimed at improving work processes and products." The process helped every employee understand the role of his or her group in the organization and built a fundamental commitment to the charter of each unit. Employees came to trust that the group's goals were sound, and were therefore more motivated to achieve them.

The major point of this section: You can teach people the attitudes and skills they need to collaborate. In fact, you probably *have* to teach them. It is a serious mistake to assume that when people are put in a flattened organization or become members of self-managed teams, they will have the skills their new situation requires. To avoid false starts and demoralizing ineffectiveness in the pursuit of collaboration, evaluate what attitudes and special skills are needed for success in the new organization you are creating. And if people don't have those attitudes and skills, help them to acquire them.

### 5. EFFECTIVE DEPLOYMENT OF TEAMS

Teamitis is giving teams a bad name. But teams can be deployed effectively. To understand why some teams flourish while others fail, Forum conducted a major research project including an intensive study of teams in six companies and interviews with pairs of team leaders in twenty-seven others.

We found that to succeed, teams need specific conditions. They achieve their potential only when they can answer yes to the following six questions:

1. Do team members share the same purpose for working together?
2. Do team members have a chance to influence the goals that are set for the team?
3. Are team members in charge of the work that they do?
4. Do team members believe they have the right skill levels and skill sets to meet their goals?
5. Do team members hold each other accountable for achieving the team's goals?
6. Do individuals get rewarded based on the team's performance?

To create conditions where team members can answer yes to these questions, successful organizations maintain a team registration system. In such a system, each team's charter and formation are approved by a senior group of managers. While this may sound controlling and restrictive (just what you are trying to get away from), a requirement for registration actually empowers team members. It lets the team know their work is approved and sanctioned by management, that it's not just make-work. It ensures that the team's work is strategically important and it prevents redundancy—working on the same things that other teams are working on. Figure 4.3 is an example of a team registration form.

Of course, the team leader also plays a vital role in any team's success—but it's a different role from what most people expect. Leaders of outstanding teams don't manage their teams in the traditional sense. They spend comparatively little time telling people on the team what to do, dealing with conflicts, or even functioning as cheerleaders.

**Figure 4.3**

CUSTOMER-CENTERED QUALITY REGISTRATION

**Issue selected for improvement:** ______________________

______________________

______________________

**Sponsor:** ______________________

**Results of this improvement will impact:** ☐ Quality ☐ Cost ☐ Delivery ☐ Safety ☐ Morale

**Check:** Is this issue being worked on anywhere else in the organization?

**Team leader:** ______________________

**Previous Training**

**Team members:**

1. ______________________
2. ______________________
3. ______________________
4. ______________________

**Manager approval:** ______________________ Name ____________ Date

**Council approval:** ______________________ Name ____________ Date

Our research discovered that leaders of outstanding teams spend a great portion of their time managing the *linkage* between the team and the rest of the organization. And these leaders often viewed the way they had managed this linkage as having facilitated the team's success. "In any of these new initiatives, you need to have sponsors," says Eric Shuler, a successful team leader at DuPont. "You need to continually find new sponsors because sponsors come and go. Especially because when a new initiative is kind of embryonic and fragile, a key role is to go out and build sponsorship continually. With these new things, some of the people who are raising their hands to sponsor initially don't know what they're getting into."

Leaders of outstanding teams are cautious skeptics, understanding the strengths and weaknesses of teams as a way of organizing. "If managed properly, teams are the best thing there is," said one. "If not, they can be an easy way to kill something." Another was even more graphic:

> A team is like having a baby tiger given to you at Christmas. It does a wonderful job of keeping the mice away for about twelve months, and then it starts to eat your kids.

---

**The Ultimate Team**

Recently we were making a presentation to a senior management team in Italy. The session was difficult because people didn't listen, talked at and interrupted one another, and were generally restless and competitive, each following a personal agenda.

Suddenly one of them leapt out of his chair as if someone had given him a hot foot. Excitedly he shared his revelation with the group: "We go around telling everyone that teamwork is important. It's even one of our company values. But look at us. We're one of the worst examples of teamwork anywhere. No wonder there's no universal collaboration here!"

Absolutely right!

Check in with the management team of which you are a part. What does your team behavior signal to those who are watching? Are you a prime model of universal collaboration, or are you teaching something else?

---

Another important finding about effective teams is that a team's capacity to handle complex problems grows over time. What this means is: Don't assign a brand-new team that is just learning how to be a team the task of fixing a chronic historical malfunction like the billing system.

As people learn your organization's problem-solving process and become comfortable in the team environment, teams will be able to take on bigger and more pervasive problems.

For "neophyte" teams, look for three key indicators of success.

First is *enthusiasm.* When a new team has completed its work, you want its members to be excited about what they've accomplished. Enthusiasm is evident when team members volunteer for the next team assignment or ask to lead a future team. This is important because the rest of your organization will look for their reaction. If it is upbeat, others will answer the recruiting call for future teams. If they are negative, staffing new teams will be like trying to get people to volunteer to take a cut in pay.

Indicator number two is *learning.* What have the initial teams learned that will enhance the effectiveness of future teams? This question should be formally asked and answered. And the answers should lead to changes that will benefit future teams. A strategic business unit manager at Milliken & Company told us that one of his company's competitive advantages was how fast and effectively it could transfer new learning throughout the worldwide organization.

Of course, the third indicator is *results.* Effective teams work on problems that are linked to the customer or company direction. While the scope of their work may not be massive, it must be relevant and important. What color to paint the company cafeteria hardly qualifies as a serious topic for team consideration.

## 6. Organizational Structure

Universal collaboration requires an organizational structure designed for smooth service to, and intimacy with, customers. This sounds obvious, yet organizations have found a plethora of ways to create structure that defeats people's efforts to serve.

Until Thomas Ryder arrived as president, American Express Establishment Services had been divided into eight functional groups such as "sales" and "accounting." In some respects this may have been convenient for American Express managers. All transactions were handled by one group. But for customers, the system was a nightmare. They couldn't figure out who in the organization to approach with any particular question. And people in the organization, all handling the needs of an incredibly diverse collection of customers, couldn't get to know any of them well.

Ryder and his managers charted interactions from one point to another to show the complexity of relations between customers and the Establishment Services' functional groups and between the groups themselves. For obvious reasons, this resulted in what was dubbed "the spaghetti chart."

In order to streamline operations and focus on the customer, the spaghetti chart had to go. The team reorganized into four groups to serve specific industries:

- travel,
- retail,
- restaurants and entertainment, and
- "emerging markets" (new industries like mail order).

With this reorganization, the group created line-of-sight service for its one hundred or so largest merchant clients in each of the industries.

Now American Express people were aiming at customers rather than at managers in the hierarchy. This structural change clarified and simplified interactions. Instead of serving itself, the organization could put full energy into serving its customers.

Similarly, CUNA Mutual simplified for greater collaboration and customer support. It put decision making close to the customer, created a single point of contact for customers, and consolidated over two hundred services into three clusters. Executives decentralized market decision making and authority by creating eight regional offices, each run by a senior marketing officer (SMO). In the past, different offices had marketed different products. These new offices can deliver almost any CUNA Mutual resource to the customer.

In an internal move that mirrors the field reorganization, clusters of products are administered by a newly named market segment manager. When field employees need help they can go to a single point of contact for a large array of products. Now the entire organization is aligned with customer needs. CUNA Mutual is also carefully developing influence skills in people. Together with its strong internal-customer orientation, these enable CUNA Mutual to deliver genuinely seamless service to its customers.

The principle behind this structural work was stated simply by one executive: "We start with our customers and build the organization from the outside in, not the other way around."

The company that is unable to hold this point of view reminds us of the man who was dropping off two suits to be dry-cleaned. As he drove up to the cleaner, he noticed a bold sign in the window: IN BY 9:00—OUT BY 5:00. It was 8:45 A.M. when the customer entered the store, put his suits on the counter, and said, "I'll be back for these at five." To which the clerk behind the counter said, "You're not going to see these suits till next Tuesday!" "I don't understand," replied the man, "Your sign says in by nine and out by five." "Oh no, fella!" responded the clerk, "That's not the suits, that's me. *I'm in by nine and out by five!*"

What we have in this vignette is a company that is designed to serve itself rather than its customers. It is self-centered rather than customer centered. What are the indicators that your company's structure might be designed to serve the hierarchy instead of your customers? There are five questions which can help give you the answer. They are:

1. When you trace the interactions between different groups in your organization and your customers, does it look like a spaghetti chart? If yes, what lines can you eliminate?

2. How many levels are there in your hierarchy? Some very large companies have as few as four. Determine what value each level contributes to your customers and eliminate those that contribute marginally or not at all.

3. Is the primary orientation of your organization vertical (functions, hierarchy) or horizontal (process and collaboration)? How can you restructure to create more horizontal thinking and behavior?

4. Where is the focus of decision making in your company? What can you do to move it closer to your customers?

5. When your customer has a problem, how many departments must he or she contact to get it solved? Is there a way for the customer to get help with only one phone call?

## 7. INFRASTRUCTURE

Finally, to support universal collaboration an organization needs to change the infrastructure that underlies its daily work. For many, the existing infrastructure—the physical layout of facilities, compensation system, perhaps even computer systems—was probably created to support an obsolete, more hierarchical way of working. New systems to support collaborative, horizontal ways of serving customers are needed.

Key infrastructure elements include:

- physical layout,
- technology,
- internal communication systems,
- compensation, and
- recognition systems.

### *Physical Layout*

The physical space your organization occupies can significantly affect collaboration. Ask yourself whether your office layout impedes or encourages collaboration, and what you can do about it.

When the office furniture manufacturer Steelcase videotaped how office work is actually done, it found that people who collaborated effectively needed different kinds of space for their personal work and their group work.[4]

Hewlett-Packard changed several production lines from a straight to a horseshoe configuration so employees at the beginning of the line could actually see what was coming off the end. This very shape symbolized collaboration, and productivity jumped because of it.

Applied Materials, the world's largest maker of semiconductor manufacturing equipment, promotes collaboration by banning people from having individual offices or even significantly differentiated work areas. Everyone from the newest salesperson to the CEO has a nearly identical cubicle.

Another simple but symbolic aspect of physical layout can be found at Saturn. So often parking spaces around a company are reserved and numbered to indicate a parking pecking order. Usually the CEO is closest to the main entrance, followed by the COO, EVP, etc. Not so at Saturn. In their Spring Hill, Tennessee, offices and plant there are no designated parking spaces. It is strictly first come, first parked. This signals to every employee that the ones who arrive early deserve the premier spaces. Hierarchy has nothing to do with it.

### *Technology*

Today's technology makes collaboration easier, but only if it's used properly.

The author Michael Schrage points out that technology can create a "shared space" inside which groups can collaborate. One of the oldest kinds of shared space is the blackboard. By putting ideas on a shared board, people can think together. Voicemail, electronic mail, and videoconferencing can extend a shared space across continents. It's as if people in New York, Paris, and Bangkok can all share a blackboard at the same time. Schrage describes electronic whiteboard technology that actually allows people in several different sites scattered around the world to write on a board and have their messages appear on similar boards at all the sites at once.[5]

We don't need the technology of the future to create global shared space. Today, we can use voicemail boxes to help a team work together. We can even give a customer a voicemail box on our company system for dependable communication with the team.

Electronic mail by computer and videoconferencing can have a similarly powerful impact. U.S. Bancorp would have had a far more difficult time gathering one thousand employees' reactions to its vision statement without its electronic mail system. And the system allowed managers to effectively communicate what they were doing about the responses.

Be alert for technologies that help you collaborate better with your customers. Astra Merck, a pharmaceutical marketing joint venture of the Swedish pharmaceutical company Astra and the U.S. giant Merck, puts a desktop publishing system called Express Link in each of its thirty-five customer units. The system allows local staff to produce high-quality custom versions of all sales materials on Astra Merck products almost instantly. For example, they can quickly customize a brochure featuring an Astra Merck drug by putting the logo of a local health maintenance organization that wants to promote the drug to its own physicians.

The approach makes sales presentations "much more powerful"

than traditional sales literature, says Astra Merck president Wayne Yetter. "Now, when we talk to a physician about Plendil (an Astra Merck drug), the information that we are using, the page that we are sharing, bears the name of the plan that this physician belongs to."[6]

The important question regarding technology always is: "Will it help us serve our customers better or is it the latest fad?" The Astra Merck system makes collaboration easy and adds significant value for customers.

### *Internal Communication Systems*

In Chapter 3 we saw how the best companies manage the process of hearing the voice of the customer. Similarly, the best companies also have a strategy to both hear from and speak to their employees. Their internal system of communication forms an important part of the organization's infrastructure.

Dr. Edson de Godoy Bueno of Amil recognizes the importance of communication when he puts "Chairman/Training Manager" on his business card. By regularly teaching courses to his "collaborators," he both communicates his messages to employees and gets an unusual opportunity to hear from them.

John Ward demonstrated a strategic way of communicating after he took over as chief executive of Chase Manhattan's credit card business in 1993. It was clear Chase Bankcard Services' business suffered from serious morale problems, since turnover had nearly doubled to 38 percent a year. In the recession of the early 1990s, the bank had neglected the credit card business while using its profits to cover losses in other parts of the bank. Clearly employees had been hurt, but it wasn't clear just what was wrong.

Ward and Pat Rowell, his human resources chief, decided to base their communications strategy on the bank's annual climate survey, which asks simple multiple-choice and 1-to-5-scale questions. Employees had been answering the survey since 1989, but it had had little impact.

The 1993 survey showed only 50 percent of employees were satisfied with the bank—at a time when organizations Chase benchmarked itself against were reporting more than 70 percent. Communications and pay were the key gripes.

Rowell built a communications program around the survey. She organized seminars on the results for all Bankcard Services managers that allowed them to report on why they thought communications and pay were issues. Each manager then presented the results of the survey to his or her people, with the message that the bank was working on solutions. Then it developed new communications programs and a new, systematic approach to pay.

The new approach allowed Chase Bankcard pay to take aggressive salary action for its employees—particularly top performers. But the key change was that Chase explained its pay programs through its emerging communications methods. Pamphlets, newsletters, and seminars all dealt with pay. Ward and other senior executives participated in "town meetings" at each Bankcard Services facility.

Result: The following year employee satisfaction rose twenty points, to 70 percent. Turnover declined, and the Bankcard unit was able to resume rapid growth.

The key lesson: The Ward-Rowell approach to communications worked because it was strategic. It built on an existing but previously neglected communications channel (the climate survey), and simply responded logically to the information already coming in. To support

---

**Ambassadors to Employees, Serving Customers**

Listening to the voice of the employee is as vital as listening to the voice of the customer. One complements the other. In Delta Air Lines' Integrated Customer Service (ICS) initiative, the company has chosen 120 "ambassadors" as a communications channel throughout the organization. The ICS program is a comprehensive effort to improve service. Delta leaders reasoned that if anyone knew where reforms were needed, it would be the frontline employees who face hundreds of problems daily. Ambassadors were recruited carefully. Only those respected by their peers as strong, customer-focused performers made the cut. Ambassadors included both customer contact people like pilots, flight attendants, ticket agents, and reservationists, and internal people such as mechanics, baggage handlers, and human resources specialists. To get ideas for ICS, the ambassadors interviewed over 7,100 Delta employees. Delta is creating its new customer service plan from these interviews and from new voice-of-the-customer data. And, because of such widespread employee involvement in its creation, its successful implementation is more likely assured.

---

collaboration, the communications infrastructure needed to be adjusted, expanded, and attended to.

When designing a communications strategy, opt for face-to-face interactions whenever possible. A senior executive, manager, or supervisor speaking with employees, talking about facts—not promises—and responding to questions with candid answers is superior to a memo, phonemail, or E-mail communiqué every time. One large bank audited the effectiveness of its communication program by stopping each element, then documenting employee response. Only four of its 40,000 employees asked what had happened to the monthly video, 36 asked for the twice-monthly newspaper, 890 asked for the Social Committee publication, and 2,112 asked for the monthly listing of job vacancies, promotions, and transfers.[7]

The point is obvious. How effectively we communicate is not a function of how many channels we have. It is determined by which channels work best. All others are waste.

### *Compensation*

A compensation system that supports collaboration can play a key role in allowing collaboration to develop. At Saturn, the compensation format is identical for everyone from the person who sweeps the floors to the president. It has three elements: economic performance of the company, quality/service performance of the company, and attainment of individual personal development plan (e.g., completion of training or acquisition of expertise). This compensation plan strongly supports Saturn's values: making the numbers, providing outstanding service and quality, and developing people. There are no personal performance objectives, which in many companies spur intramural competition.

CUNA Mutual was able to introduce team incentives in a unionized environment. The union had traditionally opposed individual incentive pay for fear of the effects of management's subjective ratings of employees. As they tried to make the workplace more collaborative, managers realized that they wanted to introduce more of a group-oriented incentive pay plan. Both sides were happy to settle for a 5 percent incentive opportunity based on company performance and on the employee's work group achieving agreed-upon goals.

At MBNA America Bank, the outstanding credit card company, sixteen key customer variables are measured daily. The performance on each factor is posted on a large tote board in the company lobby with an overall average positioned at the top. For every day that the average is above 95 percent, money is placed aside and distributed to employees every quarter. In this ingenious system, employees are in effect actually being paid by their customers!

***Recognition Systems***

To support universal collaboration, recognize those who do it. For example, give teams special emphasis in recognition programs. Recognition efforts that only acknowledge individual performance get just that—individual performance. At one company, no team was ever given its prestigious Chairman's Award before 1989. In 1995 half of the awards went to teams.

American Express' Establishment Services unit not only makes a point of recognizing teams but even gives awards to people from other parts of American Express who collaborate effectively with it—an unusual boundary-crossing practice that should become more common.

Many sales organizations are moving from individual to team bonuses as the complexity of matching a provider organization's resources to a customer's requirements increases. One company which customarily sent its quota-busting salespeople to far-off exotic resorts has started including sales-support people as well. Now they travel to closer, top-quality resorts and during their celebrations actually build the basis for future and better collaboration.

Some companies even get their customers into the act, asking them for the names of employees who provide extraordinary levels of service.

There's no question that when you observe a world-class company, an air of celebration exists. Teams and those who collaborate well are honored and feted. The number of ways that exist to recognize someone is limited only by the imagination. But one which has worked for centuries and is perhaps the most projected of all is a simple and sincere "thank you."

## A DISCOVERY MORE POWERFUL THAN THE COMPUTER

*Real learning gets to the heart of what it means to be human. . . . Through learning, we extend our capacity to create, to be part of the generative process of life.*

—PETER M. SENGE, *THE FIFTH DISCIPLINE*

Many organizations do manage effectively for universal collaboration. Consider how the creation of an America's Cup Syndicate works as it seeks to win the most coveted prize in yacht racing. The organizers have to start with a strategy: how they'll build the boat and then how they'll sail it. They need leaders— one in command on the water, and another who leads off the water.

But you can't get anywhere without a crew. Leaders recruit the best crew they can and then they train, drill, and develop. They work with the crew members to ensure each knows how to work with all the others. Each crew member is a partner of every other crew member.

In the 1995 America's Cup races, it became apparent that New Zealand had achieved collaboration a bit more universal than the collaboration in U.S. America's Cup syndicates. By most accounts, America had the best boat design technology and an excellent crew. But New Zealand had something else. Its designers collaborated better with its crew.

Rather than simply designing a boat and turning it over to the team, the New Zealand designers involved the crew and listened to them on every aspect of design. The result: a boat designed by sailors. U.S. designers used the best computers, but didn't hear the crew members quite so well.

Ultimate outcome: The New Zealand team beat the U.S. computer wizards, 4–0.

## ACTION POINTS

- Does your organization have an effective vision? Before saying yes, try this. Randomly select ten nonmanagerial employees. Ask each: Do we have a vision? What is it? Does it have meaning for you? If employees are confused about the vision or it has little meaning to them, your vision doesn't have the power it needs. To fix this, create a process to reaffirm or modify the vision.

- To what extent do your employees feel actively involved in the workings of your enterprise? In small focus groups, ask employees this question and others of concern to you or them. How would they like to be involved? What supports and inhibits their involvement? Of course, running these focus groups is an act of involvement in itself. **Warning:** Do this only if you are willing to listen and be open to change.
- Create a vital internal-customer process. Formalize it by having internal suppliers actually "call" on their internal customers. Establish internal-customer measurements that align with external-customer requirements. Create consequences and payoffs for achieving the measurements.
- How well do people in your organization collaborate? If improvement is needed, ask three questions: (1) Do they actually have skills? (2) Do excellent collaborators get rewarded and does disruptive behavior get corrected? (3) How effective is your most senior team at creating universal collaboration among themselves? After answering these questions, fix what needs to be corrected.
- Do you suffer from teamitis? Ask each team in your company to audit itself using the questions on page 132. Allow any team that is not being effective to disband with thanks, not recrimination. Through this process, identify the patterns of team ineffectiveness and fix them.
- Check your organizational structure and goals. Do they support or inhibit universal collaboration? What needs to be changed?
- Do your physical layout, technology, internal communications systems, compensation, and recognition systems support universal collaboration? Assign each element to a senior executive to investigate this question and recommend improvements.

## Chapter 5

# From Customer Satisfaction to Lasting Customer Enthusiasm

*Loyalty today is no longer a function of rote or duty, but rather passion. You must do things so astonishingly well that customers become not merely loyalists, but rather outright apostles.*

—Skip LeFauve,
Chairman, Saturn[1]

If on a certain Friday in June of 1994 you were driving from Nashville toward Saturn's manufacturing facility in Spring Hill, Tennessee, you might have sensed that something a little weird was happening. First of all there was a traffic jam, and although it was raining hard, serious traffic is an almost unheard of occurrence in the remote recesses of this rugged hill country.

And if you looked in your rearview mirror, your side mirror, and beyond, you would have realized that you were surrounded. Thousands and thousands of the same little cars covered the hills of the interstate like lemmings going to the sea, and they all had little orange balls on their antennas that bravely said: "Spring Hill or Bust."

## "A Customer-Service Orgy"

Total strangers got out of their cars and started mingling with each other—hugging, shaking hands, slapping each other on the back—right there in the middle of the road. And the funny thing about these—count 'em—twenty-eight thousand vehicles was that they were simple, practical, subcompact vehicles—not Harleys or Vettes or Porsches. But for some reason, these people loved their cars—so much so, in fact, that they felt the need to come from places as far away as Taiwan and Hawaii to celebrate, consecrate, and whoop it up.

Saturn's homecoming weekend was, in the words of one journalist, "a customer-service orgy."[2] Despite high winds and rain which flooded parking lots, *more than forty-four thousand attendees* did everything from touring the assembly plant to attending the wedding of two Saturn employees.

But the main event was simply Saturn devotees sitting around telling each other "one-up" stories of what it's like to do business with Saturn.

Devotees like white-haired, seventy-three-year-old Jack Drohan from Quincy, Massachusetts. Says he: "I had told my daughter, 'You know, I like this car so much, I'd like to drive down to Tennessee to see how they make it,' and two weeks later I get an invitation to their homecoming. I couldn't believe it." Indeed, how *does* one understand such devotion to a car and the company that produced it?

## A "Lulu" of an Idea

The answer lies in the fact that a few organizations today—Saturn, to be sure—have learned how to make the interaction at the customer interface so distinctive, so superior, and so consistently anticipatory of customer needs that those customers are quite literally flabbergasted.

Saturn has revolutionized the automobile industry because, according to Chairman Skip LeFauve, who was Saturn's first president, it is more than a great little car. It is an "idea . . . a whole new way of doing things, of working with our customers and with one another. It's more of a cultural revolution than a product revolution."[3]

Think back to 1982. GM was in distress. The Japanese were killing sales with their low-cost, high-quality automobiles, and the company seemed paralyzed. General Motors' much maligned chairman Roger Smith had to do something. In his desperation Smith had an idea, and it was, in his words, a "lulu."[4]

What if GM could beat the Japanese at their own game and make a low-priced, high-quality car in America? What would happen if GM, in fact, could create an entirely different sort of car company, one that could zoom past industry goals of "customer satisfaction" to a new watermark of "customer enthusiasm"? What if the way this automobile company produced, sold, and serviced its product was so distinctive that the buzz about the new product would be as much about the way the company treated customers as the car itself?

As it turned out, Smith's idea *was* a lulu. Only five years after the first model rolled out of production, Saturn

- was number two in overall retail sales in America;
- had the lowest service cost of any car ($52, which is $32 less than the industry average);
- had the highest resale value of any car in any class;
- had the highest customer retention rate in the automobile industry (61% of customers say they would buy another Saturn); and
- had the highest sales per retailer (899 units) of anyone in the industry.

Saturn, which was formerly referred to by industry analysts as GM's "Saturn Experiment," was the top award winner in the 1995 J. D. Power and Associates car sales satisfaction index.[5] This particular J. D. Power award measures customer satisfaction in the sales and delivery process, and Saturn's total score of 160 points is remarkable for a number of reasons.

First, Saturn's sales and delivery process for its subcompact outclassed such high-priced luxury also-rans as Nissan's Infiniti (150); Toyota's Lexus (149); GM's Cadillac (149); Volvo (148); and Mercedes-Benz (147). In fact, Saturn surpassed the previous record high for any car in any class.

What's more, 90 percent of Saturn owners were "very satisfied" with the way their 1995 cars were sold and delivered. An impressive figure in its own right, but truly a major feat when you consider that the vast majority of Americans surveyed find the process of buying a car highly distasteful. According to David Aaker, professor of marketing strategy at the University of California at Berkeley, the Saturn way of interacting with customers is "a real breakthrough in the auto industry, which is bizarre. They treat the customer as a friend. They treat the customer intelligently."[6]

## Almost Embarrassingly Well Done

According to Betty Moe, who drove the forty-five hundred miles from Anchorage, Alaska, to the homecoming weekend, Saturn's selling process is "almost embarrassingly well-done."[7] Saturn treats customers as they wish to be treated and, in fact, they are called "guests" by salespeople who in turn call themselves "transportation consultants." These consultants put their emphasis on "educating" consumers about the Saturn "difference."

This Saturn difference means that customers don't feel like "victims" who, when faced with the prospect of buying a car, feel they have to do battle with glib salespeople and sales managers with a seemingly bewildering and infinite number of deals, deals, and more deals. To that end, Saturn has removed the mystery of how prices are computed and the fear of an unfair advantage by instituting a "no-dicker sticker" policy: a fixed price on the car which assures buyers that they will not be at a disadvantage by being a woman, a minority, or simply an unskilled negotiator.

Says customer Marc Gorelick of Michigan, "I honestly feel that our sales rep was sincerely interested in answering all of our questions . . . as opposed to the usual experience where the buyer is made to feel like a side of beef tossed into a pool of piranhas."[8]

Customers show their appreciation for the way Saturn manages the customer interface by rewarding Saturn with the highest customer-retention rate in the industry—and this despite less-than-perfect product quality. "When the [Saturn] product is measured by defects, repairs, and such, it's a very average product," says Daryl Hazel, director of market research at Ford Motor Company, "but when you talk to the people who own the product, there's a difference. And that difference is attributed to how they were treated."

## A Different Sales and Service Brand

Saturn is now turning a profit in an industry where profitability is fleeting and in which the barriers to entry for a new car company seem almost insurmountable. Underlying Saturn's success is its commitment to live its number one value, *customer enthusiasm*, and that one value has changed the face of automobile buying history. What could have been a typical foray into a 1980s-type of "customer satisfaction" initiative—with the goal of selling and servicing better than the competition—turned out instead to be a commitment to creating a *breakthrough* in how customers are treated. The result is a *brand*—not just of a car but of a car-buying experience.

Advertising people define a brand as an elusive quality that separates a product offering from all others. From its inception, Saturn created a brand by intentionally designing its methods to create a competitive advantage at the customer interface. In essence, the ways customers learned about, bought, and got service from Saturn would become as much a product of Saturn as the car itself.

Saturn's successful and enterprising concept of intentionally creating a proprietary, branded way of interacting with customers is working in a variety of other enterprises—with similarly stellar results.

## 3M'S CUSTOMER-FOCUSED MARKETING

Say the name *3M* and the word *innovation* is likely to come to mind. Lore has it that if you work for 3M and you have a good idea, someone will help you get the funding to make it a big product—maybe even the next Post-it Notes. Year after year 3M is lauded for its continuous stream of breakthrough technologies and products—products as varied and as useful as Scotch tape, surgical masks, and traffic control materials.

3M is comprised of fifty operating units in more than sixty countries, and it turns out over sixty thousand innovative products based on eighty-five unique technologies. But this entrepreneurial fervor had a downside for those customers who needed a number of different 3M products. They likened the difficulty to "a grocery shopping disaster."

> Look at it this way. You're busy, you haven't much time for errands. Let's say you stop after work at a market, pick up milk and eggs, then look around for the bread. "Sorry," says the clerk. "You have to go down the street to the bakery." You check your list. "How about apples?" you ask. "The farmers' market is two blocks over," the clerk says. "Well, how about lunch meat?" The clerk shakes his head. "The butcher shop downtown is the only one carrying meat these days." Maddening, yes. But that's not all. Turns out the farmers' market takes only checks, the butcher is closing and says you must use your

credit card, and it's cash-only at the bakery. How are you supposed to figure out what you've spent?

A headache? Sure. By the time you get those five items on your list, you've spent hours which could have been better spent elsewhere. Until recently, many of 3M's commercial and industrial customers found themselves in a similar situation, asking questions like, "How come there are four 3M salespeople out in my waiting room?"; "Why do I need to work with three different distributors?"; "Why do I need to process twelve different invoices and twelve different sets of payment terms?" What 3M now says is, "You don't. You shouldn't. And you won't have to again."

### 3M: ONE-STOP SHOPPING

The solution was 3M's "Customer-Focused Marketing" (CFM), a proprietary process which makes it easier for customers to do business with them. Customers who once experienced the above problems now can be served by one representative of a sales team and distribution channel—one-stop shopping for all 3M products. This consolidation of resources gives the customer more purchasing power, reduced paperwork, and a more efficient use of precious time. For instance, because of CFM, all end users of 3M's Automotive Trades Division now have easy access to a full assortment of products from sixteen different 3M business units through one representative and one channel.

The results? Extraordinary. Customers cite CFM as a primary reason that they intend to do more and more business with 3M. This helps explain why over the last several years, sales via 3M's CFM approach increased *five times faster* than sales by traditional methods. Overall, they are significantly more profitable, too.

3M hadn't really listened to its customers before on this subject. When customers complained about the lack of coordination, the company typically responded with a smile and a hoped-for pacifying remark. The first customer to complain loudly and really stamp its feet was Wal-Mart, which sent a clear message that eight individual 3M reps with eight merchandising plans, eight sets of payment terms, and eight cooperative advertising proposals was just not acceptable. As it turned out, many industrial and commercial customers agreed. And many of 3M's competitors who had the exact same problems predicted that 3M would just not be able to pull off a solution. "3M Coordination" was an oxymoron, they said.

The competition was wrong. Bruce Hamilton, formerly 3M's general manager in Canada, took on the responsibility for championing the effort. Hamilton took the customer data directly to the heads of each business unit and began the process of getting unit leaders excited about the potential of the initiative. In addition to increasing the level of management support for 100 percent customer satisfaction through the CFM process, Hamilton took a wide variety of actions, from changing pricing and merchandising structures to increasing training.

Customer-Focused Marketing has allowed 3M to forge competitive advantage right at the customer interface by creating an atmosphere that makes it easy for customers to deal with 3M—and one that is not a "grocery shopper's nightmare."

## SHOCK VALUE

In truth, the standards for what constitutes excellent selling and service have risen to the extent that just doing the same thing better no longer differentiates your company. For example, if you are in an automobile accident, good service is a friendly claims adjuster who shows up within a reasonable period of time and then arranges for courteous, fast approval. Compare that to Plymouth Rock Assurance Corporation, which dispatches its "Crashbuster" to the accident scene, makes the necessary repair appraisals, and then cuts a check on the spot.

What is striking about Saturn, 3M, and Plymouth Rock Assurance is that rather than depending solely on good products and services to add value for customers, they are reinventing how they do business. The result is outright devotion, enthusiasm, and appreciation among customers and employees. Treating people fairly, intelligently, respectfully, and as *they* want to be treated ("the platinum rule") creates, to put it mildly, a bit of a stir. And a lot of loyalty.

## How to Create Competitive Advantage at the Customer Interface

*The definition has widened. A brand is no longer a synonym for something that comes in a package, can or bottle. Every product, every service, every cause that has a competitor is a brand that needs to define and defend its uniqueness.*

—Barry Day
Vice Chairman
Lintas International[9]

Most organizations have figured out how to reduce costs and install quality in the way that they *produce* products and services. Total quality management as applied to manufacturing was once a means of creating a strong competitive advantage. Today it is merely the entry card for competing in the marketplace. In our research, a secret of the customer-centered companies we studied was the way they differentiated themselves *at the customer interface.*

If your goal is profitable growth, one of the most important levers is customer retention. As Jagdish Sheth, professor of marketing at Emory University, has found, it costs five times as much to acquire a new customer as it does to get business from an existing one. Today the economics have swayed even more in favor of investing in existing accounts.

Many other studies confirm this, including research done by Fred Reichheld of Bain and Company and Earl Sasser of the Harvard Business School, which indicates that a 5 percent increase in customer loyalty can result in a 100 percent increase in profitability.[10]

Although these statistics have been well publicized, the newest research indicates that creating merely "satisfied" customers is no longer enough to ensure loyalty. Earl Sasser and Thomas Jones, also a Harvard Business School professor, discovered that there is little or no correlation between "satisfied" customers (vs. "highly satisfied" customers) and customer retention.[11] And PNC Bank Corp., a fast-growing financial services organization, recently affirmed this when it found that only customers who were "extremely satisfied" (6s and 7s on a scale of 1–7) were likely to be loyal.

The reason for creating consistently extraordinary experiences at the customer interface is to go past that bar of indifference labeled "good enough sales and service" and reach an interaction with customers that so utterly distinguishes you from others that it is a brand in itself—a unique impression that sets your company apart from others. Just such a process caused one Saturn customer to comment that she actually *looked forward* to going to her dealership. Imagine that.

The customer interface is a highly leveraged place to invest. All the work you've done backstage—research and development, strategic planning, training, process streamlining, creation of customer support services, production—is ultimately in the hands of the front line, your most direct and powerful channel to the customer. People on the front line create expectations, take the customer's pulse, get feedback on products and services, solve problems, and scout for such street-level information as how well you are performing relative to your competitors. Actions at the customer interface have the most directly measurable effect on profitable growth. As Robert Lee, executive vice president of training and development for Pacific Bell, states, "The training we give people that allows them to sell more hits the cash register right away."[12]

A piecemeal approach to sales, service, and marketing will never create the level of customer devotion that translates into highly profitable growth. That takes a strategic, holistic, and integrated approach that we call a Proprietary Customer Interaction Process: a reliable, value-added, *branded* way of interacting with customers, one as unique to your organization as your trademark.[13]

The steps to creating competitive advantage at the customer interface are:

1. Determine how customers want to do business with you.
2. Get leadership committed to a branded way of interacting with customers.
3. Install a high-value, distinctive and consistent customer-interaction process.

## Step 1: Determine How Customers Want to Do Business with You

How do organizations create a "perfect" customer-interaction process? Well, let's face the fact that "perfect" is a matter of perception unique to each customer. For example, in recent research delving into how customers define *value*—and what customers are truly willing to pay more money for—Forum found that organizations often assume mistakenly that all of their customers are interested in partnerships. Not so. As the Value Orientation Frame in Figure 5.1 illustrates, what customers value was defined along two dimensions: the need for relationship and the need for information.

Customers with a high "need for relationship" placed high value on the supplier's ability to understand them: their needs; their organization, strategy and challenges; and their future plans. Suppliers who are able to create such an in-depth relationship add value by be-

**Figure 5.1**

Value Orientation Frame

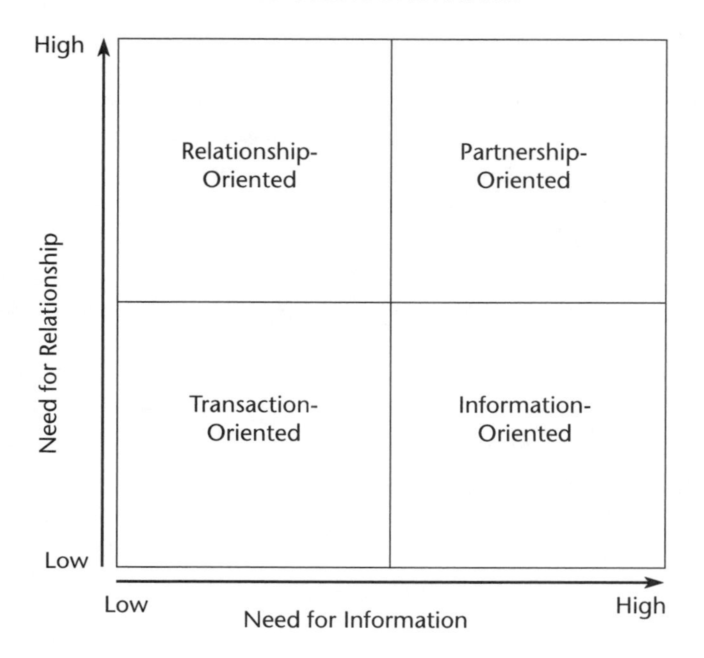

ing able to anticipate customer needs—and often play a key role in helping make the right decision for the customer. Often, buyers who are less experienced with the product they are buying will place a high value on this type of relationship. In essence, they say, "You know your products and services. I'll tell you what I need, and you make it happen for me."

The other dimension is the need for information, in which customers who fall on the extreme right-hand side of the chart say they will pay more to do business with a supplier who can keep them informed and educated about the world in which they operate. Suppliers who are able to provide easy access to information save their customers time and effort and make it easier to do business with them. Often these buyers are sophisticated, sometimes even knowing more about the products and services offered than the salespeople themselves.

The combination of these dimensions results in four types of customer buying frames. The two axes create a two-by-two matrix, or "map," which helps classify customers by what they value. Depending, then, on what customers value most, they may be classified as transaction oriented, relationship oriented, information oriented, or partnership oriented (the buyer who values both relationship and information).

In our research in North America, customer preferences arrayed equally across the four segments—in other words, about one quarter was transactional, and just wanted the right product at the right time with the lowest possible price, and so on. In Europe, the results were similar, but with more customers placing a slightly higher overall priority on the relationship. In Asia, customers were more transactional, but still arrayed in all quadrants; it also took longer in Asia to earn the right to have a long-term partnership with customers. Although there were some differences by industry, many customers who bought the same product from the same company had drastically different perspectives about what they valued. The key, then, is that each customer has his or her own perspective on value. That's why a customer-centered company selects and understands its target buyers *before* building a proprietary interaction process. In this way, it eliminates the risk of designing a creative way of doing business that no one cares much about. More detail on the Value Orientation Frame is in the Toolkit on pages 265-269.

**The Four Customer Value Segments**

Forum interviews with over 300 experienced buyers uncovered four types of customer-interaction preferences:

1. **The Transactional Buy:** Customers here have low needs for a relationship and low needs for information (e.g., vending machine purchases).
2. **The Relationship Buy:** Customers have high needs for a relationship. They need sales/servicepeople to have an in-depth understanding of their situation (e.g., many buyers of sophisticated insurance products or legal services).
3. **The Information Buy:** Customers have a high need for information and a low need for a relationship. They know what they want, and want to be informed and educated. (e.g., users of discount brokerage, doctors buying pharmaceuticals).
4. **The Partnership Buy:** Customers have a high relationship need and a high information need. They want organizations that are proactive, that inform and educate, that understand their company/needs. They need a personal relationship, mutual beneficial goals, and a sense of joint risk (e.g. Wal-Mart's renowned relationships with its major suppliers).

The first step, then, is to understand clearly what your customers value, and what is working and not working with the way you deal with customers. One of the most important rules for data collection is to get an in-depth understanding of the customer's *current* experience. Customers are not always able to articulate what your interaction process *should* look like, but they are able to help you understand their expectations and to give you deep insight into the current situation—in effect, what it is like to be in their shoes.

This step is mostly a matter of taking the procedures and tools spelled out in Chapter 3 and targeting them specifically to your customers.

**Great Questions to Ask**

1. What is it like to do business with our company?
2. What bothers you most about the way we sell and service you?
3. What is working in the way we conduct ourselves?
4. How can we make it better?
5. What can we do to save time in these interactions?
6. What is your description of an ideal interaction with a company like ours?
7. What is the company you most like to do business with? Why?

Customers' perspectives on working with you often will be a surprise—maybe a shock. When Standard Life, the largest mutual life assurance company in Europe, found itself in an increasingly competitive and demanding business environment, Group Managing Director Scott Bell decided the company needed to know what customers thought of it.

Standard Life asked customers to tell the company how it was doing with them. It expected these customers to say, "Well, as a company in an industry without a good reputation to begin with, Standard Life is the best of a bad lot." Instead, customers described Standard Life as "remote," "uncaring," "inflexible," and "arrogant." While management's initial temptation was to say that customers "don't know what they are talking about," the top team eventually accepted the objectivity of the data and began to take actions that would remedy the situation. Standard Life today is engaged in a highly successful effort to reorient how it deals with customers—one which increased the company's market share significantly in only six months. Moreover, customer surveys are showing that "excellent service" has become a key differentiator for Standard Life.

What created a fast start for Standard Life was the decision to have executives collect the customer data: a powerful way to get leaders committed to the idea of having advantage at the customer interface. In another instance, global investment banking firm Goldman Sachs recently brought together its two dozen equities division general partners for its annual meeting. In preparation, each one was asked to interview several clients. These interviews created a great deal of energy for the meeting, focused discussions on the customers, and actually led to the conception of a new product right there in the meeting.

## Step 2: Get Leadership Committed to a Branded Way of Interacting with Customers

Although there are many ways to design a proprietary customer interaction process, beginning at the top saves time. Why? Because significantly revamping the customer interaction usually requires companies to make major transformational changes. It means asking employees to change the way they sell and service, thereby asking companies to change how people are rewarded, how communication occurs, how information is shared, and, overall, how things work. At 3M, designing a collaborative customer-interaction process was straightforward, says Bruce Hamilton, "but the leverage was in getting the management commitment to make sure that it would work." To put it mildly, getting management totally committed is not always easy.

In this step, leaders need to answer such questions as: What will we commit to? What should our brand/personality be? What do we want our customers to say about doing business with us? How do we know it will be valued? What are we willing to invest to make this work? Do we want to try addressing the needs of our entire customer base, or do we have one customer segment to target that is ready to pay more for a world-class interaction process?

According to John Guaspari, vice president at the consulting firm Rath and Strong, a strong executive commitment to outstanding customer contact "aligns and energizes . . . efforts so they occur faster and stick more deeply." For example, at MBNA America Bank, a highly successful credit card issuer, each officer is required to spend four hours per month listening to customer phone interactions. British Airways management also actually handles complaints over the phones. Best Products' Partners in Service Program requires executives to work in showrooms during busy times of the year. Every two years, CUNA Mutual executives work at a customer's company for a month. Of course, involving executives directly with the customer is just one facet of the interaction process. Even when they are not in direct contact, managers can made a key difference in ensuring world-class customer interactions.

In the United Kingdom, Standard Chartered Bank's David Morgan, head of Global Corporate Banking U.K., felt that Standard Chartered's U.K. business suffered from a lack of focus and no linkage to the strengths customers perceived the bank had. Based on customer and internal data, Morgan and his colleagues hooked on to the bank's strong position in the Far East, Middle East, Africa, and Southeast Asia. They decided to target sophisticated customers who would value Standard Chartered's ability to help them trade and invest in those parts of the world. Focusing on these corporate customers meant a fundamental reshaping of the client portfolio—and a new way of managing relationships in which the relationship manager had to understand customer needs and then find a way for the bank to satisfy those needs. What Standard Chartered didn't need was what Morgan characterized as, "Here's what we've got; let's find a customer we can stick this to."

Standard Chartered's new, more sophisticated target segment was not overwhelmed. Customers saw the bank as deficient in some fundamental areas such as ability to coordinate global efforts, involvement of senior executives with customers, relationship-building skills, and follow-up. "This customer data made the process of getting leadership commitment pretty straightforward," says Morgan. "We had a customer-interaction process and had as many ways of working with customers as we had relationship managers. There was no consistency and our customers saw it."

The proof was there that big changes were needed. And it was crucial that management "own" this new way of working. Says Morgan, "Undertaking a training program where you have to take your people off-line for a week is inconceivable unless management believes in its importance. And they supported it because they knew that relationship-manager training was not going to be a nice week in the English countryside. We were trying to fundamentally change the way our people think and interact with clients."

The results to date are fantastic. Whereas only 11 percent of Standard Chartered's target customers saw their relationship manager as "best in class" at the beginning of the effort, now over 70 percent of customers believe their relationship manager deserves such a rating. And, the U.K. business has gone from operating losses to a profit.

David King, chief operating officer of John Hancock Funds, believes that one of his firm's key competitive advantages is that its customer service reps (CSRs) are better than those of anyone else in the business. One reason for this is that the customer service person is a highly respected member of King's organization, and management is dedicated to reinforcing this on a day-to-day basis. At Hancock, there are stock traders, investment analysts, and salespeople who came up through the CSR ranks. The knowledge that they are in positions where they have a chance to grow professionally—that they have a real stake in the company's success—motivates CSRs to work harder in creating a superior experience for the customer.

In general, the customer-centered organizations we studied took some similar actions to get leadership support:

1. **They did their homework up front,** using customer data to add credibility and getting leadership involved in collecting the data directly. At Standard Life, some of the leaders have spent over a month of time observing frontline people in customer interactions.
2. **They created alternative "brands"**—descriptions of what a unique customer experience would be like—based on that data. For instance, at Minneapolis-based Norwest Corporation, CEO Richard Kovacevich likes to say he is in the retailing business and even calls bank branches "stores." Norwest's sales and service process depends on frontline people giving customers "heavy doses of personal attention."[14] Some of the stories that become lore are about the teller who took a confused customer's checkbook home to balance and reconcile it, about the constant flow of thank-you notes and reminders, and about the consistent encouragement employees get from management. Norwest's return on equity ranks very high among its large-bank competitors, its net income is soaring, and its typical customer buys three times as many "products" as customers of competitor banks.
3. **They saved time by asking management to react to ideas rather than expending a lot of effort in creating the plans from scratch.** What was important was that management was involved in interpreting data, giving input, previewing ideas, testing con-

cepts, and so on, but did not start with a blank slate. As one AlliedSignal sales manager said, "The decision to have a proprietary process was pretty autocratic, but what the process looked like and how we would execute it involved many levels of management."

4. **Leaders were given specific "to-do" lists** that they needed to execute in order to demonstrate their commitment visibly. Actions included making presentations at the beginning of training programs to put the importance of the training in context; meeting with small groups of people to break down the barriers to doing things differently; actually teaching training programs; conducting follow-up interviews with customers; and holding quarterly meetings with direct reports to reinforce new approaches. At Standard Chartered Bank, David Morgan opened every training program and returned at the end to discuss "blockages to implementation" with employees. During these conversations, employees raised issues about everything from compensation to changes required in Standard Chartered's credit approval process. Based on what he learned, Morgan often was able to take immediate remedial action.
5. **Leaders played a key role in monitoring progress.** In nearly every success story, Forum found, leaders were using scorecards (see Chapter 3) and other measures to make sure that their daily actions were working. Says Morgan, "We benefited greatly from regularly revisiting our progress and adjusting along the way. Lots of small tweaks were much easier than a stop-and-go management process that required major restructuring every two to three years."

---

**What Managers Need to Know about Managing the Customer Interface**

Even in this age of the flattened organization, one of the biggest influencers of employee behavior is what they see their managers doing.

- Link the Vision to Daily Work

The manager must become the link between company strategy and what takes place at the customer interface. He or she must not only grasp the corporate vision but be able to communicate it in terms of specific effects on sales and service practices.

- Model Competence

  Those on the front line must be able to turn to their managers with confidence, calling them in as senior resources on key accounts, and as accomplished sales- and servicepeople in their own right.

- Create Direction

  Coaching a team is as important as playing on it. Managers must be able to provide a sense of clear direction with training, feedback, and support. They must become advocates for the frontline force. In fact, according to our research on sales, the most valuable management practice is "going to bat" for salespeople.

- Reward Change

  Forum research suggests that companies will see results sooner if they examine how they recognize and reward frontline performers. For example, if the corporate goal is long-term customer relationships, a company should not reward its front line solely on short-term volume.

## Step 3: Install a High-Value, Distinctive and Consistent Customer-Interaction Process

Installing your customer-interaction process is a process in itself, a series of logical steps that will enable you to make a continuous commitment to improvement. Before we outline the process, look at the story of PCA International, a model of the kind of customer interface most companies would like to achieve.

### PCA—The Perfect Picture

For most parents, taking the kids to have their picture taken doesn't rank high on their list of favorite things to do. Small wonder. The big studio companies have done a great job of making color portraits widely available and affordable to the average family, but the photographic experience often leaves a lot to be desired. People are bombarded with high-pressure sales, portrait packages that include pictures customers don't want, and impersonal production-line sittings.

PCA International, based in Matthews, North Carolina, was one of those studio companies. It focused on photographing, producing, and selling moderately priced quality portrait packages, and operated out of more than fourteen hundred permanent Kmart portrait studios under an exclusive license agreement.

Two things changed in the portrait industry to make PCA take another look at its future. First, customers in general became more informed, more demanding, and less tolerant. They wanted more control over the transaction, and they scorned high-pressure sales.

Second, there was a boom in portrait-studio capacity. Six years ago, customers had twelve hundred or so permanent studios to choose from among the big competitors. Today, PCA alone has more than fourteen hundred. The remainder of the big portrait companies operate about two thousand combined. Meanwhile, there has been virtually no increase in the number of children to be photographed. Result: an intense battle for customers.

### *The Best Experience*

In late 1992, PCA took a first step to differentiate itself from its competitors when it began testing a new, advanced in-studio system that combined traditional film-based photography with the advantages of computer-based digital imaging. The resulting $50 million investment in a digital imaging system—now installed in all of PCA's permanent studios—gave PCA's photographers the capability to instantly present, on a color computer monitor, a digital proof of each portrait taken by the photographer.

Although customers loved the control that digital imaging gave them as they made their purchase decisions, PCA's customer surveys shouted that the technology wasn't enough. Says Jan Rivenbark, PCA's chief operating officer, "The consumer told us that our technology was nice but that the competition had it too. Our system, in fact, was a better mousetrap and was much more sophisticated and cost-effective than the competition's was, but the customer just didn't care how we did it. It's just like McDonald's—the customer doesn't care how the hamburgers are made, they just want them to taste good."

What customers said they wanted were great pictures *and* a great overall photographic experience. That "best photographic experience" became the rallying cry for PCA's thirty-one hundred employees, with a long-term goal to create such a phenomenal interaction for customers that they would return frequently. Before, the idea was to get the customer to spend a lot of money during the first (and usually only) visit.

Since that decision, PCA's leaders have dedicated themselves to making quality at the customer interface its distinct competitive differentiator.

An early "installation" step was training, entitled "Achieving Service Excellence," for all regional, district, and studio management. Instead of just being lectured about customer satisfaction as an abstract principle, people were trained by their managers in key skills and watched videos of PCA's customers talking about what they want, need, and appreciate. It also touched on photographic skills and effective use of computers in the studio.

In another step, PCA crafted (1) a communications strategy to involve employees in the effort to achieve service quality and (2) a reward system to ensure that employees had the incentive to look for more than just big payments from onetime customers.

The results have been swift and dramatic. Customer complaints have declined over 60 percent—even through the hectic holiday season. The average sale has increased over 25 percent, a direct result of customers' increased comfort levels and confidence in PCA's photographers and photographic system. And corporate earnings have increased over 70 percent, demonstrating that the commitment to making PCA the industry standard was a sound, sustainable business strategy.

Creating a proprietary customer interaction process requires a blend of systematic thinking and good intuition about what will provide value for customers when they deal with your organization. The following actions can pay off handsomely:

1. Map your process to determine areas of value and waste.
2. Create world-class competence in your people.
3. Manage the crises perfectly.
4. Develop a special process for your best customers.
5. Install systems to support the interaction.
6. Create fast results with fast, intentional implementation.

## MAP YOUR PROCESS TO DETERMINE AREAS OF VALUE AND WASTE

Making a map of how you currently interact with customers provides the basis upon which to improve. Mapping means creating a flowchart of what you currently do, from the time you first target prospects all the way through your after-sale service, account expansion, and so on, similar to the diagram in Figure 5.2.

The key is to lay out the actual steps that your customers experience and then to document what the encounter is like. Figure 5.3 shows what that documentation might look like for the first three steps laid out in Figure 5.2. In essence, each step in this process represents an opportunity to increase or decrease value for the customer. For instance, in the account targeting step, you would look at whether salespeople are calling on strategically selected customers or whether their approach is random, as noted in the matrix.

---

**Try This Exercise:**

Harvard Business School professors Ben Shapiro, Kash Rangan, and John Sviokla suggest that the best way to truly understand how your customers experience transactions is to "staple yourself to an order."[15] They suggest that managers track every step of the order—where it goes, how long it stays, who handles it—as a way to get insight into the real-world life of your customer. Numerous lessons result from this exercise, including a deeper understanding of how customers' needs can "fall between the cracks" of an organization. This exercise will help you identify both ways to improve and the people in your company who need to make the improvements.

---

Next, you develop potential solutions and the corresponding ways you would measure whether your solution was working. The final task is to use this matrix to determine opportunities for creating breakthroughs at the point of interaction. You should ask: Are there rows in this matrix that represent golden opportunities for us to add value—maybe even in a way that can be proprietary to our organization? The high-value rows become your priorities for action.

PCA realized that it had a critical opportunity in the customer interaction. The business historically had been one in which the photographer would go to a retailer, put a sign in the lobby, rush the

**Figure 5.2**

A TYPICAL CUSTOMER-INTERACTION PROCESS

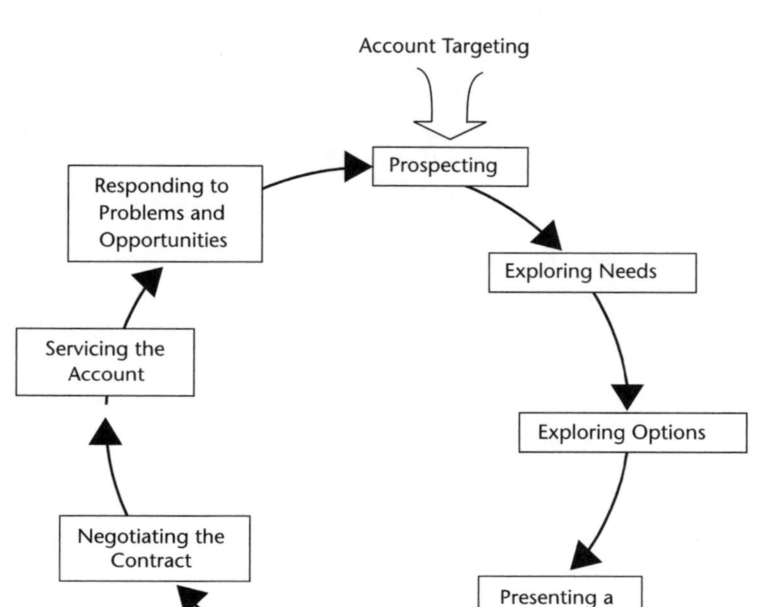


**Figure 5.3**

SAMPLE PARTIAL MATRIX OF CUSTOMER-INTERACTION STEPS

| Stage | Key Problem(s) | Prospective Solutions | Measure |
|---|---|---|---|
| Account Targeting | Random, unguided approach to marketplace | • Customer segmentation | Percent of assigned accounts with whom we have opportunities |
| Prospecting | Low "hit" rate<br><br>No referrals across geographic markets | • Referrals campaign<br>• Training<br>• Global accounts process clearer | Decrease in number of cold calls<br><br>Number of calls made within global accounts |
| Exploring Needs | Salespeople not able to create urgency | • Training in customer-centered selling<br>• Joint call support | Percent of calls advanced |

customer through the pictures, send them out, and never see the customer again—a fleeting relationship, at best. So the map might have looked like the one in Figure 5.4.

PCA overhauled its customer-interaction process by committing to deliver a phenomenal experience at each step—one that matched the way the customer wanted to be handled. The company and its well-trained personnel also tried creating a long-term relationship with the customer—making the hoped-for delightful photographic experience the first in a series of interactions that would increase profits over time. It was not designed to be a one-shot deal.

The Customer Interaction Assessment section of the Toolkit contains a description of the key skills required to effectively implement the Customer Interaction Process and an opportunity to assess your strengths on each skill. In addition, we've included fourteen other proven tools that you can use to improve your success with customers.

Another success story involves Lutron, a privately held designer and manufacturer of some of the world's most innovative, efficient, and aesthetic lighting controls. Observers thought Lutron was in big trouble when General Electric decided to enter its market for dimming controls. But in retaliation, Lutron created a process for mass customization of its lighting products. They come as snap-together modules that assemble like Lego blocks to quickly produce lighting configurations for key commercial customers in different colors and shapes. This capability to customize products easily gave Lutron a chance to simplify its customer interaction process as well. Instead of having the sales process include design and installation done by scores of engineers and distributors who needed regular training and high salaries, the expertise was designed into the product. The customer-contact people could focus on being consultants to their customers and let the customers do the actual design of the product to fit their needs. Whatever the customer wanted was easily manufactured back at the plant.

**Figure 5.4**

THE CUSTOMER-INTERACTION PROCESS IN A TYPICAL PORTRAIT STUDIO

In essence, Lutron used mass customization to reduce complexity—and create phenomenal value—at the customer interface. Lutron has been growing at 20 percent per year and is the number one producer of lighting-control equipment in the world—an extraordinary performance and one turned in under the shadow of big, powerful GE.[16]

## CREATE WORLD-CLASS COMPETENCE IN YOUR PEOPLE

To win, grow, and keep customers, you must, in the words of Milliken & Co., make your organization a "customer satisfaction system." The entire organization is needed to get business in the first place, then retain and grow it later on. That requires a reliable, unique customer-interaction process that is executed by trained people who are capable of demonstrating world-class skills at the customer interface.

A few years ago, UNUM, a five-thousand-employee disability-insurance company based in Portland, Maine, determined that providing a superior experience at the customer interface would be one of the keys to differentiating it from its competition. UNUM worked toward this goal with various employee populations, including customer-service representatives and new hires, but found a particularly fruitful opportunity for their most experienced salespeople and their managers.

People came to the training with actual customer cases to work on. As they learned new tools and skills, they applied them directly to these customer situations. The plan was to use the training as a vehicle for getting breakthroughs in key accounts, and the training investment paid off almost immediately when one senior-level salesperson applied what he had learned. By asking better questions, applying a newly formed competitive strategy, and revamping his perspective on what his customer truly valued, he won the largest piece of business in the history of the company.

---

**World class competency is built person-by-person. To build it:**

1. Identify your high performers and your moderate performers.
2. Survey their customers, peers, and managers about what they do, how they behave, and so on.
3. Use that data to determine what differentiates the best people from the others.
4. Design your training based on those differentiators.

---

***Build the Skills***

3M's often-benchmarked process— created by its Sales/Marketing Learning and Development department—for building world-class skills in its people (see Figure 5.5) is called A.C.T.—for *A*nalysis, *C*urriculum, *T*ransfer.[17] The company first *analyzes* the baseline skills of each employee to determine improvement priorities. This leads to a training *curriculum*, and ultimately, to *transfer*, via a variety of methods, to ensure that the new skills are used back on the job.

New skills are required—even of experienced people—because of changing customer requirements. Says Scott Evans, 3M's Abrasive Systems Division national sales manager, "We have to continually get better because the customer's time is extremely valuable. It's no longer Joe the purchasing agent who has half an hour to talk about fishing before getting down to business. Customers only have time for us if we know how to add value and how to solve their business problems—and this requires a new set of skills."

3M's *analysis* is typically done by surveying customers anonymously, a process which creates momentum. Adds Evans, "When frontline people hear how they need to change from their customers' perspectives, they are ready to learn." The training *curriculum* at 3M is then driven by what's important to customers and is customized to individual needs. And when its new sales training curriculum was designed, salespeople went through the programs with other key employees who were going to be involved with customers: sales managers, customer service people, technical service people, other marketing personnel.

*Transfer* is what Evans sees as the most important step, ensuring that 3M's A.C.T. process is just that—a continuous process. Training in the classroom is reinforced on the job through smaller team meetings, follow-up activities, and refresher sessions where people can practice skills. Ultimately, it loops back to another assessment so that people can see how they are doing and begin the process all over.

**Figure 5.5**

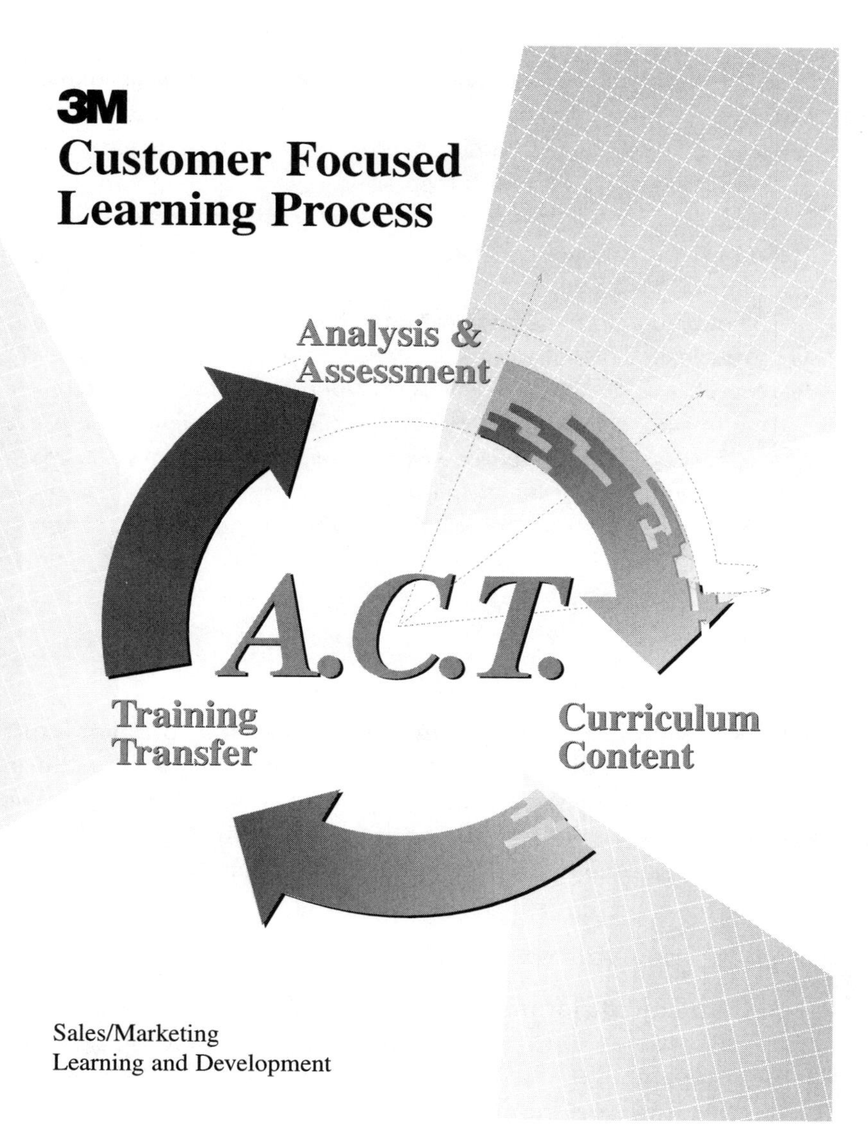


Reprinted with permission of 3M

**Try This Exercise: Get Served!**

Often when we are running a workshop on service, we will include a special "live" exercise. Here's how it works:

At the end of the day we give everyone a simple evening assignment. We ask them just to "go out and get served"—at a store, restaurant, or other establishment—and notice two things: what kind of service they are receiving and how it makes them feel.

Store clerks, waiters, taxi drivers, and hotel operators are always among those with whom the seminar participants interact between the end of day one and the beginning of day two of the seminar.

The next morning, most typically say they were not served well, and because of the service transgressions they experienced, people typically felt "upset," "angry," "not listened to," "ignored," and "ripped off."

The touch of reality introduced by this real-life experience brings the concept of good and bad service alive for everyone and creates even more eagerness among participants to learn better ways to serve.

For a one-day meeting, this exercise can be run during lunchtime.

### *Skills of High Performers*

Over the last twenty years, Forum has conducted independent research concerning the characteristics of people who are outstanding at the customer interface. These people are distinctive not only because of their skills, but because of the attitudes and beliefs they hold about their customers. The following themes have emerged.

#### *1. High Performers Are Customer Centered.*

If one term could capture what sets top performers apart, it would be *customer centered.* Our research shows that outstanding results depend on the ability to think from the customer's point of view—understanding and responding to the customer's agenda, buying cycle, and best interests. High performers have a deep understanding of both their buyers' long-term goals and the overall business climate. They see each customer as an individual and also as a part of the company he or she represents.

*2. High Performers Earn the Right to Do Business. They Don't Just Assume It.*

High performers—people who consistently turn opportunity into success—understand that at every stage of the business relationship they must earn the customer's trust, respect, and interest. In practice, that means resisting the urge to offer a solution every time, or even worse, before a customer mentions a potential need. It means limiting the role of the "trial close" (a technique in which a salesperson proposes, for example, "If I could show you how to do 'x,' would you be willing to move ahead?") to avoid pushing customers when they are not ready to move, and pacing the relationship to keep the customer responsive and engaged. It means handling objections head-on, rather than trying to diffuse them, and not assuming that the customer sees the benefit of answering your questions. Finally, it means making sure that the quality of the follow-up and service merits the privilege of further sales.

**American Express Earns the Right**

Critical to the turnaround at American Express Establishment Services was targeting and winning mega-accounts like Sears and Wal-Mart. Under the leadership of James Berrien, a handpicked team of professionals developed a specific program to approach and ultimately convince these resistant accounts to accept their charge card.

A key element of their approach was the guideline that no presentation could be made until at least one meeting solely devoted to probing was completed. In this way Berrien's crew could customize its proposal to the specific need of each prospect. As a result of such preparation, most of the "tough sells" became customers. In fact after its presentation to the long-resistant Sears executives, the AmEx team got a standing ovation!

*3. High Performers Involve Customers so that They Are Persuaded by Their Own Ideas.*

Success today demands a radical shift from the "peddler" mentality of merely demonstrating products and expounding on their features.

It requires treating the customer as a full participant in the buying process. As often as not—shades of Willy Loman—a flashy presentation alone alienates rather than persuades. High performers regard the customer interaction as a conversation, not a one-sided pitch. They encourage the customer to do the talking, and they do more than listen. They learn. By doing so, high performers allow customers to discover needs and reasons for purchasing and repurchasing on their own. In the end, customers are much more persuaded by their own ideas than by what they are *told.*

*4. High Performers Influence Internal Resources Productively.*

In most industries, customer-contact people can no longer manage customer relationships on their own. The increasing need customers have for information requires frontline people to rely on a variety of other product, technical, financial, and other specialists. Top performers know how to orchestrate these resources to make their organizations work effectively for customers. These high performers still act as the key contact for the customer, and also serve as leaders of internal teams. In fact, Forum research in this area found that high-performing customer-contact people outscored all others in twenty-one out of twenty-three dimensions of "internal influence"—meaning that the best people are as proficient on the "inside" as they are with customers.

*5. High Performers Think Longer-Term for Greater Profitability.*

Success with customers now means abandoning the once traditional idea of the "hit and run sale." High performers regard their relationships with key customers as long-term and cultivate them as such. In some cases this may even mean forgoing short-term opportunity—for example, recommending another company's product when you might be able to do the work but know it will not be in your "strike zone." When customers face tough business challenges and complex technological choices, they are most likely to rely on salespeople who can help them make the right decisions.

To determine how your people compare to high performers, turn to the Customer Interaction Coaching Guide on pages 283-286 of the Toolkit.

## Manage the Crises Perfectly

Merlin Stone, management consultant and former dean of faculty of human sciences at England's Kingston University, says: "A company can be ripped apart by complainers. . . . When customers do have poor experiences, rather than tell the supplier, they allow the situation to fester. They infect other customers with their attitudes, creating a snowball effect."

Such a crisis happened recently at a Starbucks coffee store in Berkeley, California. Starbucks, the largest chain of coffee stores in the United States, is known for "guaranteeing exceptional quality" for its customers. Still, Starbucks apparently failed to make proper amends when a customer complained about having bought two defective espresso machines. The customer, Jeremy Dorosin, subsequently experienced a series of unsympathetic interactions with Starbucks employees and eventually lashed out at the company through four *Wall Street Journal* ads, soliciting other dissatisfied customers.

Starbucks did make offers to compensate its customer. Dorosin, who thought the offers were without empathy and were "too little, too late," became a customer-turned-terrorist who eventually demanded that Starbucks buy almost $250,000 of ad space to apologize—and that it establish a center for runaway children in San Francisco.

While Dorosin might be considered a "customer from hell," this story does illustrate how time-consuming and expensive it can be to muff a customer-satisfaction crisis that needs deft handling. Research conducted by the Technical Assistance Research Programs Institute of Washington, D.C., came up with this revealing statistic: The average happy customer will tell three others about his or her experience, but the average unhappy customer will tell up to nine.

Complaints may be a pain, but they *are* valuable. The famed General Electric Answer Center in Louisville, Kentucky, receives three million calls a year. Of those, the 10 to 15 percent that are actually complaints have the most merit. According to N. Powell Taylor, the center's former manager, "We want complaints to surface because the research shows that only four percent of dissatisfied customers complain. The rest say nothing to you, but plenty to their friends and family. If you can satisfy the complainers, eighty percent of them rebuy."[18]

Sharon Whiteley, Richard Whiteley's wife, recently had an experience that probably sounds familiar to you. She returned a defective humidifier to the chain store where she purchased it. The clerk handling the complaint was most gracious: "I'm sorry you had this problem and appreciate the inconvenience it has caused you—not only of it not working but of you having to return it." *Wow.* Sharon could feel the tension melting away. "This isn't going it has caused be so bad after all," she thought.

Just as Sharon was beginning to enjoy her relief, *wham.* The clerk continued: "But this problem is not our fault. . . ." From there the conversation went downhill. No sooner had Sharon been led to anticipate one of those delightful but rare interactions at the customer interface when her fears were confirmed: *This is going to be a fight.* Sharon never claimed the problem was anyone's fault. In fact, she didn't care whose fault it was. She just wanted the problem fixed—and to get on with her life.

Those precious fifteen seconds could have made the difference between an unusually positive experience that would have cemented Sharon's loyalty, and a downward spiral of discontent, resulting in a lost customer and—if it was a common occurrence—ultimate market damage.

It seems obvious that the service provider was unskilled at handling an upset customer. Sharon was not placing blame, but the clerk heard it that way and took a defensive position. While it's true that the skills required to handle a dissatisfied customer go against our natural instincts, they can be learned—and should be.

Figure 5.6 shows how a skilled service provider could have turned Sharon's complaint into a positive experience.

### *Step One: Encourage*

The act of encouraging (nodding one's head or saying something like, "Oh? Tell me more," or "That must have been really frustrating") is a signal to the customer that you care, that you are prepared to remain present in the interaction, that you have empathy, and that you will ultimately "own" his or her problem. From the customer's point of view, a service provider who responds this way is an ally, someone who will see the issue from the customer's perspective and be a partner in finding a solution. In Sharon's situation, the service provider actually did this well and put Sharon at ease.

***Step 2: Question***

*"Can you tell me exactly what the problem is, Mrs. Whiteley?"*

The next objective is to clarify the complaint so that a proper solution can be created. Asking questions gives the frontline person a chance to understand the customer's problem in depth. For instance, if a customer complains about high prices, you need to clarify what he or she means: Is the price too high relative to the value being received? Has the customer found a competitor's price to be lower? Is it over the customer's budget? Is it higher than the last time? Does the customer have a misconception about the real price? Or is it something else? Asking questions helps you avoid responding to a problem that the customer doesn't have.

**Figure 5.6**

PROCESS FOR HANDLING OBJECTIONS

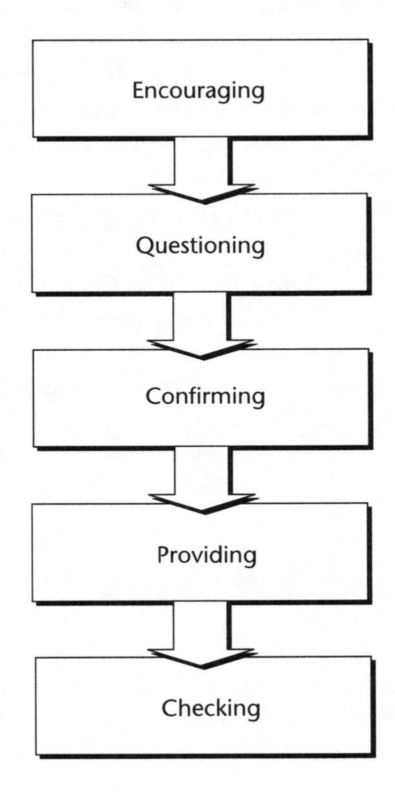

***Step 3: Confirm***

*"So, as I understand it, when the humidifier is running, it leaks. Are there other problems?"*

An often overlooked but powerful step to help complaining customers is to reiterate to the customer what you understand to be their problem. This says to them that you are not only trying to gather information but that you are trying to pinpoint the problem so that you can fix it. Most important, it demonstrates that you have listened and therefore earned the right to proceed. Confirming also gives the customer a chance to correct your understanding if you've gotten the story wrong—always a possibility.

***Step 4: Provide***

*"Mrs. Whiteley, let us replace the unit you've brought in with a new one. I'll have our people bring it right up and carry it to your car."*

Here is where the organization can break away and truly create not just a good recovery experience but one in which customers are likely to be astounded. The odds are in your favor. Customers are so used to being frustrated when they report problems that they are usually thrilled when things are handled well.

When Saab was forced to recall certain cars in Norway, the company turned a potentially detrimental customer encounter into a delightful one. Instead of doing just what they had to, i.e., fix the car, they "fixed customers" as well, by picking up their cars, correcting the defect, cleaning them inside and out, and returning each along with a gift of Norwegian salmon. Now customers say, "Hey, when's the next recall?"

***Step Five: Check***

*"Again, we apologize for the inconvenience. Will this handle the problem or is there something else I can do?"*

This step is often ignored. It is the simple act of verifying with the customer that the proposed solution will restore buyer confidence. If the service provider doesn't achieve this, it is a matter of returning to step two and trying again.

### *"Oh Please Let My Statement Be Incorrect"*

Sometimes handling a crisis well calls for more than refined interpersonal skills. One such example is a service guarantee, which will return all or part of the customer's money if he or she is not satisfied.

You can get leverage out of a service guarantee as long as you can reliably fulfill the expectations it creates. Holiday Inn's unfortunate surprise with their "No Surprises Guaranteed" program was that they promised something so general that it was too difficult to deliver on profitably—surprises happen and Holiday Inn couldn't possibly keep its promise. Offering a guarantee that is beyond your capability to fulfill creates a quality problem because you have raised customer expectations and therefore have produced an expectations/delivery gap. Reliable service guarantees, on the other hand, say to your customers and employees that you believe in your product and services and will stand by them.

John Hancock Funds is the only mutual fund group that has a service guarantee and no one has ever tried to copy it. Basically, if the company ever makes a mistake on your account, you get twenty-five dollars. Last year, according to Chief Operating Officer David King, it cost John Hancock a mere fifteen thousand dollars to cover such errors, and the marketing value is tremendous because customers see John Hancock Funds as a highly ethical company which holds itself accountable.

---

Best Products Co., Inc., the large catalog showroom company, filed for Chapter 11 bankruptcy protection in early 1991 and has since revitalized both the look of its stores and the way it does business with customers.

The company's turnaround has been dramatic. It emerged from bankruptcy in June of 1994 with a strong cash position and a strong commitment to customers. As Best looked at its customer interactions, the company learned that customers' most common complaints related to how it handles out-of-stock items. Running out of items was resulting in tremendous frustration for customers who traveled to Best showrooms expecting a particular item at a particular price.

Best developed a formal policy in response to the problem and communicated it to their customers. If, for instance, a $219 VCR was advertised to be selling at a 10% discount, and then it was out of stock in a store, Best employees could take any of the following five actions:

- Find the item quickly at another Best store
- Send the VCR via mail order and pay shipping charges for the customer
- Take the same 10% discount off another type of VCR
- Help the customer find another VCR with the same features and charge the same price
- Give the customer a rain check, which allows the customer the sale price when the item becomes available.

You might say that the above policy is not extraordinary, that it is what any excellent customer-contact person would do. By making the options explicit to employees and customers, however, Best created value and institutionalized the policy—ensuring that even the least-skilled serviceperson would handle the interaction well.

## DEVELOP A SPECIAL PROCESS FOR YOUR BEST CUSTOMERS

Sometimes organizations determine that a particular group of customers will value a proprietary interaction process specific to their requirements. Often this group is comprised of your best customers.

When David Shackleton, general manager of the Westin Stamford and Westin Plaza Hotels in Singapore, joined the organization in 1994, he targeted their top accounts and asked them what it was they valued most about doing business with his hotels. "Location" was the only thing they mentioned. "Clearly there was a need for us to change whilst we were still on top," says Shackleton, "because anybody can build a hotel, and if that was our only point of differentiation, our success could not last."

This research also revealed that a significant proportion of its business—27 percent—came from a relatively small number of large customers such as airlines and tour operators. The relationship with these customers had been awkward in the past, largely characterized by an annual negotiation session that was challenging at best as both parties looked for the best financial arrangement possible.

Shackleton and his team created twelve strategic partnerships with key accounts in Singapore. Instead of being negotiated each year primarily around price, these contracts are based on shared values and a common commitment to adding value to the partnership. As preferred partners, these Westin customers get guaranteed access to hard-to-get Singapore hotel rooms, and, in return, Westin becomes the customer's preferred supplier for all accommodation needs in Singapore for the next four to five years. Meanwhile, the partners negotiate a rate that is fair for both parties and commit to an ongoing dialogue about how the hotel can add even more value for the customer. An example of this is Westin's technology for linking its partners into its system to make their own room reservations. As a result, Westin is one of the few hotels in Singapore that is able to move discussions with its customers from a single-minded focus on rates to consideration of other important mutually beneficial aspects of the relationship.

The hospitality industry is a leader in recognizing the importance of adding value for its best customers. Consider executive floors in hotels, frequent flyer programs, special VIP privileges such as Delta's Elite Flyers card, and so on. These strategies work in other industries as well and can help you expand your customer interaction brand. At the extreme, you can follow in the footsteps of Poochies Self Service Pet Wash, a company that actually decided to go after its very best customer—the dog—rather than worry about the dog owner. Notice how the letter in Figure 5.7 is actually addressed to the dog!

## Install Systems to Support the Interaction

A proprietary customer-interaction process requires a number of systems that support its implementation. The systems we see providing the most leverage are related to technology and to rewards.

### *Use Technology to Customize the Interaction*

Customizing what customers want, according to Francis Gouillart of Gemini Consulting, means "you can invent recipes that escape the commodity trap. If you define yourself in relation to your competition, you are commoditizing your product. You are already in a copycat mode.[19]

A particularly powerful use of technology is to create what we call "institutional memory," a company's ability to keep track of customer

**Figure 5.7**

# Poochies

Self Service Pet Wash
Espresso Bar • Fine Pet Supplies
619-541-2525 619-541-BONE
Awarded 1995 Hot 100 Pet Supply Retailers

August 1995

**Dear Marcus,**

Thanks for being our customer! Please thank Carole, too, for her love and concern in providing you the very best in quality pet food and supplies offered here at Poochies. Not every dog is as lucky to have an owner like Carole that drives to a store catering to its every need. To thank her, we suggest you drive her to Poochies next time and treat her to a refreshing fresh fruit smoothie in the Espresso Bar.

Tell Carole to look at our insert for this month's pet supply price comparisons. As we continue to prove that you don't have to shop at a big store to get a great price. For example, Nutro Natural Choice 20 lb dog food is $16.13 at Pet Supply Warehouse and only $14.99 at Poochies. We mean it when we say we are the World's Smallest Pet Supply Superstore!®

Coupon for

**Marcus Mullins**

Free 24oz box of Iams Dog Biscuits for your Birthday!

000779-0895-0008
Not Valid With Other Offers - Expires 08/31/95

New Menu Items. Try our new blended Iced Whippuccino. Available in coffee and mocha varieties. This secret recipe was specially formulated by Sandy & Laura in the Espresso Bar. Also, try our new smoothies available with protein powder, wheat germ, ginseng, etc. Our fruit bowls are prepared fresh daily, too.

ATM now available in Espresso Bar. Don't have time to drop by the bank? Stop in for some of our howling great coffee and get cash back using your ATM card. Until you get a checking account, Marcus, this convenient service will only be available to Carole.

Live on Channel 7/39. Joe Lizura of KNSD News broadcasted live weather reports from Poochies on July 24th as he toured Poochies. Thanks to "Lady", Skipper", & "Samantha" who became instant celebrities.

Refill and save on many shampoos, conditioners, cat litter and stain and odor removers that we offer. Save $2 off the regular price when you bring the original container in to be refilled. Recycle and save big!

Price Matching. In case our pet supply prices are not equal or less than any competitor, or you hear a great ad special on the radio, we will verify and **match** it immediately. Since there are so many competitive offers, we'd appreciate the opportunity to earn all of your business.

Airedale Breed Night. Hey Marcus, we invite you to join us Friday, August 18, from 5-8:30 pm. Your pet wash is only $1.99 and you will receive a 24oz box of IAMS dog biscuits. Best of all, you'll meet other Airedale friends. It's sure to be a social scene.

Coupon for

**Carole Mullins**

$0.50 off on any Espresso drink (12 oz or larger)

000779-0895-0020
Not Valid With Other Offers - Expires 08/31/95

Calendar of Events:
- Low Cost Vaccine Clinic: Sat, August 19, 2-4 pm.
- Low Cost Flea Dip Day: Sun, August 20, 2-5 pm. Only $3. We do it for you. Bring a towel. Dogs on leash and cats in carriers.
- Breed Nights: Beagle's Aug 11; Airedale's Aug 18; Welsh Corgi's Aug 25; Schnauzer's Sep 1

**Custom Newsletters by Koch Business Services (619) 571-1608 (voice/fax)**

Reprinted with permission of Poochies

information and desires that transcends what any customer-contact person might know about the customer. Organizations with no institutional memory risk losing customers each time a representative leaves or is promoted.

USAA is an insurance company known for its customer retention. The company targets military personnel. In order to boost retention with such a mobile group, USAA has invested heavily in a database at its San Antonio headquarters. Wherever customers move, customer information, billing, and policies easily can be modified. This means that customers continually experience USAA as an organization that cares enough about their business to keep track of them—and to remember their history, their priorities, and their preferences. USAA provides a feeling of stability for a mobile group of customers who clearly value this treatment. Proof of the pudding? At last check, USAA's customer retention rate was 98 percent.[20]

American Express does this with the "member since" feature of its card, demonstrating the value of "we know you now because we knew you when." And Marriott's system allows employees to access information about past guest visits and preferences.

Financial powerhouse Fidelity Investments is a well-publicized example of how technology can improve customer interactions. Fidelity's 6 million customers can call for help, as the company says, "when they want to and in the way they want to." They can do it by mail, by 800 number, by visiting an investor center, or by using online services (Fidelity's customers use the Internet twenty thousand times per day) twenty-four hours per day, seven days per week.

Fidelity's research tells it that customers value assistance more than advice, and convenience more than personal services. So automation is a critical element of the Fidelity customer interaction. In fact, 70 percent of its customer calls are automated, representing a system that would require an additional four thousand employees without technology. Costs are lower, too. A call answered by a human costs Fidelity $8.90, but a call handled through technology costs only 70¢.

Adds Roger Servison, managing director of Fidelity's retail business, "Our emphasis on technology doesn't mean we don't obsess over listening to our customers. Technology has allowed us to stay continually and literally connected to customers. For instance, we had 70 million calls in 1994, 40 percent of which were made on weekends and evenings. We think this trend will continue to show up and we are constantly seeking innovative ways to anticipate these changes."

### *Reward Systems*

When 3M decided to install its highly successful Customer-Focused Marketing Process, it determined that its biggest obstacle to getting employees committed would come down to the three R's: Review, Recognition, and Reward.

*Review* meant the need to change the report card. If success was reported based on product-line revenue rather than on whether a customer's needs were getting met—and if no one got recognized or rewarded when he or she sold another division's product—then Customer-Focused Marketing would become one more well-intentioned but totally unrealistic initiative at 3M.

In response, 3M took three actions. First, to fix the review problem, the company changed the metrics. Instead of talking market share, it now is beginning to measure *customer share*—that is, how much total business 3M does with a particular customer. The planning process reinforces this so that if a customer spends ten thousand dollars annually on ceiling tape, sandpaper, and Post-it Notes, the sales representative has learned how to have a dialogue with the customer to explore how 3M can get even a larger piece of his pie.

Second, high-level business-unit leaders are increasingly committed to incorporating CFM sales into performance appraisals, recognizing their people publicly for cooperating with other divisions, and the best examples are communicated throughout the organization.

Third, the corporate CFM leader, Bruce Hamilton, has created a Dual Credit Commission System, which ensures that when one division sells another division's product, the people from both organizations get 100 percent credit for the sale. The additional cost of the dual crediting is more than made up for by the substantial sales increase realized when a customer buys eight 3M products instead of one.

## CREATE FAST RESULTS WITH FAST, INTENTIONAL IMPLEMENTATION

One of the most important factors in installing a proprietary customer-interaction process successfully is related to how fast and how intentional the implementation is. As Norwest CEO Richard Kovacevich said, "I could leave our strategic plan on a plane and it wouldn't make any difference. No one could execute it. Our success has nothing to do with planning. It has to do with execution."

Standard Life, the large European insurance company, has focused heavily on implementation, and it has paid off handsomely. The life-assurance firm's strategy has stressed four factors:

1. Critical mass implementation—Standard Life management assumed it needed commitment from at least 20 percent of its employees if any major change was to have a chance of succeeding.
2. Quick action—Management moved as swiftly as possible to get the necessary 20 percent or better on board to generate energy for the change.
3. Intensive training—This is necessary not only to build skills but to give people a chance to discuss their new roles, adopt (or resist) the change, discuss key success factors, and become involved in leading the process.
4. "Cascade-down" communication—Standard Life's implementation started at the top with the general managers and then went to assistant general managers, then to the rest of management, and so on, cascading like a waterfall and building power as each level of the organization supported the next.

The results were that Standard Life created energy and commitment, and reduced the projected cycle time of the change by half. The training resulted in constant feedback on new opportunities to create competitive advantage with customers, and the intensive implementation kept management focused on the task—much more so than a trickle-down process would have.

**Preparing for a Competitive Invasion**

Because their customers don't have much of a choice of suppliers, some institutions have historically paid little attention to them. Such is often the case with utilities.

Hong Kong's China Light & Power Company, Ltd., however, has seen the light. In an effort to thwart what they believe will be a "power invasion" from China in 1997, the leaders of this utility are instituting major change.

Their new vision, "We aim to deliver Absolute Customer Satisfaction as the Best Utility in the World" is intended to make current customers so loyal that when choice comes in 1997, there will be no contest.

To achieve this vision China Light & Power is attacking on all fronts. One important priority is its commitment to creating "customer competence" throughout the organization. In addition to ensuring that customer-contact people excel with customers, technical specialists, such as engineers, are provided with special customer service training. They have even gone so far as to change the title "chief engineer" to "general manager of distribution and customer service." The objective is to create a sustainable competitive advantage by having every employee in every function centered on the customer.

## FINAL THOUGHTS: AN EVOLUTION IN SELLING

Perfecting interactions at the customer interface can become *the* critical competitive advantage for companies. Some argue that companies in more controlled markets—utilities, for example—would be unwise to invest in creating more than basic levels of customer satisfaction, but in most highly competitive markets, excellence at the customer interface is intimately tied to the bottom line.

In these companies, the salesperson plays a special role in the very eye of the storm, targeting and retaining accounts, coordinating shipping schedules, negotiating terms and partnership agreements, mediating problems, understanding customer needs, providing technical support, and so on, all the while uplinking critical street-level information back into the organization.

Salespeople have always been pivotal to the success of their organizations, but their role has been changing as dramatically as the business environment itself. For years companies sold from the inside out, using self-serving, sometimes manipulative techniques to push product. This **Product-Oriented Sales Process**—get in the door, move product, go on to the next sale—defined the sales force as simply the distribution arm. The overriding question in salespeople's minds was "How can I get the customer to say yes?" They used words like "pitch," "hook," and "land" (a customer). The salesperson-customer relationship was basically an antagonistic one.

By the 1980s a **Consultative Sales Process** became popular. A consultative sales approach sought to address the destructive aspects of a zero-sum, often "out to get you" product-oriented approach. Now instead of salespeople asking "How can I get you to say yes?" they wondered, "How can I get you to want what I have?" The insurance industry, for example, began to understand that while some insurance salespeople would be able to win over a few friends and family members, more often than not, a pushy approach ended up alienating many potential customers. Consultative selling took away much of the sting of hardball tactics by helping people understand that it was a good idea to assess what customers' needs were prior to recommending a solution. The initial focus shifted slightly from the product to the customer, but ultimately it was just a more gentle way to make inroads to push product.

Today, most good sales organizations have a more customer-centered process. The overriding questions now are, "How can I create a solution that truly meets my customer's needs? How can I build a long-term relationship?" A **Customer-Centered Sales Process** is an empathetic and committed process in which salespeople creatively partner with customers to meet common goals.

World-class customer-centered organizations regard selling as a key strategic weapon. These companies are able to integrate their marketing, sales, and service processes together so securely that they answer questions such as, "How can we get the company to have what the customer wants? How can we differentiate ourselves with impact and value at the customer interface?" Or, "How can we create a way of interacting with customers that is a key source of competitive advantage?" Such questions are the basis of a **Proprietary Sales Process.**

The sales task becomes highly intentional, highly reliable, and customer-value-creating, propelling these organizations to customer-centered growth.

---

**You'll Know You Have a Proprietary Customer-Interaction Process When . . .**

A truly proprietary customer-interaction process goes beyond just doing a little better than your competitors. Here are the most frequently found characteristics of a proprietary customer-interaction process:

- **Links to Customer Needs**

A proprietary interaction process mirrors what customers themselves would describe as the ultimate experience at the interface.

**Example:**

Nabisco's 4,000-person sales force has a customer-interaction process wholly dependent on making "life easier for the retailer."[21] Its process intentionally seeks out ways to make that happen: whether it's removing minor nuisances, such as simply delivering to a back door rather than traipsing through a retailer's warehouse, or removing a retailer's more major headaches, like running a retailer's entire biscuit department.

- **Links to Company Culture**

A proprietary interaction process is wholly consistent with other aspects of how the company does business and its values.

**Example:**

IBM's signature starched white shirts in the 1980s or UPS's award-winning sales force trained to be as efficient, reliable, and team-oriented as the total company is.

- **Patented/Secret**

A proprietary interaction process is a highly valued aspect of a company's competitive advantage and is therefore often regarded as a secret weapon.

**Example:**

Dow Chemical believes its recruiting of salespeople to be "one of our best-kept secrets."[22] Likewise, Kodak says it wants its customer-interaction process to be as distinctive as its technology.

- **Links to Target Segmentation**

A proprietary customer-interaction process is often segment specific. That means that it adapts to the specific needs of target customers.

**Example:**

A large European brokerage firm identified the top 8% of its customers, which represents 54% of its profits, and designed a segment-specific interaction that was especially tailored to meet the needs of its most profitable customers. Similarly, Taco Bell determined that its "heavy users" were not just going a few times per month, they were averaging 17 visits! Data from these customers drove changes in how its fast-food operations worked.

- **Links to Critical Leverage Points**

Proprietary customer-interaction processes zero in on key profit levers. Through its design, the process ensures that people spend their time in the right places and with the right people.

**Example:**

Westvaco, "a large paper manufacturer," interacts directly with those who write original product specifications on bids (e.g., the designer of an annual report often specifies the type of paper to be used) as well as directly to buyers; Reynold's Metals sales force has been enlisted not only to sell existing products, but also to serve as "knights in the crusade against competing materials"[23] by working to discover further ideas for the development of aluminum-based products right in the customer's office; and GD Searle found a critical leverage point in their team-based customer-interaction process when, as in basketball, it began compensating employees for "assists" at the interface.

- **Integrates Measurement**

A proprietary customer-interaction process is a systematic process with measureable results.

**Example:**

Xerox's Account Management Process (XAMP) relies heavily on measures to track employees' performance at the interface before, during, and after the call. Both Apple and Eli Lilly rely on measures to reinforce the training they do: Apple checks off boxes on employee T-shirts as they pass through each of one of Apple's eight training programs, while Eli Lilly incorporates measures within a formal certification process.[24]

- **Not Just For the Front Line**

A proprietary customer-interaction process is potent only when its key attributes are saturated throughout the organization.

**Example:**

Hyatt trains its senior management in its customer-interaction process and those managers put their skills to work: Each month they are required to call on five potential accounts that are currently stalled as "tentatives."[25] Amil installs its process throughout the organization via training that is personally taught by top management to all employees.

## ACTION POINTS

- Rather than treating everyone the same, determine how your customers want to do business and match your approach to what they want. Pay particular attention to each customer's need for information and relationship.
- Know your customers' businesses better than they do. Know what the customers they serve expect, and collaborate with your customer to exceed those expectations.
- Get senior managers committed to a branded way of dealing with customers. To do this, get leaders involved at the customer interface. Coach them with plans to which they can react and help them develop clear "to do" lists. Encourage them to monitor progress and recognize improvements.
- Create a proprietary customer-interaction process. To do this:

  –map your current customer-interaction process
  –train your people to world-class levels of competence
  –manage crises perfectly
  –consider special processes for your best customers
  –install systems to support interaction
  –implement fast for fast results

- Compare your high-performing frontline performers with mediocre performers. What do the successful ones do that the others don't and vice versa? From this create a profile of the high performer and train your people to master those special skills that account for success.
- In dealing with an upset customer, rule number one is to always understand that his/her inalienable right as a customer is to be upset. He/she may be upset for the wrong reasons, but to be denied the right to his/her perceptions and the emotion that flows from them is nothing short of pouring gasoline on a fire. Create a complaint and objection handling process that always starts by acknowledging this with the customer.
- If you are training your sales and customer service people, ask if others in the organization should learn the same skills and train those people as well.

Chapter 6

# FROM FACILITATIVE LEADERSHIP TO CONTACT LEADERSHIP

*Most employees want to do a good job. How they perform is simply a matter of whom they work for.*

—DARRYL HARTLEY-LEONARD
PRESIDENT, HYATT HOTELS CORPORATION

"WE ARE GOING TO WIN in this business. That is why I came here—to blow out the competition—and I am not going to back away from that."

With that announcement, Victoria Rickey introduced herself as the new managing director, Europe, for NACCO Materials Handling Group (NMHG), the second largest forklift-truck manufacturer in Europe. The employees knew change was happening when they'd first heard of Victoria Rickey. For one thing, she was the first woman ever appointed to any high-management post in the organization.

But they weren't ready for the change they got. After her initial, clear declaration of purpose, Rickey seemed to be everywhere. Almost before she'd gotten off the plane from the home office, Rickey had moved European headquarters of the group from London to the site of its large factory in Irvine, Scotland. She believed she and her other top executives should be closer to the heart of the organization. Rickey was constantly on the front line—in the factories, the dealerships, and customers' offices, asking questions and pushing people to understand and do more for customers. "In the old days you had a hierarchy of supervisors who either passed information up the line or soft-pedaled that information if the news was bad," Rickey notes. "Today in business we've cut a lot of that out, so you have to do a lot more managing-by-walking-around, and spend more time communicating with the workforce."

## LEADERSHIP IS A CONTACT SPORT

Rickey represents a new style of management that we call "contact leadership," which has emerged only recently. A few years ago, the key idea in leadership was the leader as facilitator. Leaders ensured that things were happening but still tended not to get their hands dirty. Even many of the best leaders kept themselves a little bit at arm's length from their people. They "empowered" others by scrupulously avoiding interference with their work. For many leaders, that meant they didn't spend too much time at the front lines—hanging around might stifle employee initiative. So they stayed in their offices.

In the most customer-centered organizations today, by contrast, people like Victoria Rickey are hands-on, close-up, down-in-the-trenches, and deeply involved with their day-to-day businesses. With her first words, Rickey communicated a new sense of what it meant to work for NMHG, which had been troubled for so long that people thought mediocre performance and low morale were the norm. Rickey made it clear that the group intended to serve the customer in a world-class way. She launched a program to create a customer-satisfaction index that would hardwire the voice of the customer into the organization, and she sent all senior officers out calling on customers. Every three months, Rickey held an all-employee meeting at each factory to report on progress in and threats to the business as a whole, and to hear the voice of the employee.

### THE BURNING PLATFORM

It hasn't been all fun. Rickey had to relay bad news to the front lines. "The first job of a leader, when you're managing change in an organization today, is to 'create the burning platform,' " says Rickey. That meant she had to focus employees on the fact that survival was at issue. The message was that employees were on a blazing deck, that she is standing on it with them, and the task was to put out those flames or perish.

In 1995 the European economy was recovering from recession and companies were buying more forklift trucks. Most employees saw little reason to worry. So at every company meeting—even as the good times returned—Rickey focused on NMHG's failures in serving its customers, its production weaknesses, and the constant threat posed by competition. Linde and Toyota had far greater financial strength than NMHG, and low-cost Korean products would soon invade the European market. Rickey also pointed to an uncomfortable precedent. Fifteen years earlier, Clark Equipment had been the market leader in forklift trucks. But it had failed to provide the improvements its customers wanted. By 1995 Clark's sales had shrunk from $1.42 billion to $875 million.

Rickey didn't have to tell NMHG employees what would happen if their company followed Clark's lead. In meetings all over the company, she made sure no one forgot how complacency had led to Clark's downfall.

But even while openly confronting the dangers, Rickey showed confidence in her people. She urged those working on the key improvement initiatives to come directly to top management for help—if they found their paths blocked.

## Taking It to the Top

She appealed to the hearts and minds of all NMHG people with her vision of NMHG as the world leader. And she developed and inspired people by dramatically increasing training, by assigning people to newly created jobs that stretched their talents, by prominently recognizing contributions leading to improvements, and by taking every encounter with customers and employees as an occasion for building enthusiasm.

The previous management had commissioned plenty of teams to improve quality and efficiency. But after their initial commissioning, top executives weren't involved with them. Some teams had been meeting for as long as two years without significant accomplishment. Others had made improvements that didn't seem to matter to customers.

Rickey pulled the highest-potential managers in the company out of their existing jobs and assigned them to lead new teams to attack key problems. Then she assigned one high-ranking manager to each team as a sponsor. This was a clear and unmistakable signal of this mission's importance.

In just eight months, Rickey achieved remarkable progress. The new improvement teams were so effective that many produced impressive results several months ahead of schedule.

One team was assigned to examine the options the company offered on its trucks. The team discovered that one line of forklifts offered ninety-eight different lengths of fork, and ninety-six different instrument panel configurations. Within months, the team had developed a plan to standardize a smaller number of forks and introduce a few full-featured but less costly instrumentation configurations. "I'm sure no customer said, 'I'd like that truck, but would you please make the fork one-inch longer,' " Rickey comments. The new plan will give customers what they want while saving money.

Another team focused on redefining quality in terms of customer needs. As discussed in Chapter 3, the factor most important to customers was related to service: how fast a truck could be returned to use when it broke down. Only 15 percent of customer concerns were on price, which NMHG executives had traditionally considered to be paramount. As a result of these discoveries, NMHG improved training at its dealerships and created the Master Parts system, which guaranteed that every dealer would always keep the one hundred most-requested parts in stock. Additional teams began improving sales and production forecasting and reworking the options NMHG offered.

Sales continue to soar. In 1995 they were up 40 percent from two years earlier. Rickey says that it's too early to give her credit for that growth. But we think Victoria Rickey represents an important phenomenon—a new kind of customer-centered leader emerging for the twenty-first century.

## THE TWENTY-FIRST CENTURY LEADER

As a leader, Rickey bears a striking resemblance to virtually all of the most effective leaders in the customer-centered organizations we researched. Throughout the world, we found the same patterns appearing. The best leaders are far more directly involved, side-by-side with their people, while at the same time never micromanaging or stifling enthusiasm.

No one who's seen the best leaders at work today would describe their style as "arm's length." They're constantly on the front lines—talking to customers, talking to employees, reminding people what the plan is, helping them understand new developments, checking on people's level of confidence, helping them to believe in what's possible.

### EMPLOYEES ARE EMPOWERED BY DEFAULT

The accelerating pace of change today demands this approach. Several of these people told us that if they went away from their companies for even a two-week vacation, they felt on their return that they no longer understood the business. In such a world, how can a leader afford *not* to be on the front lines?

In addition, today's fundamental changes in the structure of world business demand this new style of leadership. When managers started to talk about "empowerment" in the early 1980s, companies had complex structures of supervisors and middle managers, all assigned to tell lower-ranking people what to do. Today those hierarchies have been radically streamlined. Where perhaps five people once reported to one leader, today the number may be twenty or more.

So "empowerment" is less of an issue. Today's frontline employee is "empowered" almost by default. There's no one around to give assignments and check whether they're done. The employee must make dozens of daily decisions that "bosses" once took care of. And he or she needs to understand the crucial role of the customer in the equation.

## WHAT LEADERSHIP CAN ACCOMPLISH

"Every single day we lead by being out there communicating what's really important—taking personal responsibility for the customer," says Tom O'Brien, chief executive officer of PNC Bank Corp. in Pittsburgh. "One key role of senior management is to create other leaders throughout the organization who reinforce the direction and the vision. It's not a grand statement or something that you put on a wall. Instead, it's helping people know what to expect, what will happen tomorrow, why we are making certain decisions, and how they fit into the plan."

PNC Bank Corp. is a powerhouse that has grown rapidly into one of America's largest banks. It has prospered through careful attention to customers, wisely managed mergers, close monitoring of its revenue/expense relationship, a commitment to adding value for customers and shareholders, and strong leadership at all levels of the organization.

The bank has taken unusual care in studying what produces successful relationships with its hundreds of thousands of customers. In doing so, it has made some important discoveries. It measures customer satisfaction by calculating only the percentage of its customers who are "extremely satisfied" with the bank—a top-tier number that has been increasing steadily each quarter. Executive Vice President Susan Bohn and Vice President/Director of Marketing Research Jim DiCostanzo discovered that the overwhelming majority of the reasons PNC's customers say they're "extremely satisfied" relate to a cadre of knowledgeable, attentive employees who make it easy for customers to do business with the bank—rather than to its pricing or policies. Bank employees going out of their way to manage customer relationships well account for over 70 percent of the reasons PNC's corporate customers are "extremely satisfied." And among retail customers that proportion is over 80 percent.

This result isn't surprising. But what causes employees to treat customers so well? Figure 6.1 shows the answer. Bohn and DiCostanzo's research found that exceptional treatment of customers correlated most closely with the *behavior of their leaders*. If leaders were accessible, willing to listen, and fair, and if employees generally believed in the

**Figure 6.1**

THE SUCCESS SEQUENCE

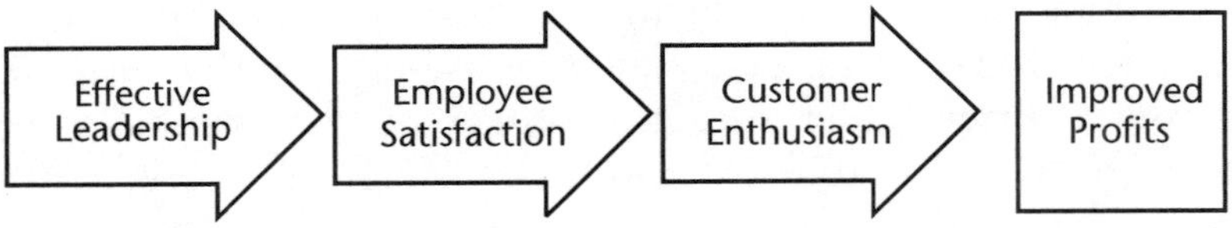

Effective Leadership → Employee Satisfaction → Customer Enthusiasm → Improved Profits

*Source*: Research Conducted by PNC Bank Corp.

bank's top management, then they in turn delivered higher quality service to customers.

So a kind of trickle-down theory is at work. At PNC and other thriving organizations, great contact leadership produces world-class employee performance, which in turn produces loyal customers. And those customers in turn are the foundation of exceptional profitability and rapid growth.

## FOUR ELEMENTS OF CONTACT LEADERSHIP

A Forum Corporation study recently investigated one hundred successful leaders and five hundred of their peers, and identified four qualities (or "clusters") that mark the most successful, customer-centered leaders. These qualities are:

1. **A passionate connectedness to customers and employees.** The most effective leaders are no longer content to just analyze market data or hear from others what's going on. They are physically, visibly, directly, constantly obtaining information firsthand.
2. **A deep commitment to creating meaning for people in clear, concrete terms.** A lofty customer-centered vision is no longer sufficient. Today's best leaders translate their dreams into day-to-day reality, making sure people understand what it all means and how they fit in.
3. **An ability to mobilize people and help them see progress—with a mix of both challenge and support.** The new leader doesn't just practice empowerment and delegation, but shows an ability to get people aligned and working toward the same goal. Taking personal responsibility, challenging people to do their best, demonstrating confidence in their abilities, and providing support, the new leader helps everyone in the organization to see progress.
4. **The capacity to inspire and develop others to be leaders.** This is not "motivating" in the traditional sense of the term, but giving people the capability to inspire themselves—not creating followers, but other leaders throughout the organization.

Like Rickey at NMHG and O'Brien at PNC Bank Corp., Larry Bossidy, chief executive of AlliedSignal, is a superb contact leader who demonstrates the four qualities. When Bossidy arrived at AlliedSignal, a giant maker of automotive, aerospace, and chemical products, it was not a happy place to work. No wonder—earnings had been on a six-year plateau. People were dispirited. They had no clear idea where the company was going.

## FROM BAD GUY TO HERO

Bossidy couldn't immediately make the place happier. He knew that to become competitive AlliedSignal had to shrink, and quickly reduced head count from 105,000 to 85,000. But Bossidy was no mere cost cutter. He immediately began the work of aligning AlliedSignal and focusing it more on the needs of customers. In his first sixty days as CEO, Bossidy spoke with nearly 5,000 employees and scores of customers about what was wrong and what actions he should take.

He found, for instance, that AlliedSignal's information systems were misleading the company. While internal data showed an order-fill rate of 98 percent, customers reported that Allied was filling only 60 percent of orders. "I got a real earful from customers in the beginning," recalls Bossidy. "If you don't satisfy customers, you can pull the curtains. It's over."[1]

It was far from over. In the three years since Bossidy arrived at AlliedSignal, profitability has soared, the stock price has risen from thirty dollars to nearly eighty dollars, and the company is back on the growth track. Larry Bossidy is perhaps the most popular man on Wall Street, and *Financial World* named him Executive of the Year.

## CONTACT LEADERS CONNECT

Bossidy's constant visits to customers and employees demonstrate his deep desire to *connect*. He notes:

> Customers always have events and they need speakers, and no one wants to speak. I raise my hand. Why? Because I'm Mario Cuomo? No. Because it gives me two hours to spend with a customer's organization. That's a chance of a lifetime. . . . You know, they are the only customers we have, so we'd better love them. . . . As we get more and more customer focused, we don't have to preach about the need to change. People know it."[2]

Bossidy's success is in part explained by research conducted by the consulting firm Rath & Strong. A survey called Connecting Customers and Change, which includes responses from two hundred senior managers from Fortune 500 companies, indicates that executives are more satisfied with their organizations' change efforts when the breadth, depth, and frequency of their customer contact is high. In particular, there was a strong correlation between the amount of executive customer contact and the speed of organizational change. "A strong customer connection seems not only to give people information to support change efforts, but also to align and energize those efforts so they occur faster and stick more deeply," says Rath & Strong vice president John Guaspari.

## Contact Leaders Create Meaning

Bossidy *creates meaning* by developing clear values and a clear vision of the future of AlliedSignal. When he first arrived, he took his top twelve managers off-site and spent two days arguing about what was really important for the organization. The group came back with seven simple values that give people a view of what is expected of them: customers, integrity, people, teamwork, speed, innovation, and performance. Says Bossidy:

> If you are a leader in this company, you risk being a hypocrite if you don't behave according to our values. And you're going to get some heat—and I think that's terrific. . . . People need to know where they are going, what victory looks like, where AlliedSignal is going and how we are going to get there . . . and they have to have a reason to get there and some help along the way.[3]

## Contact Leaders Mobilize

Bossidy also knows how to mobilize people by hearing, communicating clearly, challenging, and supporting them. He deals with tough questions honestly. He creates forums that enable him to listen to people at all levels. And he lays out with clarity, to the whole organization, the formidable tasks Allied faces. He seems to understand what management consultant Curt Berrien meant when he said, "Vision is a communication challenge, not a design challenge."

If someone is critical of the company during a public meeting,

Bossidy thinks it's a positive event. He says, "That gets it on the table and permits response. . . . It's good if people go home at night and say, 'I told that son of a bitch what I thought about him today.' "

But Bossidy also creates more private forums where he can hear what ordinary employees are saying. Whenever he travels, he meets with groups of about twenty employees, without name tags and without their bosses present.

"We want to create an environment in which people will speak up," Bossidy says. "When I conduct interactive sessions, I don't walk out after three questions. I make it clear that I'm going to be there until the last question is asked."

### *Showdown with American*

Bossidy showed he could get people on board in the aftermath of a 1992 meeting with Robert Crandall, president of American Airlines and a key customer for AlliedSignal's navigation, communication, and other aerospace systems. Crandall made it clear that he didn't believe AlliedSignal was driven by the marketplace—as American was—and if he weren't locked into a long-term contract he would take American's business elsewhere. AlliedSignal bureaucracy was costing American Airlines money. And in the months since Bossidy had joined the organization and launched sharp cutbacks, service had gotten worse, not better. At that point, employees were in a state of shock, wondering how far cutbacks would go.

Bossidy did something unusual but wise. He let every employee know about the bad news he'd heard from Crandall. The message, coming directly from the customer, seemed to galvanize important parts of the organization. Management adopted a plan to serve customers like Crandall better, then executed it. Attacked first were internal problems in manufacturing and R & D—the problems the company thought it could solve quickest. Then executives put their energy into understanding their remaining employees and training them to create an organization that could deliver growth by performing better for customers.

Today, AlliedSignal is a significantly different company. In 1994, Crandall had become a happy customer and told Bossidy he had never seen such rapid improvement by a supplier. Bossidy had effectively mobilized the organization for real change.

### CONTACT LEADERS INSPIRE

Finally, Bossidy knows how to *inspire.* To inject both discipline and teamwork into the organization, and to help people become better at leading with him, he mandated that each employee attend a four-day training program about how to deliver quality for customers. (Bossidy attended, too.) "This is not one of those short-lived quality initiatives," he said. "And it takes more than putting up posters and hugging each other. It is about making people work more closely together to continuously look outward to satisfy our customers. . . . At the end of the day you bet on people rather than on strategy because the issue is always whether you can execute."[4]

As with many of the other successful leaders we observed, Bossidy is moving his organization quickly—focusing less on helping people *cope* with change and more with showing them how to *get used to* a new way of working. In his contact leadership, persuasion and coaching have replaced barking orders; candid, concrete communication has replaced ethereal vision; personal responsibility has replaced the kind of "empowerment" that people saw as abdication; and standing up for what is important has replaced the "what-would-you-like-to-do-and-how-would-you-like-things-to-be?" style so popular a few years ago. As Susan Beckmann, the highly successful manager of the Boston office of MCI's Business Markets Division, says, "When things are fuzzy and uncertain, you'd be surprised how much people like being told what to do every once in a while."

Leading in a fuzzy and uncertain environment is just the challenge Bossidy, like Rickey and O'Brien, has mastered. "Yogi Berra was wrong," he states. "It ain't over when it's over because it's never over."[5]

## HOW TO LEAD A TRANSFORMATION

Popular mythology treats leadership as something nebulous, perhaps inherent in a few people who have a mysterious gift. It's seen as a matter of style, charisma, and intense personal magnetism.

That's the Hollywood version, perhaps. But in reality, good leadership is very different. Our research into one hundred successful leaders and five hundred of their peers found that those who are

---

**Self-Test: The Myths of Charisma**

Most people still believe that leadership has something to do with charisma. We don't. So we ask people to take this simple test:

1. Write down the names of the three best leaders you ever worked for.
2. On a scale of 1 to 10, 10 being the highest, rate each one for his or her charisma.

In our experience, chances are that your favorite leaders weren't very charismatic. (Most people rank favorite leaders somewhere between 5 and 6.)

---

leading high-growth, customer-centered organizations behave in clearly definable ways—ways almost anyone can learn.

These behaviors and characteristics create a compelling picture of what is needed from those who run customer-centered organizations. Rather than depending on charisma (a remarkably scarce commodity), the best leaders demonstrate passionate connectedness and take specific actions that enable them to create meaning, mobilize people, and inspire their organizations to move forward in focused ways. The rest of this chapter will show how it's done.

## CONNECTING WITH A PASSION

Forum's research found that the most successful leaders were almost compulsive in the way they connected with both employees and customers. You could say that they had a basic need for better information—especially about customers, but about everything else that related to their business, too. The goal was not information for its own sake, but to make sense of the world. An out-of-touch leader is just not a leader.

When we first met Steve Bonner, president of the Construction Information Group (CIG) of McGraw-Hill, Inc., we immediately noticed the enormous stack of business books on the corner of his desk—at least eight, including works on total quality management, leadership, and how to be customer-driven. One of us commented, "That's a pretty hefty reading challenge you've got ahead of you."

"Oh, I've already finished those," he said while pointing to another skyscraper on his credenza. "That's my reading list."

But reading was only the beginning of how Steve connected. We soon learned that he had created a group of thirty-five senior managers whom he'd named "ambassadors" to interview people throughout the organization and bring the "voice of the employee" to top executives' attention. We learned that he carefully reviewed a well-chosen list of industry periodicals and research services to understand the dynamics of CIG's industry, and that he constantly studied other companies' approaches to strategy formulation as a way of benchmarking his own. In addition to these activities, Bonner stayed in direct touch with customers to ensure that his insights were focused and on target.

Leaders who spark renewal are spending less and less time behind closed doors and more and more time out in the world of their customers, their suppliers, their employees, and their competitors. This may even frustrate those who work for them. Indeed, the people who report to one auto executive complained they could never find him in his office. His response: "Well, the last time I checked, we weren't making cars in my office."

The old advice about "management by wandering around" is only the beginning. GE's CEO Jack Welch and others make a fetish of using E-mail to keep in touch. Regular visits to customers, both internal and external, play a key role in the strategies of the most successful executives. In the fast-food industry, some executives get out to restaurants and flip hamburgers just to stay connected.

Most executives haven't yet developed a full version of the "dynamic scorecard" we discussed in Chapter 3, but a crucial part of many strategies for getting in touch is gathering customer data at least as regularly as you gather financial data. While he was chairman and managing director of British Airways, Sir Colin Marshall received a complete report on customer ratings of his top-rated airline every month. In addition, Marshall connected by spending a lot of time at airports. He was known for showing up at 5:00 A.M. to meet the first flight arriving for the day. That not only kept him in touch, but encouraged his fellow managers to become early risers as well. "We've all found ourselves getting up a lot earlier since Sir Colin joined the organization," says Chris Byron, British Airways' senior general manager for manpower, "and we've become much more visible, and we've learned to listen."

Connected leaders help other leaders to connect, too. When George Fisher left Motorola to become chief executive of Kodak, he wanted to make sure everyone knew customers. One way he did that was to schedule the board of directors meeting not, as tradition had it, in cozy, cloistered Rochester, New York, but in Las Vegas in the midst of the national Photographic Marketing Association convention. Fisher wanted the board, which includes a former governor of Kentucky and even a former chairman of the Securities and Exchange Commission, to walk the halls in the convention center and personally meet with some of the twenty-seven thousand customers and customers-to-be.

At MBNA America Bank, the large credit-card marketer, each officer spends four hours per month listening to customer phone interactions. British Airways executives are actually required to handle complaints periodically. Through its Partners in Service program, executives of catalog retailer Best Products, are in the stores during the busy seasons to experience crunch time for themselves.

### *What? No Executive Bathroom Key?*

Many wise businesspeople are even physically restructuring the layout of their offices to get them better in touch. By breaking down walls or putting executive desks in the middle of the action, they eliminate the insularity of the "executive wing."

As newly installed chairman of UARCO, a large document-technology-solutions provider, Bob Harbage immediately removed a wooden wall that created a narrow corridor to the executive offices. "To accelerate the change in our business, we've got to work in clusters, task forces, and teams of people," Harbage says. "We moved seven executives out of the west wing offices to create war rooms, not unlike Winston Churchill's bunker war rooms of fifty years ago. In these centralized spaces are posted the latest information about customers, competitors, employees, and business results."

Harbage has also sent his executives off to the front lines. After listening patiently to the long, boring, mostly financial reports at his first officers' meeting after his arrival in 1994, Harbage announced: "That's the last of that kind of meeting. We don't want a history lesson about what's in the rearview mirror." The new policy was for every nonselling officer (e.g., the chief financial officer, the director of purchasing, the head of human resources) to go out into the field, prior to meetings, to

- Ask customers: "What are you not getting that you'd like to have?"
- Ask salespeople: "What would you like to have to sell that you don't have to sell?"
- Ask managers: "How can we double our value to customers in this area?"

Figure 6.2 describes the practices comprising the Passionate Connectedness cluster. Take a moment and assess where you stand on each.

**Working Your Way Down the Ladder**

Appearances are deceiving. What guests staying at the Westin Stamford and Westin Plaza hotels in Singapore don't know is that the bellhop carrying their luggage may just be the general manager, David Shackleton. Shackleton believes that he needs to literally walk in the shoes of his employees and interact with customers in the real world if he is to fully comprehend their needs and frustrations. He believes that ivory towers can often become gallows chambers. According to Shackleton: "Too often senior management gets caught up in administrative matters and loses sight of what the customer really wants. By putting myself in the shoes of our staff and working side by side with them, I get a better picture of how we are really meeting the expectations of our guests."

Shackleton's hands-on experiences have resulted in numerous, seemingly trivial changes that taken en masse make an enormous difference to customers. He learned as a waiter that mornings are especially difficult for guests and has instructed employees to help ease their anxieties with a sincere smile and "good morning." His experience as a bellhop revealed to him that, "We must try harder to greet our guests by name. We have many opportunities . . . to recognize them properly and appropriately."

Another potent side effect of Shackleton's connectedness is that it goes a long way to improving management and staff cohesiveness. "It also provides," says Shackleton, "a very useful lesson in humility, as well as reinforcing the fact that the real work in a hotel is not done behind a desk."

**Figure 6.2**

LEADERSHIP PRACTICES THAT WORK:
A PASSIONATE CONNECTEDNESS

The five practices that our research demonstrated to be correlated with exceptional performance in this cluster are:

- Seek information from as many internal and external sources as possible
- Analyze how well group members work together
- Know the capabilities and motivations of those in the work group
- Know how what you do supports and drives the organization's strategy
- Know your own capabilities and motivations

## A DEEP COMMITMENT TO CREATING MEANING

Today's customer-centered business leader helps to create and keep a positive, exciting picture of the future that lies before the people in his or her organization. It's a picture that gives meaning and direction to everyday work, that takes corporate goals from the rarefied air of the boardroom and makes them clear and binding to everyone in the company.

The task of creating meaning is more than just having a vision, and it is much more than a set of principles hammered out at a remote conference center. It is a guide—the imperatives of the company—and to be successful it must be reinforced every day by a leader who gives it life and breath on a personal basis; who makes sure everybody understands what he or she is doing and why; who involves other people in giving daily direction to this vision; and who, in fact, lives it.

Contact leaders do much more than craft profound phrases about the future. They enlist employees in a cause, if you will, a reason for existing, a reason for excelling—interpreted and modeled every day by the successful leader.

### *A Good Cause*

Working for one of these leaders can be somewhat like working for Apple Computer in its legendary early days. It wasn't the weekly paycheck that drove employees there to work late and wolf down meals at their desks. It wasn't maximizing profits or even the possibility of far-off riches from stock options or a promotion to a better job.

What was it? It was the overriding power of the "idea"—the belief that this company and these people were going to create a computer for Everyman. That was the point.

In a similar manner, the working environment under customer-centered leaders provides purpose, direction, and meaning. People know what the challenges are, why they're worth taking, and how they, the people, personally fit in. The vision may not even be articulated, but it is there and it is alive and robust.

### *Making It Their Idea*

Today's business leaders—the ones who are customer centered—help their people to understand their company's goals by involving them in their creation. In fact, of all the actions leaders took in this area, the one that correlated most with "creating meaning" was the degree to which the leader involved employees in shaping the direction.

UARCO's Bob Harbage asked his upper middle managers to create a vision for the future, a future where business forms would be computerized rather than produced on paper. Top management stood aside and let them work. That vision, Project Phoenix, was given to top management, which (1) embraced it, and then (2) communicated the vision throughout the company with very few modifications. Project Phoenix called for a total reinvention of how UARCO brings products to market and how it provides customer service.

Emma Lou Brent, president of tiny Phelps County Bank in Rolla, Missouri, saw involvement as a way to emphasize her institution's goals and aspirations—in effect, to translate its vision for employees. She created charts that showed exactly how the bank made every penny it earned, then invited all fifty-three of her employees to a goal-setting meeting. Her belief was that a small bank could survive in an era of megamergers only if it gave such superior service that it was clearly perceived as helping the citizens of Rolla and its environs to better manage their lives. Emma Lou Brent helped every employee to share her vision and to understand what each person had to do to help achieve it.

The result? Her Phelps County Bank has decisively surpassed big competitors in its region.

Perhaps the biggest mistake a company can make is to assume that writing a vision statement automatically takes care of problems. Like customer information that sits unused and ignored, a sense of direction that isn't carried to the front lines—that merely rests on a plaque on some boardroom wall—is essentially worthless.

Sometimes leaders don't involve the right people in creating a vision. Sometimes they don't involve anybody. In a worst-case scenario, perhaps, the president of one hotel company called in his ad agency and had the account team write the vision. That action went over with his employees like the proverbial lead balloon.

A vision is a powerful instrument—as long as it is practical, reasonable, and suffuses the organization, and as long as it is translated and made concrete in daily contacts. In fact, James Collins and Jerry Porras, a pair of Stanford University professors, report in their book *Built to Last* (1995) that the stock market returns of "visionary companies" are nearly seven times those of nonvisionary companies.

### *Walking the Talk*

Finally, leaders create meaning by visibly modeling it: standing up for what they tell others is important. David Weekley, president of highly successful David Weekley Homes, was living his company's vision of building beautiful, flawless homes when he personally called on customers who didn't like what he had built, who had said they would not recommend his company to anyone else.

"At first," says Weekley, "I was devastated because we had all worked for four to six months doing everything to make the customer happy. And we had failed. The fact is it's a lot of very little things that mean success or failure in this business."

By visiting the very small share of home buyers who weren't satisfied, Weekley took a powerful stand in favor of 100 percent customer satisfaction. He was out there, calling on dissatisfied people, giving meaning to his company's direction, sending a message to each and every employee. Fortunately for Weekley, there weren't many such calls to make—the percentage of customers who would recommend his homes to prospective buyers is consistently in the high 90s.

To succeed, a company today needs a driving, overriding, collective purpose that is understood throughout the organization. Today's customer-centered leader understands how to create one. He or she is no stranger to the practices listed in Figure 6.3.

**Figure 6.3**

LEADERSHIP PRACTICES THAT WORK:
A COMMITMENT TO CREATING MEANING

The five practices that our research demonstrated to be correlated with exceptional performance in this cluster are:

- Communicate the strategy of the organization as a whole
- Involve the right people in developing the work group's strategy
- Create a positive picture of the future of the work group
- Stand up for what is important
- Adjust plans and actions as necessary in turbulent situations

## MOBILIZE PEOPLE AND HELP THEM SEE PROGRESS

*My job is to create an environment where individual excellence can emerge.*

SKIP LEFAUVE
CHAIRMAN, SATURN

How do you mobilize people when the company you are charged with leading is fending off bankruptcy and you need to lay off 40 percent of your workforce? Ask Stewart Kasen.

Kasen, president of the catalog retailer Best Products Co., Inc., somehow found a way to beat nearly insurmountable odds. Kasen was brought in by Best's owners, the New York buyout firm of Adler & Shaykin to rearm the neglected retailer against aggressive competition. Kasen, a sports enthusiast who frequently uses sports terminology to make a point, left the top position at the $750 million California department store chain, Emporium Capwell, because he loved the idea of winning an underdog game. "From a merchandising and marketing standpoint," says Kasen, "it was a classic repositioning challenge for me."[6] Repositioning, it turned out, was an understatement.

Best was in for more serious trouble than Kasen expected. The company had defaulted on $1.5 billion worth of debt, and anxious creditors refused to ship. During the 1990 holiday season, 25 percent of customers were turned away because Best no longer had the goods. By January 4, 1991, little more than a year after Kasen signed on, Best filed for Chapter 11 bankruptcy protection.

### *The Worst of Times, the Best of Times*

The next few months consisted of store closings, layoffs, and interminable meetings with lawyers and creditors. A Best lawyer, trying to locate Kasen at a restaurant during the reorganization attempt, told the maître d', "to search for a haggard looking man with white hair." The maître d' made a beeline right to Kasen.[7]

Word had begun to trickle down about Kasen's sacrifices. He was obviously taking personal responsibility for a debt that truly was not his, and employees deeply appreciated it. They realized that they had a leader in Kasen, who was not only an astute businessman but one who would remain with them through the long ordeal that was to follow. They were ready to fight back. But how?

Kasen's determination resulted in confidence from creditors, and with Chemical Bank in the lead, the company arranged for a line of credit that it could use while it was reorganizing. One of the first things Kasen did was to protect the dispirited retailing business by isolating it from unsettling legal maneuvering, ensuring that day-to-day operations wouldn't be distracted by the financial restructuring. He focused exclusively on the most profitable products, spiffed up interiors and displays, reformatted store layout, and brought in the technology needed to improve customer service.

But what people remember most was how Kasen became a coach and champion for his people. He spoke of Best's difficulties directly and honestly, and he kept both employees and vendors apprised of the changing situation with weekly progress reports. He began an open-door policy where employees were free to come to him to discuss any and all problems, and he specifically encouraged controversy. According to Kasen, "I told [one group of employees] that if they couldn't meet their deadline, to fall on their sword." They met it and honored him with a plastic sword that now sits on his conference table. That sword has become a potent symbol of the level of commitment expected.

Kasen made sure the organization showed confidence in the abilities of its people at all levels, introducing morning huddles between managers and staff in every store. He closely tracked how each store was doing by carefully surveying groups of customers every week in every single store.

The result? On June 14, 1994, Best left New York bankruptcy court free from the legal surveillance of Chapter 11. Kasen raised his arms straight up as if signaling a touchdown. The next day, Kasen entered the lobby of his corporate offices to seven hundred or so cheering, enthusiastic employees, balloons, confetti, and the theme song from *Rocky*. He had this to say: "This is as good as it gets in life. This isn't the end, this is the beginning."

This win, according to Kasen, was because of his team: "If I can take credit for anything, it is attracting, recruiting, and developing a team of people who together have developed the strategy and have implemented it. The coach oversees it all, he challenges the players. He initiates the strategies."[8] Best's previous owners think much of the credit goes to Kasen. He was referred to as "a sharp businessman and a real human being" and those are just the qualities needed to motivate a team to overcome nearly insurmountable odds.

Best's first profitable year was 1994: a $23 million gain versus a $21 million loss in 1993. It was a successful repositioning, but the heroics of Kasen and his team indeed make that an understatement.

Says senior legal counsel Teresa Hanger: "My grandmother still doesn't get why I left a successful private practice to go to an insolvent company, but this is an amazing learning experience. Under Stewart's leadership, we are inventing a brand-new company."

### *Leadership for Fourteen Hundred Locations*

Jan Rivenbark, chief operating officer of PCA, the portrait studio company that is making photo-taking sessions into memorable experiences, has learned the essence of creating the well-led organization today. In 1994 Rivenbark, was relaxing after a Scottsdale, Arizona, meeting where he'd left his top one hundred managers enthusiastic and ready to commit to creating "a phenomenal experience" for customers. He felt elation and anxiety. The meeting's success caused the elation, but a nagging fear caused the anxiety. Rivenbark worried that the meeting's effects would be short-term. He wondered: "How do I keep up the intensity?"

Rivenbark faced an especially daunting communications challenge because PCA's "front line" of three thousand studio photographer-associates was spread out in more than fourteen hundred locations. Says Rivenbark, "I can't exactly mobilize the troops by having them gather in the cafeteria and sing the company song."

He had an idea. He decided to appoint a senior member of his management team to take responsibility for making the vision of "best customer experience" a reality. But then he reconsidered:

> I realized that if this direction was critically important, then I was not going to be able to delegate it. If we had to integrate the importance of customers into the fabric of the company, someone was going to have to expend enormous energy to keep it alive, and that person was going to have to be me. I had to take personal responsibility for this and for removing the obstacles. And I had to communicate the message every single day.

***Behaviors to Learn***

Our research indicates that of the behaviors we consider critical for growth today, leaders are least proficient at those related to mobilizing people. The old leadership paradigm called for a loner/leader, a Gandhi-type who autonomously developed goals, persuaded others to share them, took huge personal risks, achieved the goals, then walked off into the sunset.

Virtually no one can achieve business success that way today.

Forum has found that effective leadership like Kasen's and Rivenbark's has less to do with individualism than with the ability to build and maintain relationships across the organization. Consider the behavior of Sir Colin Marshall, chairman of British Airways, after some British Airways staff members obtained internal data on competitor Virgin Atlantic and used it to lure some of Virgin's customers away. Virgin sued, and British Airways lost.

For certain this event greatly discomforted Marshall. But he did much more than authorize the payment of the damages and deal with the offenders. He showed he understood the lawsuit's impact on every British Airways employee by immediately going to Heathrow Airport and meeting with groups of employees, explaining what had happened and apologizing for this lamentable action. His empathy for his people was evident when he expressed concern that their company had embarrassed them.

This kind of care for the members of the work group is among the most powerful traits a manager can possess. In fact, in every study Forum has conducted, the "soft" relationship skills rate significantly higher in importance than do more traditional practices such as "consistently emphasizing progress against goals."

Another key part of mobilization is a leader's ability to demonstrate confidence in people. Benjamin Zander, director of the Boston Philharmonic Orchestra, demonstrates confidence in his students at the New England Conservatory of Music by announcing on the first day of class that he will give each one of them an A. All he asks is that they record in writing what they will have achieved by the end of the semester with Zander's guidance. The students respond with superior performance.

That paragon of traditional leadership, Henry Ford, once said: "Why is it I get a whole person when all I want is a pair of hands?" Today's best leaders know they need—and truly want—the energy of the whole person.

Figure 6.4 describes the practices that make up the Mobilize cluster.

**Figure 6.4**

LEADERSHIP PRACTICES THAT WORK:
AN ABILITY TO MOBILIZE

The five practices that our research demonstrated to be correlated with exceptional performance in this cluster are:

- Demonstrate confidence in the abilities of others
- Communicate clearly the results expected from others
- Demonstrate care for the members of the work group
- Appeal to people's hearts and minds to lead them in a new direction
- Let people know how they are progressing toward the group's goal

**Ensemble Leadership: When More People Are Better than One**

It's difficult for any one individual to perform all of the behaviors of leadership. And yet they're all essential. How can you do it?

Many of the effective models recently involve executives *sharing* the task. Bernie Marcus and Arthur Blank of Home Depot are two opposite kinds of leaders: Marcus a relaxed jokester and Blank a supremely organized accountant. The result: Between them, they can accomplish all the tasks of customer-centered leadership.

Bill Gates tried to find someone to be president of Microsoft, but somehow he was unable to find just the right person. So he and his three top executives joined together to form "the BOOP": **B**ill and the **O**ffice **O**f the **P**resident. It's a team of separate, but complementary, spirits.

The top 15 executives that make up General Motors's North American strategy board get together once a week, or as needed, to hash out solutions to problems quickly. What used to take weeks or even months to codify is now argued and agreed upon immediately over a table in the "war room."

If this sounds less than revolutionary, it is because the instinct and experience that it taps is very old. You can see it in virtually every healthy family business. Perhaps Dad is chairman, big sister is president, and brother is executive vice president. But where does power lie? In reality, it's shared according to people's skills.

## INSPIRE AND DEVELOP OTHERS

> *You can hand your staff a map and tell them to go to the mountaintop. Or you can give them boots, a compass, the desire to climb, and an invitation to come with you . . .*
>
> —UNKNOWN

For inspirational leadership, look at Home Depot. This chain of home-improvement centers has grown from nothing to $7 billion in sales in just fifteen years. When Chairman Bernie Marcus appeared on *Moneyline,* host Lou Dobbs said he thought he'd never before interviewed anyone with a comparable record: thirty-four consecutive quarters of record earnings.

The most obvious distinguishing feature of Home Depot management is the nature of their contact leadership: the amount of time the leaders spend in the stores monitoring their people and building a new generation of leaders. Not only do Marcus and president Arthur Blank each spend 40 percent of their own time in the stores, but they require every executive and even every member of the board of directors to spend time there, too. Each board member has to visit seven stores each quarter, first wandering around as a shopper and then introducing him- or herself to employees on their breaks and asking what changes they'd like to see in the way the organization is run.

Marcus and Blank demonstrate every one of the leadership practices described in the three previous clusters. They connect, create meaning, and mobilize. But perhaps they are most remarkable in the way that they inspire. They do it by constantly focusing on the contributions of the employees, promoting the development of people's talents, stimulating the thinking of both grassroots employees and headquarters staff, and building enthusiasm about each of the constant changes that Home Depot must make.

Bernie Marcus is literally a stand-up comedian. He worked his way through Rutgers University in the 1940s by doing comedy routines at hotels in New York's Catskill Mountains. So one way Marcus and Blank inspire employees is through a quarterly live television show, *Breakfast with Bernie and Arthur*, broadcast before a live audience of Home Depot staffers at one location to the other 230-plus stores.

Home Depot promotes people's talents with training that's far more extensive than that of its competitors. And Marcus and Blank focus on those who will be leaders. Everyone training to be a manager or assistant manager at Home Depot trains directly with one of the founders.

## Leadership at All Levels

As organizations get flatter, the need for this kind of leadership grows even more central. Leaders must create new leaders. Victoria Rickey notes that until recently a middle manager could be *just* a manager. A factory manager, for instance, merely had to coordinate the work of subordinates.

Today, contact leadership must take place at all levels if an organization is to become truly customer centered. The business environment has simply grown too complex for a few "heroic" individuals at

**The Best Leaders Are the Best Teachers**

"The very best leaders," according to Jeffrey Timmons, professor of entrepreneurial finance at Harvard Business School, "are not only the very best learners. They are also the very best teachers."

Take Red Auerbach, for example. The legendary Boston Celtics basketball coach was renowned because those he coached as players went on to teach or lead themselves: Bob Cousy, Bill Russell, Tom Heinsohn, Bill Sharman, K.C. Jones . . . all were star basketball players and all went on to coach professional teams.

Leaders make allowance for failure. According to Timmons, they reject a "zero-defect mentality" because zero defects can occur only where there is no risk.

Leadership occurs at all levels only when risk is rewarded and where there is a forgiveness of and allowance for stumbling. Fabio Cammarono, the president of Saritel, a subsidiary of Italy's national telephone company SIP, wants to change his company's rigid, monopolistic mindset. To do this he is encouraging risk: "We have two assets, our know-how and the mistakes we made during the first seven months [of building a new organization]," he says.

the top to lead the organization alone. This is especially true as people work in more remote locations without close supervision.

Bill Gates's charisma alone did not create and certainly could not maintain Microsoft's epic growth. Microsoft has created a powerful culture by intentionally fostering leadership at all levels and across functions. According to Apple founder, NeXt CEO, and Microsoft competitor Steve Jobs:

> Bill has done a great job of cloning himself as the company has grown. Now there are all these aggressive "Little Bills" running the various product groups and divisions, and they keep coming at you and coming at you and coming at you, just like the Japanese. They're not afraid to stumble . . .

Leadership at all levels is sometimes easier said than done. Many managers continue to fear that "too many chiefs" will mean anarchy. They feel that power is a zero-sum game: that giving authority to a colleague necessarily means giving up your own. In reality, for people who follow the leadership practices we're discussing, power multiplies itself. As these leaders give away authority, they become ever more productive, effective, and powerful.

## Integrity and Humility at the Heart

The cornerstone of inspiration is integrity. This means that leaders need to be honest, forthright, and humble. It sounds, well, corny, perhaps, but these qualities are essential.

Humility is often in short supply when a business is successful. Chicago-based Learning Curve Toys is growing at 60 percent per year by creating an innovative line of products that occupy children for hours. Performance is not perfect, though. When one of Learning Curve's product lines was significantly under-performing initial expectations, CEO John Lee could have pointed fingers at any number of managers. Instead Lee accepted responsibility for missing the mark. Admitting his mistake mobilized people—and also freed them to work on fixing the problems instead of worrying about who was to blame.

Unfortunately, traditional business education often doesn't focus on how to admit mistakes to people— or demonstrate confidence in their abilities. But without it, "lean and mean" organizations can't develop the new leaders they need.

## The Opportunity for Change

"As one of my mentors told me," says Susan Beckmann, director of sales and service for the Business Markets Division of MCI Boston, "the hardest thing to do is to change on an uptick. But that's what we are doing. We figure that we won't have to worry about bad business results if we do the changing now. The time to fix the roof is when it is not raining."

Beckmann has demonstrated that when managers know how to inspire employees, there's hardly any limit to the changes they can take on. Beckmann acted immediately to focus the Boston office on its customers when she was named to her job. She created a customer-focused coverage strategy that segmented customers into "growth," "investment," and "strategic" accounts and then worked with salespeople to decide which they would call on. She made sure that people would have clear development paths and clear measures of performance, and made a strong point of supporting her first-line managers rather than trying to make all the decisions herself.

The result has been excellent sales growth. But Beckmann decided she didn't have to stop there. When MCI management was looking for offices to volunteer to pilot two new concepts (virtual offices and sales automation), Beckmann immediately signed her team up—as if the new structure and redefined jobs weren't enough to handle.

"I thought that the experiments would be a great development opportunity for my people," she says. "I think that people really want to see themselves as leaders and this was a chance for them to help the whole company move ahead.

Beckmann adds, "If you can set people up for success and get everyone singing from the same song sheet; if you can create an environment that allows people to lead and to say what they think and to help make it happen for the customer; and if you can provide a clear, consistent message every day, you can really take off. That is what we are trying to do." So far, Beckmann's office is succeeding: sailing past its quotas, turning in record profits, and reversing the increases in turnover.

Figure 6.5 describes the practices that make up the Inspire cluster.

**Figure 6.5**

LEADERSHIP PRACTICES THAT WORK:
THE CAPACITY TO INSPIRE

The five practices that our research demonstrated to be correlated with exceptional performance in this cluster are:

- Recognize the contributions of others
- Promote the development of people's talents
- Stimulate others' thinking
- Build enthusiasm about projects and assignments
- Enable others to feel and act like leaders

**Learn Leadership from a Wizard**

Traditional-style leaders need a lesson from the Great and Powerful Wizard of Oz. Here is a story of how a traditional leader, the phony Wizard, was forced to become more vulnerable, more accessible, and more human—and much more effective at inspiring others.

Remember how the Wizard's legendary reputation for supernatural power and wisdom instilled fear in his subjects? Dorothy and her companions were filled with trepidation as they tentatively inched forward toward the awesome Wizard in search of his special wisdom. They came to him for answers and were willing to suffer a dangerous pilgrimage to get them.

But then the dog, Toto, pulled the curtain. And there was the Wizard, just an ordinary guy. We were relieved to find a mere mortal frantically working those levers. The Wizard was exposed. As a traditional leader, the Great and Powerful Wizard of Oz had held sway over his people via a well-orchestrated persona. He was more than human.

The defrocked wizard, who ultimately became much more powerful than his larger-than-life predecessor, resembles the new leader. While there is no supernatural wisdom, the new leader is expert at equipping others to provide leadership and do the work.

He or she knows how to identify, develop, utilize, and promote the talents of others and pass out the power needed for them to accomplish their goals. New leaders encourage timid lions to try new skills and ask scarecrows with low self-esteem for advice. And, especially, they teach people like Dorothy how to use their own two feet to get to a destination.

Employees today need leaders who will inspire them and enable them to feel like leaders.

## Final Thoughts on Leadership: The Cultural Moments of Truth

There are certain times when a leader's impact on creating and reinforcing a particular culture is greatly magnified. You might call these cultural moments of truth. When these moments occur, it is as if the leader is at a fork in the road. If he or she takes the path to the right, the culture is reinforced and strengthened. If the path to the left is taken, the culture is undermined and weakened. These moments of truth are highly visible to employees, frequent in occurrence, and vital to the creation of culture. A smart leader knows this and will use them to shape the customer-centered culture.

A dramatic and visible moment of truth outside of the business world occurred during World War II. The Nazis had occupied Denmark and announced that by a specific date all Danish Jews would be required to wear an armband bearing the Star of David. On the appointed date, Danish King Christian X, during his daily early morning horseback ride around the streets of Copenhagen, surprised his nation by wearing an armband with the Star of David.

The entire country took his cue. That very day thousands of Danes, irrespective of religion, put on the armbands. This allowed Jews to comply with the Nazi directive and still remain anonymous. With this one act, this moment of truth, King Christian set the tone for what would be one of the most effective resistance efforts of the war. Danish citizens later sheltered thousands of Jews whom they sneaked into neutral Sweden.

Understanding the power of such moments of truth can be a leader's most effective way to influence an organization's culture. There are several which are generic to any leader. Dr. Edgar Schein at MIT's Sloan School has identified five. They are:

1. What a leader pays attention to, measures, and controls.
2. How the leader reacts to critical incidents and organizational crises.
3. The leader's role-modeling, teaching, and coaching.
4. The criteria the leader uses in allocating rewards and status.
5. The criteria the leader uses in recruiting, promoting, selecting, and deselecting.

## MOMENT OF TRUTH: WHAT A LEADER PAYS ATTENTION TO, MEASURES, AND CONTROLS

In the early 1980s Xerox was losing market share to Canon at a fearful rate. As a critical element of the recovery, Xerox executives realized that they had to recapture the loyalty of previous customers and bring new ones on board. Purely and simply, this meant putting greater emphasis on customers . . . even ahead of profits!

Reflecting on that time, then chairman David Kearns says:

> One mistake we did make was the idea of having three objectives equal in importance: improving return on assets, increasing market share, and bettering customer satisfaction. . . . I refused to single out any one goal. One day, Wayland Hicks said to me, "I have a suggestion. It may be hard for you, but I think we should say that customer satisfaction is the number one goal." To affect a culture change, I realized, you have to zero in on the customer above all else.[9]

Xerox veterans say that this was a turning point in Xerox's recovery. It sent a strong message to every employee that permission was automatically granted to put the customer first. By intently measuring customer satisfaction first, a now legendary turnaround was accomplished.

Contrast this with a large high-tech company that claims to put customers first. Sounds good, but one of its field managers confided that because of the intense pressure to make the quarterly numbers, *he actually authorized the shipment of defective goods to customers.*

## Moment of Truth: How the Leader Reacts to Critical Incidents and Organizational Crises

In 1991 Saturn brought its new car to market and the unthinkable happened. The company had to recall 1,850 of them! The company's number one value is "commitment to customer enthusiasm," and this problem tested it severely.

What to do with the 1,850 cars? Because of bad antifreeze from a supplier, the engines were being damaged. The dilemma? Replace the engine gaskets and seals and send them on their way . . . or replace the entire engine . . . or replace the entire car?

Skip LeFauve, then Saturn's president, said:

> Our team got on it and within a week had identified what the problem was, and the only solution was to replace the car. Now there's where your values come into play. Are you going to go for customer enthusiasm? You're talking about the reputation of a company and now we're going to replace a car. We had 1,850 cars . . . about a $35 million decision. Within twenty minutes we made the decision to do the right thing for the customer. But it was simple because all we had to do was look at our values and say, "We're going for customer enthusiasm and that goes for the 1,850 people who bought cars with the wrong coolant."[10]

When this embarrassing and reputation-threatening incident occurred, Saturn stood by its values. The result? The company's employees, customers, and the car-buying public lauded the organization for such a clear commitment to its beliefs. And what could have been a disaster was, in effect, turned into a public relations coup.

## MOMENT OF TRUTH: THE LEADER'S ROLE MODELING, TEACHING, AND COACHING

We find that leaders in most companies are more than willing to jump on the customer-centered bandwagon. For many, regrettably, this means attending a few company rallies, spinning out customer-oriented slogans, delegating the work to be done, and waiting for the reports of increased market share. In other words, there is a huge gap between the "talk" and the "walk." An employee who worked in such an organization stated that his leaders "mumble the stumble." Not so at Baldrige Award-winning Milliken & Company. A moment of truth occurred early on when senior executives tested Roger Milliken. In his book *The Baldrige Quality System,* Stephen George writes:

> Roger Milliken decided that the first four hours of every policy committee meeting would be devoted to quality. At the first meeting after this decision, each of the four division presidents was asked to talk about his quality initiatives. One by one they discussed a few steps being taken in their divisions and what they expected to be done. Each had an hour to talk. Each was done in minutes, after which there was silence. One person in attendance, who didn't even have to speak remembers how excruciating the silences were. The senior executives quickly got the message that this quality business was not going away.[11]

Here Roger Milliken was teaching his executives a clear lesson. The lesson: Quality is here to stay, it will not go away, and I expect you, the leaders of this company, to master and model the quality principles.

## Moment of Truth: The Criteria the Leader Uses in Allocating Rewards and Status

Most people in organizations today obviously want a productive and successful career. For them this means greater challenge, meaning in their work, a continuing sense of growth and contribution, greater status and recognition, and, in most cases, more money. Because of this, who gets status and rewards in an organization—and why he or she gets them—becomes a powerful lever for shaping a company's culture. It's fundamental: I want a successful career, which means I want status and rewards. I look around and see who gets status and rewards and mimic that person's behavior so I can get them too . . . a sort of monkey see, monkey do.

The midwestern regional manager of a small software company whose responsibility was to acquire, deliver to, and maintain targeted accounts decided to reply to a request for proposal for a significant piece of business in the automotive industry. This was risky because, with limited resources and considerable pressure to "make the numbers," he would have to divert key staff members to create a coherent offering. What made it particularly daunting was that his company had zero experience in the automotive industry.

After three weeks of intensive interviewing, study, and competitive analysis, the proposal was submitted. The sales team waited and waited. Finally the decision was rendered, and of the eight competitors who had submitted bids, this group's proposal came in second. They lost the business.

When the president of the software company was advised of the loss he did an extraordinary thing. *He actually rewarded the manager and his team for losing!*

The president authorized a bonus to be paid the team because he realized that this effort and the education that came from it represented a gateway into the biggest industry in the midwestern territory. And he was right. Within two years, the automotive industry represented over 40 percent of the revenue earned in the midwestern region.

In this case, not only did one region benefit, but the entire organization saw in the president's act that it was not only permissible—but expected—that people should take a calculated risk.

## MOMENT OF TRUTH: THE CRITERIA THE LEADER USES IN RECRUITING, PROMOTING, SELECTING, AND DESELECTING

In his typically direct fashion, AlliedSignal's Larry Bossidy says, "Another tendency we've changed was to take people who weren't cutting it and move them somewhere else in the company. We've stopped doing that. I think you have to get those people out of the organization."[12]

Bossidy's philosophy here is both clear and correct. To allow people who don't measure up to the company's core values to remain in the organization is as good as saying, "Whether you choose to live these values or not is a matter of personal discretion." Dealing with these people represents a different kind of moment of truth.

Perhaps Bossidy borrowed this approach from his former boss, Jack Welch at GE. Welch is attributed with the thinking reflected in Figure 6.6.

**Figure 6.6**

CREATING MEANINGFUL PERFORMANCE AND VALUES IN YOUR ORGANIZATION

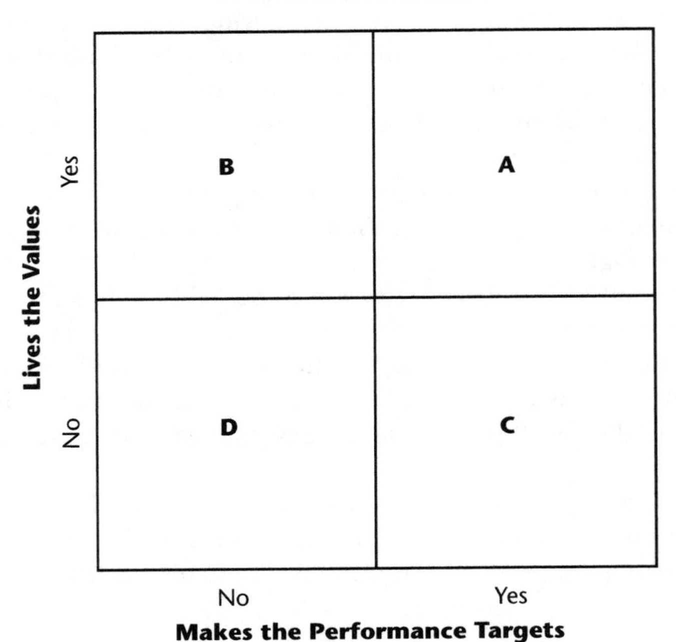

Using this simple analytic device will enable you to assess individuals on two important dimensions: how they perform and the extent to which they live your company values. The ideal, of course, is a high performer who is a model of the values. When this isn't the case, the framework can provide guidance for corrective action.

"Lives the Values" refers to the extent to which the individual's behavior is consistent with the company's ideals. If "teamwork" is a core value, this person would be seen as collaborative. If the person lives the values, he or she fits into a "yes" matrix; if not, a "no" matrix is where he or she belongs.

"Makes the Performance Targets" refers to productivity. Performers fall into a "yes" box; nonperformers a "no."

The matrix gives us four profiles to assess:

BOX D: This person neither makes the numbers nor lives the values.
RECOMMENDATION: Unless the situation changes, get this person out of your company.

BOX A: This is the ideal performer, a role model for others.
RECOMMENDATION: Reward, recognize, and promote. Others will see this success and emulate the successful behavior.

BOX B: The person's behavior and values are consistent with what is expected—a big plus. The minus is that the performance is missing.
RECOMMENDATION: Give a second chance. Coach and develop this person to higher levels of performance.

BOX C: This is the tough one. The high performer who ignores the values. With so much emphasis on short-term performance, this high performer has a lot of leverage. These people typically believe that because they perform well they don't have to adhere to organizational norms. This is the quota-busting sales person who, for example, berates internal support staff even though one of the company values is collaboration.
RECOMMENDATION: Give a second chance. Coach around the values. If there is no change, ask this person to leave your company. This takes courage because no one likes to lose a high performer, but to ignore the negative behavior is to make a mockery of values. In effect you are saying, "If you perform

well you can do anything you want." This is truly a moment of truth the entire organization will watch very carefully.

As evidenced from these moments of truth, leaders who are clear about their organization's purpose and direction actually shape the culture that is required to support such a journey. Consciously or unconsciously, they see these turning points as powerful levers that send important messages to employees, suppliers, customers, and shareholders about what really matters. These leaders know that by consistently living the purpose and values of their organizations they constantly point to and reinforce "what is important around here."

When a leader's behavior consistently conflicts with the stated vision and values of his or her company, it is seen for what it is—meaningless rhetoric that undermines the confidence in, and credibility of, the leader.

**The "Are you willing . . ." Acid Test of Executive Commitment**

To judge your level of commitment to customer-centered leadership, ask yourself these questions:

- Will you fire the high performer who does not live the values of the organization?
- Are you willing to devote a minimum three-year commitment to making the creation of a customer-centered organization happen?
- Are you willing to be visible in the effort by attending workshops, personally participating in recognition events, and spending considerable time with customers?
- Are you willing to put customers and personnel on virtually every operating meeting agenda and discuss them first?
- Are you willing to put customers first even when it might mean that short-term numbers will be missed?
- Are you willing to promote a person who embodies customer-centered concepts over an uncommitted manager?
- Do you insist on having customer-satisfaction numbers as well as the financials in your regular reporting scheme?

If you answer no to two or more of these, review your own commitment carefully before moving forward. For you, attempting a customer-centered transformation is most likely an expedition into the Great Waste: an undercommitted initiative.

## ACTION POINTS

- To determine where you can improve your leadership skills, complete the "How Good Are Your Leadership Skills?" self-assessment exercise on pages 287–297 of the Toolkit.
- Make certain that every leader in your company understands the linkage between financial results, enthusiastic customers, enthusiastic employees, and themselves.
- Get connected and stay connected to your customers and employees by spending high-quality time with them. Know what's happening from real contact versus executive reports.
- People want more than fair pay. They seek meaning in their work. It is the leader's job to put it there. Use vision, values, and personal behavior to create and sustain such meaning. Stand up for what is important and seek every opportunity to involve employees in the decisions that affect them.
- Mobilize your entire organization to achieve its purpose by clarifying the challenges and results expected and then letting these people go about the task of achieving them. In so doing, appeal to both their hearts *and* minds.
- Forget charisma. Inspire others by creating circumstances in which they actually inspire themselves. Invite their thoughts on issues, promote their special talents, and encourage every employee to be a leader in his or her own right.
- As a leader, be aware of the impact your behavior has on whether people believe your words or not. Consider every decision, every deed a potential cultural moment of truth. Always ask before deciding or acting: "How will this affect our direction, purpose, and values?"

Epilogue

# LIGHTEN UP

*To Business that we love we rise betime, And go to't with delight.*

—SHAKESPEARE

WHEN SOUTHWEST AIRLINES WON the coveted U.S. Department of Transportation's Triple Crown award for customer satisfaction not long ago, competitor Northwest Airlines did not accept the decision gracefully. Northwest continued to advertise that they were number one in customer service, reasoning that Southwest was not a big-time player.

And what was Southwest's reaction? Fury? Bombast? A thick fog of righteous indignation? An all-out effort by a SWAT team to prove the seventeen reasons why Southwest is the best? Well, not exactly.

Instead, the company ran an ad nationwide. It read:

> After lengthy deliberation at the highest executive levels and extensive consultation with our legal department, we have arrived at an official corporate response to Northwest Airlines' claim to be number one in customer satisfaction. **Liar, liar. Pants on fire.**[1]

## HUMOR AS A WAY OF LIFE

Southwest and its gregarious chairman, Herb Kelleher, understand that while business and reputation are terribly important, they aren't brain surgery either. Kelleher has led his airline to remarkable success, and in the process his organization has managed to demonstrate a sense of humor and realistic perspective that captivates customers, financial analysts, and business writers alike.

Libby Sartain, Southwest's vice president of people (an unpretentious title right there), explains her company's attitude this way: "Fun and humor on the job is a way of life at Southwest. By consistently poking fun at ourselves, we build a strong sense of community, which acts to counterbalance the stresses associated with hard work and competitive pressure. This is a key to achieving high productivity, high profitability, and high-quality customer service."

And achieve them Southwest does. While its competition has been losing billions of dollars, Southwest has been consistently profitable and sales have exceeded the $1 billion mark. It services twice the number of passengers per employee of any other airline. Not only is Southwest the only airline to have won the prestigious Triple Crown for service—most on-time flights, best baggage handling, and fewest customer complaints—but it has done so three years in a row.

And all this while doubling its operational revenue every five years. Southwest's belief that humor and proper perspective help make a company even more customer centered ties in with the facts revealed by our research. In researching this book, Forum talked to nearly two hundred companies, most of them undergoing dramatic changes: downsizing, reengineering, restructuring. In those that seemed in the worst shape, employees characterized their environments using terms such as "sad," "shell-shocked," "cynical," and "pessimistic." There was no laughter, no humor, no sense of balance.

And there is little chance that people who are internally focused and tense can turn their care and attention to customers. Says the head of a Canadian manufacturing company, "Our bad mood shows up every day in how we interact with customers. At worst, customers see us as disinterested in their needs and at best they see us as disconnected."

On the other hand, a number of organizations have run the gauntlet of perilous, trying times, and emerged with a positive, optimistic energy—an energy that could be directed toward exceeding customer expectations and toward growth. These companies are not run by stand-up comedians, but they do have the ability to lighten up a bit, to know who and what they are, as well as whom they serve.

Says an executive with a Midwest insurance company, "We realized that it would be bad business to take ourselves too seriously. After all, this is not the space shuttle gone amok. This is insurance. We are a great insurance company. At the same time, we will make a much bigger difference for our customers and be much more productive if we put things in perspective."

## COPYCAT

Such an attitude can be contagious. When Kurt Herwald, head of $75 million Stevens Aviation of Greenville, South Carolina, learned that Southwest Airlines' "new" slogan, "Just Plane Smart," might have infringed on his slogan "Plane Smart," he challenged Herb Kelleher: "Forget the lawyers, Kelleher. Let's make this simple. How about you and me arm wrestling for the rights to the slogan?"

Southwest Airlines responded to Herwald's challenge: "Our chairman . . . is a fearsome competitor who resorts to kicking, biting, gouging, scratching and hair pulling in order to win. . . . Can your pusillanimous little wimp of a chairman stand up against the martial valor of our giant?"

To which Stevens Aviation replied: "What does pusillanimous mean?"[2]

## MALICE IN DALLAS

The event was held at the five-thousand-seat Sportatorium in Dallas. The burly Herwald, a thirty-eight-year-old bodybuilder, entered the ring, opened his briefcase, and dumped out raw meat, beer, hot sauce, raw onions, and a stiletto.

Kelleher entered and announced that the Supreme Court of Texas had granted him the right to use a substitute arm-wrestler if he so desired. When the match was finally over (it involved two substitutes, world arm-wrestling champion J. R. Jones and petite Annette "Killer" Coates, as well as Kelleher and Herwald), the challenger from Stevens Aviation had won.

Herwald, magnanimous in victory, allowed Southwest to continue to use his company's slogan, and both parties donated proceeds from the event to the Muscular Dystrophy Association and a Ronald McDonald House.

Ed Stewart, Southwest's manager of public relations, estimates that the match, dubbed the "Malice in Dallas," saved his company $500,000 in legal fees and generated publicity worth at least $6 million. The dollar impact of the pure spirit created by the event, of course, is incalculable.

## GOING TO EXTREMES

In some company cultures, like that of Southwest, the ability to put things in perspective and not take life too seriously is almost a core competence. It's not necessarily easy—particularly when people are losing jobs, when companies are shrinking, when mergers are threatening the status quo, when people are being asked to do more with less, when womb-to-tomb job security is only a faint memory.

But what we learned through our research—and maybe we knew it anyway—was that companies and their leaders who are having tough times need to find ways to create a silver lining, to look at adverse conditions in a positive light. Sound syrupy? Pollyannaish? Maybe, but it works. Just as many freewheeling, creative organizations have had to learn to pay attention to process and discipline, so organizations that are serious and disciplined and sometimes humorless need to learn to lighten up a bit.

Be warned, however, that lightening up and having a self-directed sense of humor can't be forced. It can be planned and executed and stretched to the limit, perhaps, but it must be natural for your organization. And it must be appropriate. You don't have a phone-booth stuffing contest on the same day that twenty employees are laid off.

Lightening up is not a management initiative. It's a symptom, a spirit. As in the old navy story of the captain's announcement that "no one will be allowed to leave the ship until the morale improves," no one likes to be *told* their mood has to change. Similarly, organizations that try too hard to foist "fun" on employees often find them resistant and cynical. Lightening up is *not* sitting around in a circle, holding hands, and singing "kum-ba-ya"; or having an event called Fun Day and hoping it solves all your problems; or having fun because you're supposed to be having fun; or pretending to be upbeat when you're not.

Lightening up is stopping to have a pizza with people you work with; developing a can-do attitude; stepping back and getting some perspective on your problems; being a little crazy if it suits you; cracking a joke; laughing at yourself; stopping to acknowledge it when people make a difference for customers; celebrating successes, even small ones; and focusing less on "how bad things are" and more on "how far we've come."

## PUTTING THINGS IN PERSPECTIVE

Humor is a great way to get people's attention. Take the case of Southern New England Telecommunications (SNET). Change is the name of the game in the telecommunications industry, as telephone companies begin to face new and increased competition. Yet, when Barbara Gatison, president of SNET America (SNET's long-distance business) and Peter Bassermann, president of SNET Mobility (SNET's wireless business) were asked to address their peers at an officers meeting in 1994, they were expected to do what Gatison calls the "same old boring presentation, chock-full of numbers and key trends and analysis."

Gatison and Bassermann decided that they needed to send a different kind of message, one that would acknowledge the difficulty of their current business environment, but which would also add some balance to a situation that people were taking quite seriously.

The following morning they found themselves on the Atlantic Ocean, filming a video for the meeting. The video, which others characterize as "one of the most memorable few minutes of any officers meeting we've had" shows Gatison and Bassermann in a rubber raft, reading newspapers that warned of competitive threats in their industry. Outside the raft, plastic purple sharks highlighted with the names of competitors infested the rough waters. As a narrator talked about the competitive landscape, these two subsidiary presidents proceeded to scream and beat the sharks with their newspapers. At the end of the video, the sharks were gone and Gatison and Bassermann were slapping their hands and proclaiming victory. After the video debuted, the would-be sailors made a brief business presentation wearing straw hats, sunglasses, leis, goggles, and flippers. According to Gatison, the reaction was "lots of energy, lots of applause, and lots of laughter, bordering on hysteria."

Did Gatison and Bassermann do this just to have a good time? Not really, says Gatison—in reality, she is afraid of water, and the screams in the video were mostly related to her fear of drowning during the filming. "That video helped SNET's leaders understand our real business issues more than any serious presentation could have," she explained. "Moreover, our business environment feels like guerrilla warfare. It is so stressful that people cannot possibly produce if they don't have a way of relieving the pressure they feel. We need to have staying power—and if we can't stop and put things in perspective, we just cannot win." SNET America is winning: Gatison's staff has signed up more than 250,000 customers in just two years, customer satisfaction ratings are at an all-time high, and the subsidiary is ahead of virtually every target it has set.

Perhaps one of the most important benefits of this event was the signal it sent. Doing something different—maybe even a little outlandish—in the serious SNET culture was the main point. In the new environment, the organization needed radically new ways of operating—and these changes needed to be modeled by the leaders.

Continuing on this theme, during one recent off-site meeting, Gatison, in full business attire, challenged her staff to jump into a swimming pool as a symbol of the fact that everyone would need to behave differently in the new competitive environment. Gatison saw huge payoff in what most leaders would label useless frivolity: "When I jumped in the pool that day, my staff saw me as human. My being human means that if a frontline person sees a problem in the business, he will be more likely to make sure that I know what is going on around here. An executive who is not approachable is out of touch; if people keep problems away from me, I cannot possibly do my job successfully for customers."

As the SNET story illustrates, it is easier to lighten up when a company's leaders set the tone. Leaders like Doug Bergum, head of highly successful Great Plains Software of Fargo, North Dakota, a company named by *Inc.* magazine as one of the best in the nation to work for. At one Great Plains annual dealer meeting, known as "Stampede to Fargo," Bergum stood up during the keynote address and went into great detail regarding a defect that had been shipped in a software program update. Bergum humbly explained to the dealers that it was caused by Great Plains' failure to test the problem sufficiently and that Great Plains was willing to accept full responsibility. That alone might have been enough. But Bergum belongs to the

Ernie Kovacs school, which says, "If you're going to tell them the truth, make them laugh, or they'll kill you."

He finished his confession by smashing three fresh eggs on his head. Everyone got the "egg on my face" message and couldn't help responding graciously to such humility and humor.

We found other leaders personally setting a "lighten up" tone in their companies:

- Steve Sheetz, CEO of Sheetz Convenience Stores, willingly competed against his upper management in an employee-designed "Beauty Contest." He states that every year at their three-day convention the employees' biggest challenge is to "see how ridiculous they can make senior management look."
- Sam Bryant, director of human resources, and his six other fellow team members at Applied Materials, a high-tech manufacturing firm, stood before the entire company and humbly asked their forgiveness for failing to bring an important project to completion as promised. Bryant then asked employees to please follow him and his team outside. Each member of Bryant's team sat patiently atop a carnival dunking tank while employees let them have it.

Moments like these can become defining ones for a company and its culture. They are repeated to new hires as legends, and legends create meaning and identity that says it's okay to relax around here. We're not a bunch of stuffed suits. We're in this together.

## Celebrate the Wins

A company that has lightened up seldom misses a chance to celebrate little and big wins whenever possible. When Anne Sweeney, CEO of fX Networks, heard about a particularly hardworking employee, she sought him out to thank him personally. When in his presence, she took a few steps backward and proceeded to bow deeply as in reverence, turning a thank-you into a mini-celebration.

Southwest Airlines celebrates the extra efforts of its employees by such practices as painting the faces of the best service providers for the previous year on the exterior of its airplanes. In fact, there is so much formal celebrating that each year Southwest publishes a calendar just to keep track of all the activity. The employees love it.

The top two executives at Levi Strauss, Bob Haas and Tom Tusher, celebrated a fabulous year by calling a surprise all-company meeting where a magician entertained their employees with a magic show. Bob Haas then went on to thank those employees for "creating magic that led to such a great year," singling out those with particularly "magical" results. Later, at their desks, employees found a small stipend in a cutout 501 Jeans pocket. It came with the admonition that employees should not use it toward something serious but rather should take a "significant other" out to dinner or in some other way thank those back home who had supported their efforts.

Tom's of Maine, producers of natural personal-care products, believes so much in the importance of celebrating that they shut down their manufacturing once a month for a "Celebration Break." It is a chance for people to get reacquainted, to let off steam, and to take time to thank themselves for hard work. Although shutting down the factory can cost up to forty thousand dollars, Tom's believes that it's an absolute requirement. According to CEO Tom Chappell, these celebrations help to foster and cement relationships that go a long way to make his company more productive.

## The Payoff

The payoff for having a healthy, balanced, customer-centered perspective is starting to be appreciated: "Is there going to be any competitive advantage if your employees are excited about coming to work," asks Matt Weinstein, "emperor" of Playfair, a humor consulting company, "if they're continually surprising each other by leaving fun gifts around the office, if they're answering the phone like they're happy to be there? Of course, there's a tremendous competitive advantage. . . . People like to do business with people who like to do business."[3]

Southwest's competitive advantage has led other companies to its doorstep in droves. They are searching for a method, a formula, an incantation, perhaps, that will revive their employees. According to Southwest's Libby Sartain, Southwest's culture "is difficult to duplicate or define because it is constantly being refined." It is like trying to import what Tom Chappell describes as the "Soul of a Business," something that he says is a matter of "trial and error learnings" and that takes the kind of "time, patience, and scrapes that come from growing one's own identity from within."[4]

"Growing an identity from within" happens in numerous ways: in the type of people you hire; in what gets rewarded; in how you dispel fear and encourage risk; in your ability to be humble and laugh at yourself; in the way you remember a name or the way you honor and celebrate even the mundane; in the way you treat people day in and day out; and, ultimately, in the way you deal with your customers.

Over time the little things, when they are the right things, roll into a culture of deep concern for people and a balanced understanding of what is really important in the long run. That culture helps promote the idea of a customer-centered organization, one in which work is balanced and in which employees have enough perspective to be able to focus on people other than themselves, such as their customers.

Eventually the culture becomes bigger than those who initiated it. Kelleher believes that when he eventually leaves Southwest, the culture will live on without him. Says he: "Now, say, someone came into Southwest Airlines and said, 'Herb Kelleher is gone, and I don't subscribe to anything he did. Power is my bag. Hierarchy, bureaucracy, those are the things I love.' I think he'd last about a month. He'd be overthrown by the people because the culture is stronger than any individual."[5]

And perhaps more important, his employees wouldn't pitch in for a sixty-thousand-dollar ad in *USA Today* to thank him—as they did for Herb.

*For remembering every one of our names.*

*For supporting the Ronald McDonald House.*

*For helping load baggage on Thanksgiving.*

*For giving everyone a kiss (and we mean everyone).*

*For listening.*

*For running the only profitable major airline.*

*For singing at our holiday party.*

*For singing only once a year.*

*For letting us wear shorts and sneakers to work.*

*For golfing at The LUV Classic with only one club.*

*For outtalking Sam Donaldson.*

*For riding your Harley Davidson™ into Southwest Headquarters.*

*For being a friend, not just a boss.*

*Herb Kelleher, Chairman, President, and CEO of Southwest Airlines*

**HAPPY BOSS'S DAY FROM EACH ONE OF YOUR 16,000 EMPLOYEES.**

*This Boss's Day ad was entirely paid for through the contributions of Southwest Airlines' Employees.* 

# TOOLKIT FOR CUSTOMER-CENTERED GROWTH

THE FIFTEEN TOOLS THAT FOLLOW have been specifically selected or developed to reinforce the core concepts presented here. Using these tools can help you gain the most benefit from this book.

To get the most out of this Toolkit, review the list of tools that follow and select those relating to an area you wish to explore.

After completing the work prescribed by the tools you have selected, you may wish to use the last tool, the Personal Development Plan. This is designed to help you convert what you have learned into concrete action plans that will get results.

# CUSTOMER-CENTERED GROWTH: TOOLKIT

## SUMMARY OF TOOLS

| Focus | Tools | Description | Page No. |
|---|---|---|---|
| **Hardwiring** | Analyzing Customer Information | How to ensure you are getting the most out of your voice-of-the-customer investment. | 242 |
| | Value Chain | How to understand your customers' business better by creating a value chain from their perspective. | 244 |
| | Competitive Win/Loss Protocol | How to debrief a customer buying decision so you can improve future efforts. | 245 |
| | Customer Relationship Matrix | How to identify your customers' views of your company, your products, and you. | 247 |
| **Universal Collaboration** | Resource Matrix and Resource Action Plan | How to create high value for an account by ensuring that the right resources are dedicated to it. | 250 |
| | How Good Are Your Influence Skills? | How to improve your Influence skills through self-assessment. | 255 |
| **Customer Strategy & Planning** | Value Orientation Frame | How to increase the yield from an account by determining the specific relationship and information requirements of each customer. | 265 |

| Focus | Tools | Description | Page No. |
|---|---|---|---|
| | Relationship Goal Analysis | How to strengthen key customer relationships by moving them more toward partnership. | 270 |
| | Territory and Account Matrix | How to analyze the top accounts in your territory (company) to determine the level of importance of each and how to improve. | 274 |
| | Competitive Matrix | How to improve your competitive win ratio by analyzing your customer and competition *before* the competition begins. | 276 |
| | Competitive Account Strategy Criteria | How to evaluate and enhance your strategy for any competitive situation. | 278 |
| **Customer Interaction** | How Good Are Your Customer-Interaction Skills? | How to improve your customer-interaction skills through self-assessment. | 279 |
| | Customer-Interaction Coaching Guide | How to identify the customer-interaction strengths and developmental needs of the individuals on your team. | 283 |
| **Leadership** | How Good Are Your Leadership Skills? | How to improve your leadership skills through self-assessment. | 287 |
| **Personal Development Planning** | Your Personal Development Plan | How to convert the strategies discussed here into specific growth on the job. | 298 |

## ANALYZING CUSTOMER INFORMATION

At the start of an effort to listen to customers and hardwire their voice into the organization, it's important to ask what your existing customer information is telling you. The following worksheet will help ensure that you are transforming the data provided by your listening tools into meaningful action.

**Your work unit:**

**Source of information:** ☐ Survey ☐ Interview ☐ Other:

**Data collected (month/year):**_________/_________

**Type of customers:** ☐ Internal ☐ Intermediate ☐ External

1. **Expectations:** What does the data suggest is most important to your customers regarding service?

______________________________________________

______________________________________________

______________________________________________

______________________________________________

______________________________________________

______________________________________________

2. **Perceptions:** To what extent does the data suggest you are meeting these expectations?

   ☐ Exceed ☐ Meet ☐ Do not meet

   What information does the data provide that supports this response?

______________________________________________

______________________________________________

______________________________________________

______________________________________________

______________________________________________

3. **Improvement Opportunities:** Review the six service quality factors (RATER—see Chapter 3). According to the data, which areas represent the greatest gaps between customer expectations and service provided? Does the data suggest why?

☐ **R**eliability ☐ **E**mpathy

☐ **A**ssurance ☐ **R**esponsiveness

☐ **T**angibles ☐ Other ______________________

______________________________________________

______________________________________________

______________________________________________

______________________________________________

______________________________________________

______________________________________________

4. **Suggestions:** Based on this analysis, how can your work unit improve its service to your customers?

______________________________________________

______________________________________________

______________________________________________

______________________________________________

______________________________________________

______________________________________________

## VALUE CHAIN

To understand your customer's business environment, complete a value-chain drawing. In the value chain below, start with the arrow labeled "Your target account." First, identify your buying center within the target company—the people who actually purchase your product or service—*(a)*. Next, identify that buying center's major internal suppliers and internal customers *(b)*. Then, at left, identify some of the company's major external suppliers, including your own organization. At right, identify the company's major intermediate customers and, finally, its end users or final consumers.

The completed drawing will help you better understand your company's relationship with this customer and how you can help improve its performance with its customers.

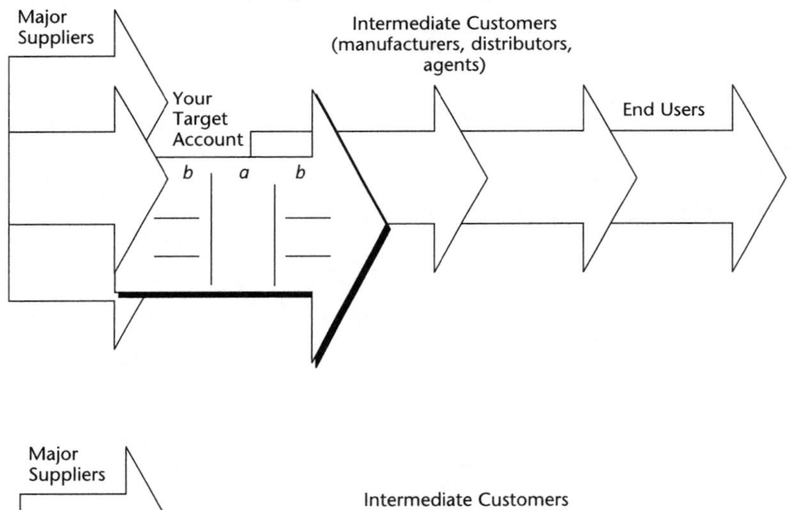


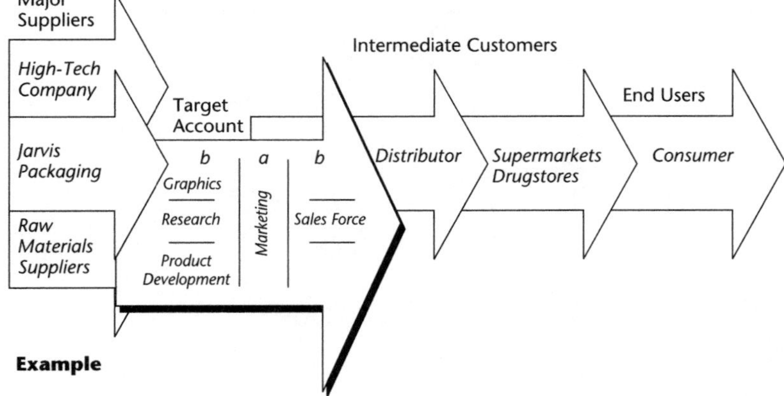


**Target Account:** Consumer products company (marketing department)

## COMPETITIVE WIN/LOSS PROTOCOL

As discussed in Chapter 3, a customer is usually "smartest" right after making a major purchasing decision. Interviewing the client just after you've won or lost a major piece of business will enable you to learn more than at almost any other time. Here is a protocol for conducting such an interview.

I. **Before the interview.** It's usually best for the win/loss interview to be conducted by a senior executive who was not the key contact person during the selling process. This executive should be briefed on the situation background, have reviewed this protocol, and prepared additional questions relevant to the situation at hand.

II. **During the interview.**

(A) Introduce yourself and thank the client for his or her time. Note that the purpose of the interview is to understand as much as possible about the customer's perceptions and experiences during the recent sales process, so that your organization can continually improve.

(B) Discuss confidentiality up front. Say that ideally you would like to be able to share all feedback throughout your organization. However, if the client feels that certain items are too sensitive, he or she should mention them during the conversation.

(C) Ask the following questions:

1. We'd like to start by just making sure we have a clear understanding of what the opportunity was. As I have heard it . . . [Start by summarizing the situation (the need, the competition, etc.) and asking the client to expand on it. Ask, "Is that correct?" and "What would you add?"]
2. Which other firms were competing for the business? How did you find out about them? Why did you consider us for the business? Why did you make it competitive?
3. Overall, why did [your company] win/lose?
4. Could you tell me something about how your decision-making process worked? Who made the decision? What were your key criteria?
5. I'd like to ask you about some specific aspects of the

selling process. [Probe for what, how, and why on the questions below.]

a. How did you feel about the quality of your salesperson's management of the relationship?
b. Did you meet other people from our organization during the sale? If yes, what were your impressions of those people? Did you feel that we used our resources appropriately?
c. What about the quality of our proposal to you? Our presentation?
d. What about the quality of our capabilities?
e. How did you feel about our pricing? Did the pricing reflect your sense of the value we were proposing to provide?

6. Overall, how would you compare us to our competitors? What are our strengths and weaknesses relative to other firms you saw? What were the competitors' strengths and weaknesses?
7. Did you call our references? Were they helpful to you?
8. What were your impressions of our organization before this selling process? To what extent have they changed?
9. What advice would you give us for working with you in the future?
10. Anything else?

III. **After the interview.** Write up the interview and distribute it, if that is consistent with the customer's wishes. Send a thank-you note to the client.

## CUSTOMER RELATIONSHIP MATRIX

Relationships that have developed over a period of time between suppliers and customers can become complex. They involve numerous individuals in both the customer's organization and the supplier's organization. It is useful for you periodically to assess the relationship with important customers, to address any weaknesses or vulnerabilities. The Relationship Matrix provides a convenient framework for such an analysis.

Using the Relationship Matrix, you can assess the views of a customer organization's key decision makers with respect to:

1. **You.** How do the account's decision makers view the individual or team conducting the analysis? How are you meeting their individual requirements?
2. **Your products and services.** What do the decision makers see as the pros and cons of the products and services they presently use? What products or services might they anticipate needing?
3. **Your company.** How do the account's decision makers view your company? What are your company's strengths and weaknesses, and how do these relate to the needs of each decision maker?

*Instructions*

To fill in the Relationship Matrix on page 249, complete the following steps:

**Step 1: Identify Decision Makers**

In column 1, enter the names of those who will make or influence the buying decisions in the account you profiled.

**Step 2: Rate Each Decision Maker's Viewpoint on Each Element**

Using the scale below, rate each individual's viewpoint on each of the elements in columns 2 through 4.

**Rating Scale**

\+ = Positive
0 = Neutral
− = Negative

**Step 3: Identify Areas of Vulnerability**

Total the ratings in columns 2 through 4 vertically. For example, a column with five pluses and two minuses would add up to "3+." Low ratings represent areas of vulnerability in the account.

**Step 4: Assess Each Decision Maker's Overall Viewpoint**

Total the figures in columns 2 through 4 horizontally to assess the viewpoint of each key decision maker and influencer. Enter the totals in column 5. This identifies the decision makers with whom you need to work more effectively.

**Step 5: Develop Ideas**

In the space below, develop ideas to address your areas of vulnerability in the account. You should include both decision makers and influencers in your plan to improve the relationship.

Ways to improve the customer's perception of you:

________________________________________

________________________________________

________________________________________

________________________________________

Ways to improve the customer's perception of your products and services:

________________________________________

________________________________________

________________________________________

________________________________________

Ways to improve the customer's perception of your company:

________________________________________

________________________________________

________________________________________

________________________________________

## CUSTOMER RELATIONSHIP MATRIX

**Customer:**________________________________________

| 1 Decision Makers and Influencers | 2 You | 3 Your Products and/or Services | 4 Your Company | 5 Total |
|---|---|---|---|---|
| | | | | |
| | | | | |
| | | | | |
| | | | | |
| | | | | |
| | | | | |
| | | | | |
| | | | | |
| | | | | |
| | | | | |
| | | | | |
| | | | | |
| | | | | |
| | | | | |
| | | | | |
| | | | | |
| **Total** | | | | |

## RESOURCE MATRIX AND RESOURCE ACTION PLAN

A resource matrix (p. 252) can help you understand whether you have the skills you need on your team and the appropriate level of commitment to your work. Then the resource action plan (pp. 253-254) can help you eliminate any gaps.

To fill in the Resource Matrix, take the following steps:

**Step 1:** In the left-hand column, list team members and their roles.

**Step 2:** In the next four columns, rate each team member's level of skill in each category and total the skill levels both vertically and horizontally.

- **Functional expertise:** The "hard" skills an individual needs in order to do his or her job (such as technical skills and product knowledge).
- **Problem-solving and decision-making skills:** The ability to identify problems, gather relevant facts, evaluate options, and make decisions.
- **Communication and team-building skills:** The ability to question, listen, encourage, build trust, resolve conflict, and promote innovation.

**Step 3:** In the next column, rate each person's *current* level of interest in and support for the project. Record the total.

**Step 4:** In the last column, rate each person's *required* level of interest and support. Record the total.

**Step 5:** Using the Sample Resource Action Plan as a guide, complete the blank Resource Action Plan for one of your accounts. Ask yourself the following questions:

**Complementary Skills**

- Are all three types of skills present on the team?
- Are any skills critical to team performance underrepresented? (Is one of the column totals much lower than the others? Are there a lot of 1s and 2s in any column?) How can you develop those skills on the team?
- Is any one team member particularly weak overall? (Is one of the row totals much lower than the others?) How can you help him or her develop the necessary skills?

**Level of Interest and Support**

- Are there at least two team members who strongly support the team's purpose? If not, how can you gain more support?
- Who are the most critical team members, given the customer's value orientation (see page 265)? How interested are they in the project?
- Where are the largest gaps between current and required levels of support? How can you reduce these gaps?
- What accounts for each person's level of interest? What is his or her perspective on the project?

# RESOURCE MATRIX

**Customer:** ______________________________

**Value Orientation:** ______________________________

| | **Skill Level** (1 = very little skill; 5 = very high skill) | | | | | |
|---|---|---|---|---|---|---|
| **Team Members/Roles** | **Functional** | **Problem Solving/ Decision Making** | **Communication/ Team Building** | **Total** | **Current Level of Interest/Support** (1 = very little; 5 = very strong) | **Required Level of Interest/Support** (1 = very little; 5 = very strong) |
| | | | | | | |
| | | | | | | |
| | | | | | | |
| | | | | | | |
| | | | | | | |
| | | | | | | |
| | | | | | | |
| **Total** | | | | | | |

Circle the areas that represent concerns.

## SAMPLE RESOURCE ACTION PLAN

| | Team Gaps/Problems | Most Likely Cause | What You Can Do | How You Will Do It |
|---|---|---|---|---|
| **Complementary Skills** | *Team is low on functional skills; especially basic administrative and logistical skills.* | *Two new employees on customer team.* | *Arrange for Janis to coach customer administrators.*<br><br>*Make all project logistics as simple as possible.* | *Take Janis on next call; introduce to Glen and Vera. Help her create coaching plan.*<br><br>*Ask Janis for advice on ways to simplify administrative process. Test suggestions with customer.* |
| | | | | |
| **Level of Interest and Support** | *Need to move Maurice (product engineer) from 2 to 4. His support is critical.* | *He has had bad experiences on sales teams before; has felt unconnected to the team, unappreciated.* | *Work on connecting him to the team's overall purpose.*<br><br>*Show appreciation for his contributions.* | *Explain how his contributions make a difference. Report weekly on how his efforts are paying off for the customer. Take him on a site visit.*<br><br>*Remember to say "thank you." Acknowledge his expertise in team meetings, and ask for his suggestions.* |
| | | | | |

## YOUR RESOURCE ACTION PLAN

| | Team Gaps/Problems | Most Likely Cause | What You Can Do | How You Will Do It |
|---|---|---|---|---|
| **Complementary Skills** | | | | |
| | | | | |
| **Level of Interest and Support** | | | | |
| | | | | |

# HOW GOOD ARE YOUR INFLUENCE SKILLS?

## SELF-ASSESSMENT EXERCISE

**Step 1:** Using the scale of 1 to 5 below and the space provided, please indicate the number that best describes the extent to which you apply each of the 21 influence practices below. Be candid in your responses.

5=to a very great extent

4=to a great extent

3=to a moderate extent

2=to a small extent

1=not at all

## INFLUENCE PRACTICES

**Rating**

______ 1. Looking for the causes of problems in work processes rather than blaming people

______ 2. Bringing together people with different perspectives

______ 3. Admitting one's own mistakes and uncertainties

______ 4. Demonstrating competence by bringing relevant knowledge and skill to the work to be done

______ 5. Evaluating the views of others according to logic, rather than according to personal preference

______ 6. Making decisions that are consistent with agreed-upon goals

______ 7. Creating enthusiasm about the work

______ 8. Supporting and helping associates

______ 9. Contributing suggestions aimed at improving work processes and products

______10. Encouraging others to express their ideas

______11. Following through on commitments

______12. Understanding which decisions need to involve others and which can be made alone

______13. Sharing responsibility for solving problems

______14. Promoting innovation

______15. Clarifying each person's role in carrying out the work

______16. Seeking creative ways to resolve conflicts

______17. Seeking to understand the problems of other work groups

______18. Communicating needs clearly to people in your organization who provide you with goods and services

______19. Cooperating rather than competing with others

______20. Considering requests to change plans and goals with an open mind

______21. Setting group goals as well as individual goals

**Step 2:** Note your highest ratings. These represent strengths you can rely on in influence situations.

**Step 3:** Note your lowest ratings. Work here can improve your influence skills. For suggested actions to help you improve, please consult Tactics to Improve Influence Skills, which follows.

### Tactics to Improve Influence Skills

Below is a list of the 21 influence practices, along with the tactics that correspond to each. Identify which practice you wish to improve. The tactics for improvement are listed below each practice.

1. **Looking for the causes of problems in work processes rather than blaming people**

*Tactics that have an impact on this practice:*

- Be courteous, respectful, and patient in interactions with others
- Suspend your judgment until you have heard all the facts and can restate another's perspective accurately
- Implement reliable methods and systems to improve the way work gets done
- Give recognition for identifying problems
- Focus on why things went wrong rather than on who caused the problem
- Use analytical methods to research root causes of problems
- Check alignment with agreed-upon group goals when breakdowns or errors occur
- Trust others to take responsibility for their own work

**2. Bringing together people with different perspectives**

*Tactics that have an impact on this practice:*

- Keep discussions focused on ideas rather than personalities
- Suspend your judgment until you have heard all the facts and can restate another's perspective accurately
- Ensure that opposition and minority positions are fully represented
- Show interest in gathering and developing ideas of others
- Listen for and acknowledge the feelings behind different perspectives
- Discuss how individual goals align with group goals

**3. Admitting one's own mistakes and uncertainties**

*Tactics that have an impact on this practice:*

- Let others know they can question and disagree
- React objectively when your views are challenged
- Request advice or aid from others as needed
- Say no to a request or opportunity when your skills are not sufficient
- Consider mistakes as opportunities to learn and advance
- Admit what you do not know
- Acknowledge your mistakes, but do not dwell on them

**4. Demonstrating competence by bringing relevant knowledge and skill to the work to be done**

*Tactics that have an impact on this practice:*

- Establish objective criteria for guiding decisions
- Offer advice and aid when appropriate
- Offer creative suggestions of your own
- Understand the key skills and areas of knowledge that affect your work
- Offer facts and data to support your points of view
- Strive to do things right the first time

**5. Evaluating the views of others according to logic, rather than according to personal preference**

*Tactics that have an impact on this practice:*

- Encourage in-depth exploration of novel issues and new ideas
- Test conclusions for clarity, feasibility, and commitment
- Acknowledge the unique talents and contributions of others publicly
- Suspend your judgment until you have heard all the facts and can restate another's perspective accurately
- Explore positive and negative consequences of different approaches
- Establish an objective, consistent way of evaluating ideas
- Offer facts and data to support your points of view

**6. Making decisions that are consistent with agreed-upon goals**

*Tactics that have an impact on this practice:*

- Establish objective criteria for guiding decisions
- Communicate priorities consistently
- Support others in producing high-quality work
- Create a group vision jointly and use it to focus and energize the work
- Include others in decision making
- Keep a list of project requests and specifications, and obligations and deadlines for meeting them
- Consider the effect of a decision on others before making it

**7. Creating enthusiasm about the work**

*Tactics that have an impact on this practice:*

- Acknowledge the unique talents and contributions of others publicly
- Promote the positive impact of the group's work and celebrate milestones
- Communicate results of your group's work to others in the organization
- Set up a measurement system to track visibly group goals, processes, timetables, and outcomes
- Consider mistakes as opportunities to learn and advance
- Create a group vision jointly and use it to focus and energize the work
- Develop group rewards as well as individual rewards

**8. Supporting and helping associates**

*Tactics that have an impact on this practice:*

- Offer advice and aid when appropriate
- Be courteous, respectful, and patient in interactions with others
- Support others in producing high-quality work
- Uncover and show concern about the pressures and constraints others are facing
- Be available to those who may need your advice or aid with complex issues
- Understand the key skills and areas of knowledge that affect your work
- Trust others to take responsibility for their own work

**9. Contributing suggestions aimed at improving work processes and products**

*Tactics that have an impact on this practice:*

- Implement reliable methods and systems to improve the way work gets done
- Facilitate an idea session in which you solicit ideas for improving products, services, and information

- Offer creative suggestions of your own
- Encourage benchmarking and other methods to assess performance against internal and external teams' performance
- Use analytical methods to research root causes of problems

**10. Encouraging others to express their ideas**

*Tactics that have an impact on this practice:*

- Let others know they can question and disagree
- Encourage in-depth exploration of novel issues and new ideas
- Be courteous, respectful, and patient in interactions with others
- Suspend your judgment until you have heard all the facts and can restate another's perspective accurately
- Show interest in gathering and developing ideas of others
- Encourage spontaneous expression without feelings of embarrassment or risk
- Be available to those who may need your advice or aid with complex issues

**11. Following through on commitments**

*Tactics that have an impact on this practice:*

- Share information throughout the duration of the project
- Give advance notice when a commitment cannot be met
- Get agreement for ownership of the various parts of follow-through
- Establish reliable processes, timetables, and outcomes with group members
- Keep a list of project requests and specifications, and obligations and deadlines for meeting them
- Gather up-to-date facts about the needs of other work groups
- Strive to do things right the first time

**12. Understanding which decisions need to involve others and which can be made alone**

*Tactics that have an impact on this practice:*

- Clarify the role each person will play

- Request advice or aid from others as needed
- Include others in decision making
- Define those areas in which sharing power may be productive and those where it may not
- Identify the key links needed between people and functions to carry out the task
- Consider the effect of a decision on others before making it

**13. Sharing responsibility for solving problems**

*Tactics that have an impact on this practice:*

- Share resources
- Support others in producing high-quality work
- Give recognition for identifying problems
- Include others in decision making
- Define those areas in which sharing power may be productive and those where it may not
- Trust others to take responsibility for their own work

**14. Promoting innovation**

*Tactics that have an impact on this practice:*

- Encourage in-depth exploration of novel issues and new ideas
- Promote the positive impact of the group's work and celebrate milestones
- Show interest in gathering and developing ideas of others
- Communicate results of your group's work to others in the organization
- Encourage spontaneous expression without feelings of embarrassment or risk
- Offer creative suggestions of your own
- Consider mistakes as opportunities to learn and advance
- Encourage benchmarking and other methods to assess performance against internal and external teams' performance

**15. Clarifying each person's role in carrying out the work**

*Tactics that have an impact on this practice:*

- Establish objective criteria for guiding decisions

- Test conclusions for clarity, feasibility, and commitment
- Test others for their acceptance of ground rules
- Clarify the role each person will play
- Get agreement for ownership of the various parts of follow-through
- Create a group vision jointly and use it to focus and energize the work

**16. Seeking creative ways to resolve conflicts**

*Tactics that have an impact on this practice:*

- Keep discussions focused on ideas rather than personalities
- Suspend your judgment until you have heard all the facts and can restate another's perspective accurately
- Show interest in gathering and developing ideas of others
- Test others for their acceptance of ground rules
- React objectively when your views are challenged
- Offer creative suggestions of your own
- Focus on overall organizational goals
- Explore positive and negative consequences of different approaches
- Establish an objective, consistent way of evaluating ideas

**17. Seeking to understand the problems of other work groups**

*Tactics that have an impact on this practice:*

- Give recognition for identifying problems
- Uncover and show concern about the pressures and constraints others are facing
- Define those areas in which sharing power may be productive and those where it may not
- Understand how other groups contribute to overall organizational goals
- Focus on overall organizational goals
- Gather up-to-date facts about the needs of other work groups
- Put yourself in the other person's shoes

**18. Communicating needs clearly to people in your organization who provide you with goods and services**

*Tactics that have an impact on this practice:*

- Define clearly the work to be done and the goals of the group
- Communicate priorities consistently
- Implement reliable methods and systems to improve the way work gets done
- Share information throughout the duration of the project
- Uncover and show concern about the pressures and constraints others are facing
- Keep a list of project requests and specifications, and obligations and deadlines for meeting them

**19. Cooperating rather than competing with others**

*Tactics that have an impact on this practice:*

- Be courteous, respectful, and patient in interactions with others
- Acknowledge the unique talents and contributions of others publicly
- Suspend your judgment until you have heard all the facts and can restate another's perspective accurately
- Share resources
- React objectively when your views are challenged
- Define those areas in which sharing power may be productive and those where it may not
- Check alignment with agreed-upon group goals when breakdowns or errors occur
- Put yourself in the other person's shoes

**20. Considering requests to change plans and goals with an open mind**

*Tactics that have an impact on this practice:*

- Suspend your judgment until you have heard all the facts and can restate another's perspective accurately
- React objectively when your views are challenged
- Consider facts and data, not the official status of the person requesting the change, when making decisions

- Listen for and acknowledge the feelings behind different perspectives
- Say no to a request or opportunity when your skills are not sufficient
- Be available to those who may need your advice or aid with complex issues

**21. Setting group goals as well as individual goals**

*Tactics that have an impact on this practice:*

- Define clearly the work to be done and the goals of the group
- Set up a measurement system to visibly track group goals, processes, timetables, and outcomes
- Discuss how individual goals align with group goals
- Create a group vision jointly and use it to focus and energize the work
- Develop group rewards as well as individual rewards
- Check alignment with agreed-upon group goals when breakdowns or errors occur
- Identify the key links needed between people and functions to carry out the task

## VALUE ORIENTATION FRAME

The Value Orientation Frame summarizes the preferences of different kinds of customers in relationships with your organization. It classifies customers based on the strength of their interest in a relationship with you and the amount of information they seek. The items in each quadrant of the frame represent what the customers in that quadrant value most. The Clues to Customer Value Orientation chart provides additional information about each kind of buyer. This is followed by Questions to Determine Customer Value Orientation and an exercise designed to help you apply these concepts to five key decision makers or influencers.

| Need for Relationship | | |
|---|---|---|
| More interest in relationship | **Relationship-Oriented**<br>• Advice<br>• Knowledge of customer and company<br>• Problem finding and solving<br>• Close working relationship | **Partnership-Oriented**<br>• Long-term, mutually beneficial partnership (an in-depth relationship and well-managed information) |
| Less interest in relationship | **Transaction-Oriented**<br>• Price<br>• Convenience<br>• Quality product<br>• Product knowledge | **Information-Oriented**<br>• Education on products and trends<br>• Information about your business<br>• Synthesis of complex information |
| | Less interest in information | More interest in information |

Need for Information

## CLUES TO CUSTOMER VALUE ORIENTATION

| Value Orientation | Typical Positions | How the *Customer* is Evaluated | What the Customer Says |
|---|---|---|---|
| **Transaction** | • Purchasing agent/director<br>• Lower to middle manager<br>• Assistant to a line manager<br>• Administrator | product/service quality; product/service cost; adherence to budget; adherence to specs; efficiency of processes; reliability and speed of delivery | "Can you do any better on that price?"<br>"We need it by Monday at 3 P.M."<br>"The specs are . . . "<br>"We're putting this out for bid."<br>"I faxed you my order." |
| **Information** | • Technical specialist<br>• Product specialist<br>• Researcher<br>• Engineer<br>• Consultant<br>• Financial specialist | product knowledge; industry and market knowledge; technical knowledge; R&D cycle time; product innovation; quality of information and data | "I need to stay up-to-date."<br>"Keep me informed . . . educate me."<br>"What's the latest . . . ?"<br>"What's happening at your company?"<br>"Give me the information; I'll make the decision."<br>"My E-mail is . . . " |
| **Relationship** | • Middle to senior manager<br>• Human resource director<br>• Chief operating officer<br>• Nonexpert buyer<br>• CEO | short- to long-term financial results; employee productivity and morale; market share; quality of advice; innovation; leadership | "What do you advise/recommend?"<br>"I'm interested in results."<br>"You need to understand our business/our industry/how we do things."<br>"We need to build trust."<br>"I don't want anything off the shelf."<br>"Can you come to our planning meeting?" |
| **Partnership** | • Senior managers who are very knowledgeable about your business and theirs<br>• People responsible for the long-term health of the company | relationship and information factors, *plus*:<br>choice of suppliers;<br>quality of organization-to-organization relationships;<br>profits and losses; creation and execution of corporate strategy | "Both our companies should benefit."<br>"I know you need to make some money on this."<br>"Your people need to know my people."<br>"We're in this for the long haul."<br>"You need to take the lead here."<br>"We'll rely on you for resources/training/project management . . . " |

## QUESTIONS TO DETERMINE CUSTOMER VALUE ORIENTATION

You can use questions like the following to help you determine any customer's value orientation. Questions 1 to 3 test the extent to which the customer values an in-depth business relationship with you and your company. Questions 4 to 6 test the extent to which the customer wants you to provide information.

**Relationship**

1. How important is it that people in my company know people in your company, and vice versa?

2. To what extent do you want me to advise you on what decisions to make, based on my knowledge of your company and your needs?

3. How important is it that I work to build a long-term, mutually beneficial relationship in which we work to achieve joint goals?

**Information**

4. To what extent do you want me to keep you up-to-date on details regarding new products, discontinued products, price changes, service policies, and so on?

5. How important is it that I help you gather, synthesize, and make sense of the complex information in your business, so that you can make good decisions?

6. To what extent do you want me to inform you about industry trends, competition, and new technologies that might affect your business?

***Note:*** *These questions are presented as guidelines. You should adapt them in conversation to suit you, the customer, and the situation.*

## VALUE ORIENTATION EXERCISE

This exercise will enable you to determine the specific orientation of each of your customers.

**Step 1:** Identify five key decision makers/influencers or key customer contacts in the space below. They can be from the same or different organizations.

1. ______________________________

2. ______________________________

3. ______________________________

4. ______________________________

5. ______________________________

**Step 2:** In the frame that follows, plot where each name identified in Step 1 should be. (Note: You may want to use the questions on the previous page as a guide for determining where each individual should be placed.)

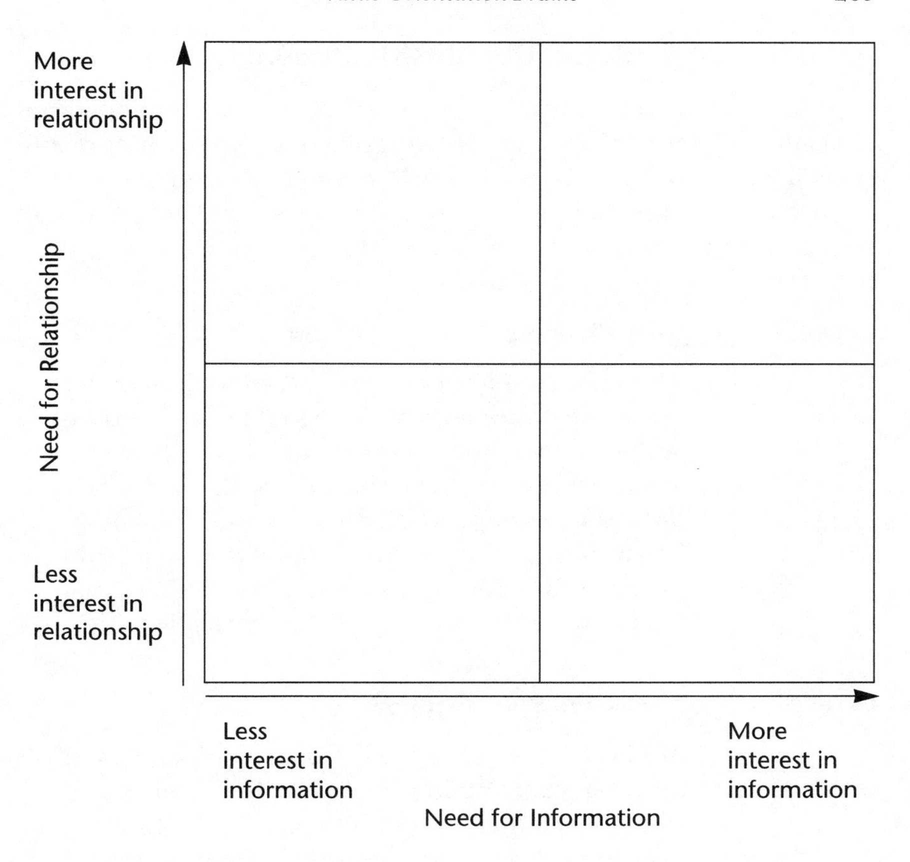


**Step 3:** Based on this analysis, how can you work with these customers to better provide what they need?

______________________________________________

______________________________________________

______________________________________________

______________________________________________

______________________________________________

## RELATIONSHIP GOAL ANALYSIS

Customer relationships that move toward the partnership quadrant typically add more value and create greater profitability for both sides. Thus, many organizations seek to move their customers toward a more partnership-like relationship. The types of relationships can be arranged in the following hierarchy:

**Level 5** **Joint Planning**

At this highest level of trust and commitment, you are at the customer's planning table. You work together to meet joint business objectives. In the extreme cases, you know what your customers need to do and how they should do it—before *they* know. You also help to determine the value of your solution and therefore its price. At Level 5, there is always a strong company-to-company relationship.

**Level 4** **Needs and Specifications**

At Level 4, the customer identifies a broad business need but calls you in to help clarify the need so that it can be adequately met. The customer regards you as an expert, and looks to you for advice on the specifications for a solution. In essence, you help set the buying criteria to which you must ultimately respond.

**Level 3** **Preferred-Supplier Status**

At this level, the customer truly appreciates the value you provide. Whenever the customer has identified a need and developed the product or service specifications, you are one of a handful of suppliers invited to compete for the business. You can spend less time proving product quality and negotiating price, thanks to an established relationship with the customer.

**Level 2** **Added-Value Services**

Here, you provide advice or other services the customer values. The buyer does not necessarily initiate contact when there is a need, but once you have the business, he or she depends on you for information and recommendations on how to use your products or services most effectively.

**Level 1** **Product/Services**

At Level 1, the buyer treats the relationship as transactional. You must prove yourself and compete on price each time out. You may have name recognition on your side, but the customer has no commitment to buy from you rather than from a competitor. To the customer, your product is a commodity. Level 1 is characterized by greater risk and higher per-unit sales costs.

Moving a customer to a higher-level relationship is an important strategic challenge, one which the Relationship Goal Analysis Matrix (on page 273) can help you undertake.

To complete the Relationship Goal Analysis, follow these steps:

**Step 1**: List all major current and potential contacts in the target organization. Note their current value orientation (transaction, information, relationship, or partnership).

**Step 2:** Assess each person's current level of trust in and commitment to you and your company (mark with an X).

**Step 3:** Determine where you might reasonably move those customers in the next 6 to 12 months (mark with an O).

**Step 4**: Step back, review your worksheet, and create a specific relationship goal for the account.

**Examples:**

- Move Ken to Level 4.
- Get Mary, George, and Tom to understand the value of joint planning.
- Move everyone in the account to Level 3.
- Get into at least two more buying centers at Level 1.
- Get Joan back up to Level 3, where she was before.

# RELATIONSHIP GOAL ANALYSIS

**Target Customer Organization:**____________________________

| **{PRIVATE}** | | **Level of Customer Trust and Commitment** | | | | |
|---|---|---|---|---|---|---|
| **Contact** | **Value Orientation** | 1. Products/ Services | 2. Added-Value Services | 3. Preferred Supplier Status | 4. Needs and Specs | 5. Joint Planning |
| | | | | | | |
| | | | | | | |
| | | | | | | |
| | | | | | | |
| | | | | | | |
| | | | | | | |

## TERRITORY AND ACCOUNT MATRIX

This exercise is designed to assess the relative importance of your key accounts and to identify what you can do to improve your relationship with each account.

On the matrix provided, please complete the following steps:

**Step 1:** In order of importance, list your key accounts in the left-hand column labeled "Initial Ranking of Accounts."

**Step 2:** Across the top of the page, list the technical and personal factors that contribute to the account. Use the scale of 1 to 10 provided on the matrix. Technical Factors represent the technical aspects of your relationship with your customer. Typically these might include: sales volume, growth potential, profitability, product fit, competitors, credit worthiness, target account/industry, strategic fit. Personal Factors represent the personal aspects of your customer. Typically they include: difficulty, quickness to close, servicing, personal rewards, referral potential, quality of relationships.

**Step 3:** Subtotal columns 1-7 in column 8. Subtotal columns 9-15 in column 16. Which set of factors is greater? Check to make certain you have not omitted any factors.

**Step 4:** Total columns 8 and 16 in column 17. Rank each account in column 18 by placing a "1" next to the largest number, a "2" next to the second largest number, and so on. Based on this ranking, should you place greater or less emphasis on any particular account?

# TERRITORY AND ACCOUNT MATRIX

| | Technical Factors | | | | | | | Sub-total | Personal Factors | | | | | | | Sub-total | Account Total | Final Ranking of Accounts |
|---|---|---|---|---|---|---|---|---|---|---|---|---|---|---|---|---|---|---|
| | 1 | 2 | 3 | 4 | 5 | 6 | 7 | 8 | 9 | 10 | 11 | 12 | 13 | 14 | 15 | 16 | 17 | 18 |
| Initial Ranking of Accounts | | | | | | | | | | | | | | | | | Add Columns 8 and 16 | |
| 1. | | | | | | | | | | | | | | | | | | |
| 2. | | | | | | | | | | | | | | | | | | |
| 3. | | | | | | | | | | | | | | | | | | |
| 4. | | | | | | | | | | | | | | | | | | |
| 5. | | | | | | | | | | | | | | | | | | |
| 6. | | | | | | | | | | | | | | | | | | |
| 7. | | | | | | | | | | | | | | | | | | |
| 8. | | | | | | | | | | | | | | | | | | |
| 9. | | | | | | | | | | | | | | | | | | |
| 10. | | | | | | | | | | | | | | | | | | |
| Totals | | | | | | | | | | | | | | | | | | |

Scale for Rating Your Account

**10 9 8 7 6 5 4 3 2 1**

Very attractive regarding this factor — Moderately attractive regarding this factor — Not attractive regarding this factor

## COMPETITIVE MATRIX

Use this matrix whenever you are in a key competitive situation. To complete the matrix, follow the steps below:

**Step 1**: In the column labeled "Buying Criteria," list the criteria the prospect will be using to make the buying decision.

**Step 2:** In the blocks under "Competitors," list the companies that are bidding for this business. Be sure to put your company in the first block because, of course, you are one of the competitors.

**Step 3:** Complete the matrix by rating each competitor on each buying criterion using the 0, 1, 2 scale provided. If you are not certain of a rating, choose the higher of the two numbers being considered.

The following questions will help you focus on and interpret the important aspects of the competitive situation you have described:

- Have you listed all of the relevant buying criteria?
- Have you forgotten any competitors?
- Where is each competitor strong? weak?
- What or whom do you not know?
- Do your ratings reflect *customer* perceptions rather than your own?
- Which factors can you influence to favor your situation? Which cannot be influenced?
- How can you strengthen your competitive position?
- How can you neutralize potential competitive weaknesses?

Refer to your completed matrix as often as required, and amend it as your knowledge and strategy develop. This analysis should become routine and should influence your activity within the account.

## COMPETITIVE MATRIX

Scale:

0 = no strength

1 = moderate strength

2 = considerable strength

Sales Situation: ______________________

Date of Analysis ______________________

Date for Follow-up Analysis: ______________________

| Buying Criteria | Competitors | | | | |
|---|---|---|---|---|---|
| | | | | | |
| | | | | | |
| | | | | | |
| | | | | | |
| | | | | | |
| | | | | | |
| | | | | | |
| | | | | | |
| | | | | | |
| | | | | | |
| | | | | | |
| | | | | | |
| | | | | | |
| **Total** | | | | | |

## COMPETITIVE ACCOUNT STRATEGY CRITERIA

Use the following chart to evaluate and enhance your strategy for any competitive situation.

| In What Ways Does Your Strategy: | Your Strategy |
|---|---|
| 1. Relate your product/service and its strengths to your customer's current and future needs? | |
| 2. Capitalize on unusual circumstances in the account situation, including any past experience you have had with this account? | |
| 3. Identify the decision makers and influencers and the process they use to make their buying decision? | |
| 4. Anticipate and address the buying criteria of the decision makers and influencers? | |
| 5. Differentiate you from actual or potential competition? | |
| 6. Respond to the motivation of your buyers? | |
| 7. Take advantage of the data, services, and staff from your home office or other sources? | |
| 8. Help establish specific objectives and plans for your next call? | |
| 9. Anticipate your customer's objections or possible delays and include specific ways to respond? | |

## HOW GOOD ARE YOUR CUSTOMER-INTERACTION SKILLS?

### SELF-ASSESSMENT

Complete this self-assessment exercise and choose one or two skill areas on which to focus during the next month, either to improve or strengthen your performance. Note those skills where you are strong. They support you in your interactions with customers. Also note where you need to improve. What can you do to accomplish such improvements? Who can help you?

To ensure your plan's effectiveness, discuss it with your manager or one of the other salespeople in your office. You should review your plan on a monthly basis and, if there are any situational changes, revise your plan accordingly. Try to review and test your monthly plan with another salesperson each time you revise it.

| Mastery | Average | Need to Improve, Learn, or Use More Frequently | |
|---|---|---|---|
| ☐ | ☐ | ☐ | **1. Connecting**<br><br>Using verbal and nonverbal techniques to establish a personal bond with the customer. For example, you might maintain a high level of eye contact, modulate your voice to a compatible tone, or make small talk. |
| ☐ | ☐ | ☐ | **2. Encouraging**<br><br>Giving verbal and nonverbal signals to encourage the customer to keep participating in the sales discussion. For example, you might nod, lean forward, say "uh-huh," or use supportive questions and phrases such as, "Can you tell me more about that?" and "I'd like to know more." |

| Mastery | Average | Need to Improve, Learn, or Use More Frequently | |
|---|---|---|---|
| ☐ | ☐ | ☐ | **3. Questioning**<br>Asking thoughtful, open-ended questions to uncover in-depth, high-quality information from the customer. |
| ☐ | ☐ | ☐ | **4. Confirming**<br>Gaining agreement on what the customer has said by listing important points, pulling together related issues, summarizing the customer's statements, and checking for the customer's agreement. |
| ☐ | ☐ | ☐ | **5. Providing**<br>Providing information about yourself and your organization to create a positive image of your organization, its products, and its services. You can do this by stating benefits, speaking concisely, and showing enthusiasm. |
| ☐ | ☐ | ☐ | **6. Handling Objections**<br>Handling objections in a manner that helps move the sales call forward without ignoring real problems or irritating the customer. |
| ☐ | ☐ | ☐ | **7. Using Capability Statements**<br>Describing the benefits of working with your company and relating them to the probable needs of the customer. |

| Mastery | Average | Need to Improve, Learn, or Use More Frequently | |
|---|---|---|---|
| ☐ | ☐ | ☐ | **8. Opening Sales Calls**<br>Stating the call's purpose and what you can do for the customer, then gaining the customer's agreement to your agenda at the beginning of the sales call. |
| ☐ | ☐ | ☐ | **9. Concluding Sales Calls**<br>Ending sales calls by suggesting an action step and checking for the customer's agreement to that step. |
| ☐ | ☐ | ☐ | **10. Exploring Needs**<br>Getting information about the customer's situation, problems, and needs. |
| ☐ | ☐ | ☐ | **11. Exploring Consequences and Payoffs**<br>Heightening needs by getting the customer to talk about the consequences of not solving a problem and to express the benefits of solving that problem. |
| ☐ | ☐ | ☐ | **12. Exploring Options**<br>Having an in-depth conversation about different ways to meet the customer's needs. This conversation should include a candid evaluation of the benefits and drawbacks of the choices available to the customer. |

| Mastery | Average | Need to Improve, Learn, or Use More Frequently | |
|---|---|---|---|
| ☐ | ☐ | ☐ | **13. Discussing Benefits**<br>Providing to the customer clearly recognized product benefits that address his or her previously expressed needs. |
| ☐ | ☐ | ☐ | **14. Presenting Solutions**<br>Describing your product or service in a convincing manner and relating it to the customer's needs. |
| ☐ | ☐ | ☐ | **15. Closing**<br>Asking for the order in a simple, direct manner and at the right time. |

## CUSTOMER-INTERACTION COACHING GUIDE

The questions below are derived from Forum's research on effective interaction with customers. This research indicated that high-performing sales and servicepeople operate effectively in five key areas. They are:

- Being customer centered
- Earning the right to do business
- Persuading through involvement
- Influencing internal resources
- Having a customer-retention mindset

In order to focus your coaching efforts with a salesperson or service provider in your organization, answer the 30 questions that follow with this particular individual in mind, and check the appropriate box.

Note this person's strengths. These represent a platform from which to build other skills. They also represent areas where this person might be able to contribute to the development of other people on your team.

Note where improvement is needed. What can you do to help this individual improve in these areas? Who else can contribute to this person's development?

Individual's Name:______________________________

***Are Your Frontline People Customer Centered?***

| | very good at this | average at this | needs improvement |
|---|---|---|---|
| Do they know how to do what is in the customer's best interest? | ☐ | ☐ | ☐ |
| Do they interact based on the customer's agenda rather than their own? | ☐ | ☐ | ☐ |
| Do they create trust by having genuine empathy for customers? | ☐ | ☐ | ☐ |
| Do they match "their" selling and servicing process with the customer's buying process? | ☐ | ☐ | ☐ |
| Do they treat promises very carefully? | ☐ | ☐ | ☐ |
| Do they adapt to a customer's changing agenda? | ☐ | ☐ | ☐ |
| Do they explain pertinent product drawbacks? | ☐ | ☐ | ☐ |
| Do they understand customer perceptions? | ☐ | ☐ | ☐ |

***Do Your Frontline People Earn the Right to Do Business?***

| | very good at this | average at this | needs improvement |
|---|---|---|---|
| Do they resist the urge to solve all their customer's problems? | ☐ | ☐ | ☐ |
| Do they know how to pace the relationship and limit the role of the "trial close" ? | ☐ | ☐ | ☐ |
| Do they handle objections head on, rather than try to diffuse them? | ☐ | ☐ | ☐ |

| | | | |
|---|---|---|---|
| Do they ensure that the quality of the follow-up and service merits the privilege of further sales? | ☐ | ☐ | ☐ |
| Do they turn their company's products into real solutions for specific customer needs? | ☐ | ☐ | ☐ |
| Do they respect the importance of a customer's time and priorities? | ☐ | ☐ | ☐ |
| Do they make progress with virtually every customer contact? | ☐ | ☐ | ☐ |
| Are they honest, frank, and trustworthy? | ☐ | ☐ | ☐ |

***Do Your Frontline People Persuade through Involvement?***

| | very good at this | average at this | needs improvement |
|---|---|---|---|
| Do they regard customer contacts as a conversation? | ☐ | ☐ | ☐ |
| Do they encourage the customer to do the talking? | ☐ | ☐ | ☐ |
| Do they gather high-gain information by asking better questions? | ☐ | ☐ | ☐ |
| Do they welcome opposition as a positive sign of involvement and an opportunity for productive interaction? | ☐ | ☐ | ☐ |
| Do they share half of their "air time" with the customer? | ☐ | ☐ | ☐ |

### *Are Your Frontline People Able to Influence Internal Resources Productively?*

| | very good at this | average at this | needs improvement |
|---|---|---|---|
| Do they build and sustain an internal network of relationships? | ☐ | ☐ | ☐ |
| Do they communicate their vision of the customer relationship to the internal staff? | ☐ | ☐ | ☐ |
| Are they team players and trusted leaders? | ☐ | ☐ | ☐ |
| Do they capitalize on the expertise of others? | ☐ | ☐ | ☐ |
| Do they take responsibility for orchestrating the entire sales relationship? | ☐ | ☐ | ☐ |

### *Do Your Frontline People Have Customer-Retention Mindsets?*

| | very good at this | average at this | needs improvement |
|---|---|---|---|
| Do they strike a balance between achieving immediate results and preservation of the relationship? | ☐ | ☐ | ☐ |
| Do they handle the full range of variables, from service contracts to delivery and payment schedules? | ☐ | ☐ | ☐ |
| Do they know how to advocate two-ways and not "give away the store"? | ☐ | ☐ | ☐ |
| Do they not push for partnership if the customer doesn't value it? | ☐ | ☐ | ☐ |

## HOW GOOD ARE YOUR LEADERSHIP SKILLS?

### Self-Assessment Exercise

Below are listed the 20 practices which correlate with effective leadership. By rating each practice in the space provided, identify your leadership strengths and where you can improve. To assess your strengths and developmental needs, rate yourself in the space next to each practice.

**Step 1:** Rating Leadership Practices.

5 = Very strong
3 = Moderate strength
1 = Little strength

*A Passionate Connectedness*

— 1. Seeking information from as many sources as possible.
— 2. Knowing how your own work supports the organization's overall strategy.
— 3. Analyzing how well the members of the group work together.
— 4. Knowing the capabilities and motivations of the individuals in the work group.
— 5. Knowing your own capabilities and motivations.

*A Commitment to Creating Meaning*

— 6. Involving the right people in developing the work group's strategy.
— 7. Standing up for what is important.
— 8. Adjusting plans and actions as necessary in turbulent situations.
— 9. Communicating the strategy of the organization as a whole.
—10. Creating a positive picture of the future for the work group.

*An Ability to Mobilize*

—11. Communicating clearly the results expected from others.
—12. Appealing to people's hearts and minds to lead them in a new direction.
—13. Demonstrating care for the members of the work group.
—14. Demonstrating confidence in the abilities of others.
—15. Letting people know how they are progressing toward the group's goals.

*The Capacity to Inspire*

—16. Promoting the development of people's talents.
—17. Recognizing the contributions of others.
—18. Enabling others to feel and act like leaders.
—19. Stimulating others' thinking.
—20. Building enthusiasm about projects and assignments.

**Step 2:** Note your highest ratings. These represent strengths you can rely on for effective leadership.

**Step 3:** Note your lowest ratings. Work here can improve your leadership skills. For suggested actions to help you improve, please consult Tactics to Improve Leadership Skills, which follows.

## TACTICS TO IMPROVE LEADERSHIP SKILLS

**Practice** 1. *Seeking information from as many sources as possible.*

**Tactics**

- Use the media, including trade publications and other references in your industry, to stay informed about scientific, political, economic, and social conditions that may affect your business.
- Take time to talk directly to customers. Make it your goal to meet several times each quarter with individuals at different levels of your clients' organizations for the explicit purpose of staying in touch with customers.
- Learn your organization's budgeting and finance procedures. Talk to people in your accounting and finance departments.
- Gain additional perspectives on your industry and the competition. Talk informally with friends outside work.
- Ask for ideas and advice from people at all levels of the organization to gain a balanced perspective on issues that affect your work.

**Practice** 2. *Knowing how your own work supports the organization's overall strategy.*

**Tactics**

- Learn about the strategic areas that affect your work group. Talk to senior people in the organization. Find out what is most important.
- Review strategic plans before determining specific approaches on new projects.
- Write down in your calendar the strategies that most relate to your daily tasks, as a constant reminder of how your work contributes to the overall strategy.
- Hold discussions in which members of your work group can ask questions about the strategic intent of your organization.
- Set priorities based on the most important strategic initiatives.

**Practice** 3. *Analyzing how well the members of the group work together.*

**Tactics**

- Set aside time to talk individually with members of your group to determine how they are assessing the group's ability to function effectively.
- At meetings, add a group evaluation to the agenda so that people can discuss their opinions of how well the group is working together.
- Monitor the group's progress and achievements. Is it meeting deadlines?
- Observe the interactions within the group. How do members talk to one another? Watch for signs of dysfunctional behavior, and ask members for ideas for improving the situation.
- Apply technology critically. Take advantage of technology—for example, project planning and spreadsheet software—that can help analyze situations and help you evaluate the group's performance.

**Practice** 4. *Knowing the capabilities and motivations of the individuals in the work group.*

**Tactics**

- Make a habit of speculating about the impact of outside events on your organization and work group. Become practiced and polished at asking, "If ______ happens, how will the group respond?"
- Use available personality and aptitude assessments to learn more about the values and skills of the members of your group.
- Take time to know each member of your group. Learn what appeals to individuals in their work. Determine the differences and similarities among members of the group.
- Observe how the group functions under pressure. Be clear about the limits of the group's ability in the midst of adversity.
- Organize informal events outside work at which members of the group can talk about personal interests, use different skills, and build rapport.

**Practice** 5. *Knowing your own capabilities and motivations.*

**Tactics**

- Look for opportunities to learn more about what challenges you. In high-pressure situations ask, "What's the best thing about this?"
- Designate specific times to personally evaluate your performance in work situations. Note what seemed easy and what seemed most difficult.
- When you are feeling frustrated about specific issues or circumstances, ask yourself, "Why is this important to me?"
- Review events in your career in which you felt particularly successful. What were you doing in those situations that led to positive outcomes for you or your group?
- Seek feedback from others on what you do well and where you could improve.

**Practice** 6. *Involving the right people in developing the work group's strategy.*

**Tactics**

- Recognize people's different styles of thinking and learning. Use a variety of images, metaphors, and ideas.
- Explain why something is to be done. "Why" is as important as "what."
- Create opportunities for people to contribute to the vision of the work group.
- Discuss how specific tasks relate to the larger strategy.
- Conduct sessions in which members of your group respond to your ideas about the direction of the work and suggest other ways to accomplish goals.

**Practice** 7. *Standing up for what is important.*

**Tactics**

- Be willing to take risks to clarify and support what is important to you and your work group.
- Help people see the value of their work, beyond the immediate task. Emphasize the fulfilling aspects of work and the positive effects of their work on others.
- Confront ideas and opinions that conflict with your values.
- Provide supporting information to substantiate your point of view.
- Represent the interests and needs of others accurately.

**Practice** 8. *Adjusting plans and actions as necessary in turbulent situations.*

**Tactics**

- Monitor the rate and volume of changes to determine the level of turbulence the work group is experiencing.
- Think about the effect of schedule changes on the people involved.

- Consider what parts of the work can be postponed or canceled if other priorities develop.
- Increase the level of communication during periods of great change.
- Identify alternative approaches when conditions change or when people are confused and unable to move ahead. Seek innovative ways to regain momentum.

**Practice** 9. *Communicating the strategy of the organization as a whole.*

**Tactics**

- Explain how the organizational strategy is developed. Who shapes the strategy? How often is it adjusted?
- Invite a senior person in the organization to meet with your group to discuss the overall strategy.
- Before determining work tasks, anticipate how you will connect the tasks to the overall direction for the group. Ask, "How does this relate to the overall strategy?"
- Clarify the strategy for the work group by discussing it at regular staff meetings.
- Think about what means most to people in your work group.

**Practice** 10. *Creating a positive picture of the future for the work group.*

**Tactics**

- Write down the key elements of the vision.
- Take time to articulate the vision. Schedule a meeting to work it out. Do not tack it on to the end of a busy meeting agenda.
- Ask, "What would customers want us to do?"
- Use memorable images. Use different expressions and media to shape the vision.
- Encourage people during difficult parts of the job

by discussing the positive aspects of the work and how it will feel when the work is done.

**Practice** 11. *Communicating clearly the results expected from others.*

**Tactics**

- Seek out individuals' special skills. State how these skills will contribute to achieving the overall goal.
- Be precise about the anticipated results. Describe the expected outcome, and then check to make sure it is understood.
- Schedule sufficient time to talk about what is to be done and the results you want to achieve. Ask, "How do we want our customers to feel when they use this product/service?"
- Follow up general discussions with written summaries of key points. Invite comments to ensure clarity.
- Tape-record your discussions in which you describe expectations for specific projects or tasks. Then play back the tape. Is the message clear? Note areas where the communication lacks clarity, and reenact the discussion by yourself as a means of self-development.

**Practice** 12. *Appealing to people's hearts and minds to lead them in a new direction.*

**Tactics**

- Structure meetings to raise questions, concerns, and clarifications. Be prepared with the necessary factual data to respond.
- Talk to people about what excites them about their work. Relate that excitement to current projects.
- Ask people questions that help you understand what is important to them. Then think about how that information relates to proposed changes.
- Take time to analyze your own concerns about change and be willing to share your feelings about the situation. Use your discussion to identify areas of mutual concern and motivational factors.

- Look for better alternatives to current situations. Ask, "What's the hidden opportunity here?" Explain the potential benefits of the new direction.

**Practice** 13. *Demonstrating care for the members of the work group.*

**Tactics**

- Spend several minutes every morning in one-to-one conversations with people. Build networks across the organization and within your work group. Take time to learn more about people through informal conversations.
- Ask people if they need help. Provide it if they do.
- Set a goal for yourself and others in your work group to get to know people in other parts of the organization.
- Think about the effect of your decisions on others' work and home lives.
- Find out what level of resources is needed to complete projects or specific tasks. Be willing to overcome obstacles in order to provide the necessary technical resources and equipment.

**Practice** 14. *Demonstrating confidence in the abilities of others.*

**Tactics**

- When selecting people for assignments, seek out those with diverse talents, experiences, and cultural backgrounds. At the outset, take the opportunity to announce publicly what strengths they bring to the project.
- Allow people space for accomplishing work. Once they are committed, do not meddle. Negotiate deadlines—do not impose them.
- Gather background data so that you can defend the decisions of your work group if they are challenged by others.
- Learn the limits of others' abilities and consider what a reasonable "stretch" would be, so that people are challenged but not overwhelmed by assigned responsibilities.

- Encourage others to take the lead in presentations to upper management. Be available as a resource person.

**Practice** 15. *Letting people know how they are progressing toward the group's goals.*

**Tactics**

- Take both formal and informal opportunities to provide specific feedback to work-group members.
- Define standards that lead to product and service quality improvements.
- Publish customer comments that indicate how well the group is doing in meeting customer expectations.
- Publish updates that describe how ideas have led to process improvements and cost savings, and display graphs that illustrate the group's performance on specific targets.
- Incorporate financial data in other performance feedback so that the group understands how it is contributing to overall fiscal growth.

**Practice** 16. *Promoting the development of people's talents.*

**Tactics**

- At meetings, be willing to listen to others. Encourage people with less experience to lead discussions and give presentations.
- Recommend others for special projects or assignments that will help them develop new skills.
- Rotate responsibilities so that individuals have the opportunity to try new things.
- Provide training in new skills so that people can develop competencies that will move them forward in their careers.
- Give people time to read the current literature for their area of work.

**Practice** 17. *Recognizing the contributions of others.*

**Tactics**

- Give credit where credit is due. Recognize people publicly.
- Divide huge projects into milestones. Celebrate as each milestone is reached. Say "thank you"—publicly and privately.
- Reflect on work that has been done. Remind people of past accomplishments.
- Tell senior people in your company about the good work that others in your group have accomplished. Arrange for the senior people to attend meetings so that they can acknowledge the progress of your group.
- Have the name of each group member listed as a contributor to the effort. Or, if it is a product, have each one's signature or name appear on it.

**Practice** 18. *Enabling others to feel and act like leaders.*

**Tactics**

- Put people on the team. Give them a sense of belonging and equality. Say, "She works *with* me" instead of "She works *for* me."
- Share information that allows others to understand the organization's norms and values.
- Use others' suggestions and information. Acknowledge their expertise.
- Rotate the responsibility for leading group meetings or project reviews.
- Encourage others to lead by giving them the responsibility and authority to carry out the work. Then trust them to do the right thing.

**Practice** 19. *Stimulating others' thinking.*

**Tactics**

- Trigger new ideas by stating "great thoughts"—either your notions or quotes from others.

- Do your homework. Be prepared to raise questions and share information about issues that are important to the group.
- Bring in guest speakers from other disciplines to help people think in a new way. For example, invite an artist to talk about the creative process he or she uses so that group members can apply the concepts to specific problems.
- Arrange site visits so that the group can observe other successful efforts.
- Brainstorm optional approaches in high-pressure situations.

**Practice**

20. *Building enthusiasm about projects and assignments.*

**Tactics**

- Review the vision, and show why it is attractive.
- Demonstrate high energy. Model the behavior. People will see that you care.
- Organize early announcements carefully. Build momentum with energizing and positive statements about the work that is to follow.
- Provide incentives for group members beyond the usual salary and benefits. For example, hold a Friday afternoon celebration to mark the week's accomplishments and to sustain energy for the weeks to follow.
- Keep a sense of humor and demonstrate your ability to laugh in the face of adversity.

## YOUR PERSONAL DEVELOPMENT PLAN

In reading this book and working through the Toolkit, no doubt you have identified a number of ways to improve your business unit's performance. The purpose of this exercise is to enable you to develop a specific plan to implement at least two changes that will enable you to do that.

Such changes may be personal, like improving your influence skills or handling complaints more effectively. Others may be organizational, like restructuring around customers or modifying rewards to reinforce universal collaboration.

To create your personal development plan, complete the planning guide that follows.

### PLANNING GUIDE

Choose one or two areas you think would benefit most from increased, sustained attention. After selecting one or two target areas and noting them below, list measures of success beside them; that is, how you will know if you have succeeded in meeting your improvement targets. Then, develop plans for improving your performance, using the following pages.

| Targets | Measure of Success |
|---|---|
| 1. | |
| 2. | |

## PLAN FOR TARGET 1

**Steps for Performance Improvement**

List the steps required to improve your performance in Target 1, the deadlines by which you want to accomplish those steps, the obstacles that can keep you from improving, and your plans for overcoming those obstacles.

| Steps | Deadlines | Obstacles | Plans |
| --- | --- | --- | --- |

**Assistance**

List the people with whom you will need to work to achieve your performance-improvement objective (including their relationship to you), the type of help you will need, and your deadline for obtaining the help.

| People/ Relationships | Specific Help Needed | Deadlines |
| --- | --- | --- |

## PLAN FOR TARGET 2

**Steps for Performance Improvement**

List the steps required to improve your performance in Target 2, the deadlines by which you want to accomplish those steps, the obstacles that can keep you from improving, and your plans for overcoming those obstacles.

| **Steps** | **Deadlines** | **Obstacles** | **Plans** |
| --- | --- | --- | --- |
| | | | |

**Assistance**

List the people with whom you will need to work to achieve your performance-improvement objective (including their relationship to you), the type of help you will need, and your deadline for obtaining the help.

| **People/ Relationships** | **Specific Help Needed** | **Deadlines** |
| --- | --- | --- |
| | | |

# NOTES

**Chapter 1: The Challenge: Turning Turmoil into Customer-Centered Growth**

1. "Global Business Leaders See No End to Corporate Restructuring," *PR Newswire* (April 4, 1995).
2. American Management Association Survey on Downsizing (July 1994).
3. Don L. Boroughs, "Amputating Assets: Companies That Slash Jobs Often End Up with More Problems than Profits," *U.S. News & World Report* (May 4, 1992), p. 50.

**Chapter 2: From Identity Crisis to Laser-Beam Focus**

1. Quoted in George Church, "We're #1 and It Hurts," *Time* (October 24, 1994).
2. See "A Tale of Two Retailers," *The Music Trades* (August 1992).
3. Katherin Snow Smith, "Organ Breathes New Life into Fletcher Music Sales," *Tampa Bay Business Journal* vol. 14, no. 23 (June 3, 1994).
4. "Kmart Corporation," *Hoover's Handbook Database 1995* (Austin, Tex.: The Reference Press, Inc., 1995).
5. Rich Karlgarrd, "ASAP Interview: Susan Cramm and John Martin," *Forbes ASAP* (August 29, 1994).
6. Suzanne Oliver, "New Personality," *Forbes* (August 15, 1994).
7. Ibid.
8. Per Forum conversation with Christopher Samuels, managing director, Center for Strategy Research.
9. Seth Lubove, "American Gothic," *Forbes* (November 21, 1994).
10. Scott Thurston, "Southwest's Wacky, Low Cost World," *Atlanta Constitution* (July 17, 1994).
11. Ron Zemke, "Creating Customer Value," *Training Magazine* (September 1993).
12. David P. Biehn, "Which Came First? A Case for Change," *Global Marketing 1994*, Edited by Richard J. Kostyra, Sterling Publication Limited.
13. Robert Tomsho, "Real Dog: How Greyhound Lines Re-Engineered Itself Right into a Deep Hole," *Wall Street Journal* (October 20, 1994).
14. "Eastman Kodak Company," *Hoover's Handbook Database 1995* (Austin, Tex.: The Reference Press, Inc., 1995).
15. Joseph Rebello, "Radical Ways of Its CEO Are A Boon to Bank," *Wall Street Journal* (March 20, 1995), pp. B1–2.
16. Rich Karlgarrd, "ASAP Interview: Susan Cramm and John Martin, *Forbes ASAP* (August 29, 1994).

17. Thomas Stewart, "Welcome to the Revolution," *Fortune* (December 13, 1993).
18. "Trendsetter Barometer," Coopers & Lybrand, 1993, as cited in "Benchmark: Farming Out Your Financials," *INC.* (April 1994).
19. Michael F. Corbett, "Outsourcing: Redesigning the Corporation of the Future," The Outsourcing Institute, special advertising section, *Fortune* (December 12, 1994).
20. Ibid.
21. Tom Peters, "Whence Comes Innovation?" *Forbes ASAP,* (August 29, 1994).
22. Peter Jennings, "Peter Jennings Reporting: In the Name of God," ABC News Shows #ABC-58 (air date March 16, 1995).
23. James Mellado, "Willow Creek Community Church," Harvard Business School Case Study, Presidents and Fellows of Harvard College (Boston, Mass., 1991).
24. Ibid.
25. Susan Headden, "Worshipping God Big Time," *Woman's Day* (October 13, 1992).
26. Barbara Dolan, "Full Houses and Willow Creek," *Time* (March 6, 1989).
27. Roland T. Rust and Richard W. Oliver, "The Death of Advertising," a scholarly paper by two Vanderbilt University professors, as quoted in Stan Davis, *Future Perfect* (Reading, Mass.: Addison-Wesley, 1987).
28. M. R. Montgomery, "The Genie of Jeans," *Boston Globe* (January 4, 1995).
29. Marie D'Amico, "New Man and the Sea," *Forbes ASAP* (August 29, 1994).
30. See Rachel Eagel, *Daily Camera* [Boulder, Colorado] (April 4, 1995).
31. Quoted in Molly Baker, "USF&G Chief Executive Transforms an Ailing Insurer," *Wall Street Journal* (March 24, 1995).
32. "USF&G," *Hoover's Handbook Database 1995* (Austin, Tex.: The Reference Press, Inc., 1995).
33. Quoted in Rahul Jacob, "America's Most Admired Corporations," *Fortune* (March 6, 1995).
34. Michael Oneal, " 'God, Family, and Domino's—That's It,' " *Business Week* (January 30, 1995).

**Chapter 3: From "Listening to" to "Hardwiring" the Voice of the Customer**

1. Quoted in Kenneth Labich, "Why Companies Fail," *Fortune* (November 14, 1994), p. 68.
2. See Rahul Jacob, "Why Some Customers Are More Equal Than Others," *Fortune* (September 19, 1994), pp. 215 ff.
3. *Fortune* magazine Special Issue, The Tough New Consumer (Autumn 1993), p. 53, footnote 24.
4. Elements of this section are excerpted from *Forum Issues Focus: The Balanced Business Scorecard,* by William Fonvielle (The Forum Corporation, 1995).
5. Peter Drucker, "We Need to Measure, Not Count," *Wall Street Journal* (April 13, 1993), p. A18.
6. "Vistakon: Dominating the Marketplace through New Product Leadership," *Johnson & Johnson Best Practices: Profiles of Bronze-Level Companies* (Johnson & Johnson: New Brunswick, N.J., 1994), pp. 1–8.
7. David Bottoms, " 'Keeping Up with the Joneses,' " *Industry.Net* (June 5, 1995).
8. Bradford Wernle, "Hundreds Go Online to Discuss Ford Explorer Design," *Compuserve* (September 1995).

**Chapter 4: From Teamitis to Universal Collaboration**

1. *The Sunday Oregonian* article by Jeff Manning (March 5, 1995), p. F1.
2. "*U.S. Bancorp Second Quarter Earnings Reinforce Focus on the Future,*" Company Newsletter, (July 17, 1995), p. 1.
3. Dennis Kravitz, *The Human Resources Revolution* (San Francisco, Jossey-Bass, 1988), cited in Patricia McLagan and Christo Nel, *The Age of Participation* (forthcoming).
4. Justin Martin, "Ignore Your Customer," *Fortune* (May 1, 1995), p. 126.
5. Michael Schrage, *No More Teams! Mastering the Dynamics of Creative Collaboration* (New York: Currency, 1995).
6. Wayne Koberstein, "Wayne Yetter," *Pharmaceutical Executive* (April 1995).
7. "Everything We Do Is Wrong," *Across the Board* (April 1995), pp. 32–36.

**Chapter 5: From Customer Satisfaction to Lasting Customer Enthusiasm**

1. Catherine Eberlein, "Bonding with Customers," *Potentials in Marketing* (September 1994).
2. John Cortez, "Saturn to Mission Control: Anybody Home?" *Autoweek* (July 11, 1994).
3. Warren Brown, "What If You Had A Party and 28,000 Saturn Owners Showed Up?" *Washington Post* (June 26, 1994).
4. Ibid.
5. Reuters," Saturn Keeps Customer Satisfied," Chicago Tribune Company (June 25, 1995).
6. Catherine Eberlein, "Bonding with Customers," *Potentials in Marketing* (September 1994), p. 5.
7. James Bennet, "Saturn Invite the 'Family' to a Party," *New York Times* (June 19, 1994).
8. Gannett News Service, "Forging the Future," *Sacramento Bee* (June 9, 1995).
9. Barry Day, "The Brand Business," *Global Marketing 1994* (Sterling Publications Limited, Sterling Publishing Group PLC; 86–88 Edgware Road, London, W2 2YW; Tel: 071-915 9600).
10. Frederick F. Reichheld and W. Earl Sasser, Jr., "Zero Defections: Quality Comes to Services," *Harvard Business Review* (September/October 1990).
11. Thomas O. Jones and W. Earl Sasser, Jr., "Why Satisfied Customers Defect," *Harvard Business Review* (November–December 1995), pp. 88–89.
12. "Building Capability at Pacific Bell," *Training & Development Journal* (February 1995), p. 25.
13. We first heard this term (*branded*) from Dennis McGurer, VP of Global Training and Development at Moore Corporation, and Bill Wiggenhorn, President of Motorola University.
14. Bruce Knecht, "Norwest Corp. Relies on Branches, Pushes Service—and Prospers," *Wall Street Journal* (August 17, 1995), p. 1.
15. "Staple Yourself to an Order," *Harvard Business Review* (July–August 1992), pp. 113–122.
16. *Advertising Age* (November 7, 1994).
17. The creation of this process was led by Jack Tencza, 3M's manager of Sales/Marketing Learning and Development, along with Alan Giangreco, Steve Wilson, Bill Goodwin, and John Hernandez.

18. John Thackray, "GE's Service Ace," *Across the Board* (September 1989).
19. Rahul Jacob, "Why Some Customers Are More Equal Than Others," *Fortune* (September 19, 1994), pp. 215ff.
20. Ibid.
21. "America's Best Sales Forces: Six at the Summit," *Sales and Marketing Management* (June 1990), p. 74.
22. "America's Best Sales Forces," *Sales and Marketing Management* (September 1991), p. 46.
23. "America's Best Sales Forces: Six at the Summit," *Sales and Marketing Management* (June 1990), p. 74.
24. "America's Best Sales Forces," *Sales and Marketing Management* (September 1991), p. 56.
25. Ibid, p. 55.


**Chapter 6: From Facilitative Leadership to Contact Leadership**


1. Noel M. Tichy and Ram Charan, "The CEO as Coach: An Interview with AlliedSignal's Lawrence A. Bossidy," *Harvard Business Review* (March/April 1995), pp. 69–78.
2. Ibid., pp. 72–78.
3. Ibid., pp. 71.
4. Nick Gilbert, "CEO of the Year: Larry Bossidy of AlliedSignal," *Financial World,* (March 29, 1994).
5. Quoted in *USA Today* (June 23, 1994).
6. Quoted in Matthew Schifrin, "Living Nightmare," *Forbes* (May 8, 1995).
7. See Gregory J. Gilligan, "Best Man," *Richmond Times-Dispatch* (August 29, 1994).
8. Ibid.
9. David T. Kearns and David A. Nadler, *Profits in the Dark: How Xerox Reinvented Itself and Beat Back the Japanese* (New York: HarperCollins, 1992), p. 234.
10. Richard "Skip" LeFauve, "Customer Driven Quality," Fortune Magazine Video Seminars (Tape 1, 1993).
11. Stephen George, *The Baldrige Quality System: The Do-It-Yourself Way to Transform Your Business* (New York: John Wiley and Sons, Inc., 1992), p. 56.
12. Noel M. Tichy and Ram Charan, "The CEO as Coach: An Interview with AlliedSignal's Lawrence A. Bossidy," *Harvard Business Review* (March/April 1995), p. 76.


**Epilogue: Lighten Up**


1. See Kathy Thacker, "Top Guns Wrestling over Ad Slogan Rights," *Adweek* (February 17, 1992).
2. Mitch Maurer, "Airline Chiefs to Arm Wrestle for Rights to Slogan," *Tulsa World* (March 12, 1992).
3. Bob Filipczak, "Are We Having Fun Yet?" *Training Magazine* (April 1995).
4. Tom Chappell, *The Soul of a Business* (New York: Bantam, 1993).
5. "Getting High on Love and Laughter," *Reputation Management* (July/August 1995).

Appendix

# FORUM CORPORATION RESEARCH SUPPORTING *CUSTOMER-CENTERED GROWTH*

Many of the concepts and conclusions in this book are based on Forum Corporation research projects. Each year, Forum conducts several such projects to stay current with what successful companies and the people in them do to create customer-centered growth. In addition to what we routinely learn from training and development activities with over five hundred Forum clients around the world, this book is based on six research projects in particular. They are:

**1. Executive Assessment of Customer Focus (1988 to present)**

In Forum's executive-development programs, a questionnaire is often administered to company leaders and employees prior to the first workshop. This questionnaire asks respondents to rate their organization on forty-three practices that characterize world-class companies. Their responses are then compared to a database that includes all past executive groups that have responded to the questionnaire. To date, over two hundred groups have responded, from multiple industries in numerous countries. The research is a by-product of the executive training, and the database is updated whenever a new executive session is conducted. This research was used as general background for this book and is cited in Chapter 1.

**2. Team-Based Organization Research (1994-1995)**

In order to understand the dynamics and effectiveness of successful teams, Forum undertook a major research project that included case studies of thirty-three companies and in-depth interviews with 330 managers, team leaders, and team members. This research identified the environments that foster team effectiveness and the specific tasks team leaders undertake to account for such success. This research is referenced in Chapter 4.

**3. Influence Research (1977, 1982, and 1991 to present)**

The influence research conducted in 1991 was built on two previous projects in 1977 and 1982. The influence database is continuously updated every year as people from organizations around the world attend Forum's Influence seminars. To date, it includes more than fifty thousand individuals. The information yielded by this large sample of businesspeople contributed to Chapter 4 and the descriptions of specific skills routinely utilized by effective collaborators. It is the basis for the self-assessment exercise How Good Are Your Influence Skills? and the Tactics to Improve Influence Skills on pages 255–264 of the Toolkit.

**4. Customer-Centered Sales Organization (1993)**

This research was conducted to identify current buying trends and what outstanding salespeople and sales organizations do that accounts for their effectiveness in responding to these trends. This work was conducted in Europe, Asia, and North America across six different industries. It involved in-depth interviews with 341 customers and is the basis for much of the information provided in Chapter 5. It is also the basis for the self-assessment exercise How Good Are Your Customer-Interaction Skills? and the Customer-Interaction Coaching Guide on pages 279–286 of the Toolkit. This research was built upon two other extensive projects that looked at what underlies sales success—one in 1982 and one in 1988.

**5. Research Project on Business Leadership (1989 to present)**

The leadership research involved the study of 7,160 businesspeople and is described in Chapter 6 of this book. It uncovered the four clusters of behaviors and twenty specific practices that are described in that chapter. The leadership practices norm base is updated as people from around the world attend Forum's leadership programs. It is the basis for the self-assessment exercise How Good Are Your Leadership Skills on pages 287–297 of the Toolkit.

**6. Primary Research for *Customer-Centered Growth***

In this book, we aimed to discover and delineate the strategies and practices used by organizations that today are actually succeeding in moving to new levels of performance. We sought out and studied companies that went beyond the defensive strategies of the recent past to achieve impressive sales and profit growth.

To accomplish this, we called upon Forum's resources and contacts in North and South America, Europe, Asia, Africa, Australia, and New Zealand. We and others associated with Forum conducted almost two hundred interviews with people in organizations representing many different industries. Each interview was aimed at determining what was actually working to create growth and precisely how others could duplicate these practices. We studied organizations that were succeeding and others that were struggling in an effort to understand and explain what really differentiated the two.

The five strategies presented in this book and the techniques described for implementing them are the result of *all* of the research described above.

# ACKNOWLEDGMENTS

*Customer-Centered Growth* reflects the efforts of many people both from within and outside The Forum Corporation. Without their dedication, this book simply would not exist. We are grateful to have been so energetically supported in creating something that we hope will make a significant difference for individuals and organizations around the world, and we feel privileged to have had the opportunity to work with so many insightful and unselfish people.

It is only fitting that a book about customers acknowledge the customers who were vital contributors to its creation. We would like to thank the great number of our customers who so graciously contributed their time and stories so that these pages could be written. Specific company names are listed in the front of this book, and we offer special thanks to: Susan Beckmann, Jim Berrien, Susan Bohn, Steve Bonner, Bob Breslin, Phyllis Campbell, Ed Chambers, Larry Dille, Barbara Gatison, Steve Goldberg, Teresa Hanger, Jerry Johnson, Chris Knipp, Michael Lund, Denny McGurer, Duncan McWilliam, David Morgan, Victoria Rickey, Jan Rivenbark, David Shackleton, Steve Sheetz, Jim Sierk, Jack Tencza, Ed Trolley, Peter Viner, and Don Woodley.

We offer deep thanks and gratitude to the many wonderful people who are The Forum Corporation. In our research and writing we were continually inspired by the vitality, depth of knowledge, and resourcefulness of our colleagues. In a sense every person in Forum can claim a piece of this book because its content represents the very core of our daily work. Having access to the breadth of Forum's research, training, and consulting capabilities made our task infinitely easier.

Forum's chairman, John Humphrey, seeded this project and has nurtured it over the last eighteen months. For his leadership and unflagging commitment to seeing the book come to reality, we thank him.

We were the benefactors of the wisdom and support of many Forum people and received help, above and beyond what might be deemed reasonable, from the following Forum professionals: Curt

Berrien, Barry Freeman, Bill Fonvielle, John Harris, John Rockwell, and Shaun Smith. Their advice and willingness to chase down facts and anecdotes brought life and substance to the book. Other direct Forum contributors include: Anton Armbruster, Ed Boswell, Mark Brodsky, Sarene Byrne, Bob Cabot, Jane Carroll, Jim Fizdale, Melinda Gleason, Marlene Groth, Rick Harris, Kevin Higgins, Rowan Jackson, Kerry Johnson, Gerald Jones, Betsy Keady, Mike Laughlin, Mary Maloney, Wayne Marks, Dick Miller, Jennifer Potter-Brotman, Sarah Risher, Craig Smith, Bobbi Smith, Dick Snowden, Diann Strausberg, Connie Steward, and David Van Adelsberg.

We are also grateful to the following special advisers and contributors of concepts and ideas. These include Tim Boyles, Jack Covert, Jim Kouzes, Barry Libert, Anne Maers, Sandi Mendelson, José Salibi, Len Schlesinger, Jeff Sonnenfeld, Tom Varian, and the many customers of Borders Bookstore in McCandless Township, PA, who helped us select a subtitle for the book.

Susan Ludwig and Susan Quinn are assistants *par excellence.* Throughout the writing of this book they worked long hours, provided constant support and technical expertise, made hundreds of phone calls, orchestrated innumerable resources, and helped us make tight manuscript deadlines with minimal hassle and disruption. We are deeply indebted to them for their extraordinary efforts. Also indispensable with technology support were Pamela Bynum, Tanya Hayward, Cat Lang, and Mike Vigue.

One of the most critical transformations on any book occurs when the concepts, ideas, and stories are actually put into words. We were fortunate to have the same three gifted people who contributed to *The Customer-Driven Company* help us with the research, interviewing, and writing for this book. Robert Wood brought to the project both organization skills and a dogged willingness to ask the tough questions that insure that uncompromising quality is brought to the work. Annie Post is a great storyteller and a constant source of energy, and she has the uncanny ability to find the unique angle, the nontraditional perspective. Peter Hillyer is a writer with special talent who helped give one cohesive voice to our writing. He ensured that this book would be written from the reader's vantage point. In addition, when we faced a fast-approaching deadline, Peter's goodwill and calm support of the team kept the collaboration and productivity at peak levels.

The great people at Addison-Wesley are no strangers to us. After a successful collaboration on *The Customer-Driven Company,* we were pleased to work within a proven partnership. We appreciate the expertise and commitment of Bill Patrick, Ellie McCarthy, Elizabeth Carduff, and David Goehring and thank them for their role in helping to bring this book forward.

Janis Donnaud has been not just an agent but a key member of our team. She has consistently and proactively provided sound advice on all aspects of the writing, design, and marketing of the book.

Special contributors to this book were our spouses, Sharon Whiteley and Paul Garcés. Sharon has enriched this important effort with her caring support, encouragement, and discerning critique offered through the eye of the successful business executive she is. Paul has added to the book his twenty-five years of experience working with executives and has been an invaluable adviser, editor, and champion at every stage. Our families deserve particular thanks. Jeffrey, Matthew, and Philip Whiteley; Lindsay and Amanda Garcés; Miriam and Sydney Perlin; and Adelaide and Pablo Garcés gave us their love, their unbridled enthusiasm, their sense of humor, and their patience—especially over the past year.

Finally, we would like to acknowledge each other. As equal partners in this endeavor we have come to fully understand and appreciate the true meaning of the term *collaboration.* Whether hammering out the premise, organizing chapters, interviewing leaders, or writing about a new idea, our willingness to assert our views and yet keep our minds open laid the collaborative bedrock upon which this book was created. When one of us was overextended with other commitments, the other unfailingly stepped in and picked up the slack. When one was a little discouraged, the other always had the emotional reserves to pick up our spirits. While many lessons have been learned through the work underlying this book, we have learned equally powerful lessons as a result of the quality of our partnership.

Richard Whiteley
Diane Hessan
Boston
1996

# INDEX

# About The Forum Corporation

Richard Whiteley and Diane Hessan are senior executives with The Forum Corporation, a leading international training and consulting company with more than 600 clients worldwide. Forum's collaboration with clients is designed to dramatically bring about profitable growth, by leveraging the investment in people—helping them learn the skills, behaviors, and processes that put the customer at the center of all that they do.

Forum's work with clients spans a broad spectrum—from management of the entire training function, to the planning and implementation of a large change initiative, to the creation and implementation of a specific training system.

For organizations that want to implement the strategies outlined in this book, Forum has a comprehensive, research-based series of learning modules that enables clients to:

- bring the voice of the customer into the organization and use it to leverage growth
- focus the organization on what is most important to customers
- create competitive advantage with customer interactions
- work collaboratively on behalf of customers
- use contact leadership at all levels of the organization
- build a world-class service culture
- install a proprietary sales process
- institute teams that truly produce results

For more information on how The Forum Corporation can help you bring about profitable growth through the implementation of the five proven strategies, please feel free to contact us.

The Forum Corporation
One Exchange Place
Boston, MA 02109 USA

Phone: 800-367-8611
Fax: 617-973-2001
http:\\www.forum.com

# *CUSTOMER-CENTERED GROWTH*

## READER'S QUESTIONNAIRE

You are our customer. Would you please take a moment to let us know whether this book has met your expectations? It should take no more than three minutes to complete and return this questionnaire.

1. This book (check one):

   Exceeded my expectations __
   Met my expectations __
   Did not meet my expectations __

2. This book includes much information that is new to me.

| 1 | 2 | 3 | 4 | 5 | 6 | 7 |
|---|---|---|---|---|---|---|
| *strongly disagree* | | | *neither agree nor disagree* | | | *strongly agree* |

3. I find I can apply ideas from this book to my work.

| 1 | 2 | 3 | 4 | 5 | 6 | 7 |
|---|---|---|---|---|---|---|
| *strongly disagree* | | | *neither agree nor disagree* | | | *strongly agree* |

4. I expect to continue to use this book as a reference for work or as a source of ideas.

| 1 | 2 | 3 | 4 | 5 | 6 | 7 |
|---|---|---|---|---|---|---|
| *strongly disagree* | | | *neither agree nor disagree* | | | *strongly agree* |

5. The tone of this book is just about right: not too academic and not too casual.

| 1 | 2 | 3 | 4 | 5 | 6 | 7 |
|---|---|---|---|---|---|---|
| *strongly disagree* | | | *neither agree nor disagree* | | | *strongly agree* |

6. This book is laid out in a way that makes it easy for me to find the information I need.

| 1 | 2 | 3 | 4 | 5 | 6 | 7 |
|---|---|---|---|---|---|---|
| *strongly disagree* | | | *neither agree nor disagree* | | | *strongly agree* |

7. The anecdotes and examples effectively illustrate the points that are being made.

| 1 | 2 | 3 | 4 | 5 | 6 | 7 |
|---|---|---|---|---|---|---|
| *strongly disagree* | | | *neither agree nor disagree* | | | *strongly agree* |

8. I would recommend this book to others (check one).
   *Yes* ____
   *No* ____

9. In this space, please describe how you will apply the information in this book to your work situation.

10. In this space, please tell us how we could make this book more useful to you.

Please send your completed questionnaire to:

Richard Whiteley and Diane Hessan
The Forum Corporation
One Exchange Place
Boston, MA 02109
USA